THE DEVIL'S
DISCIPLE

DISCIPLE

THE DEVIL'S

DIFFERENT SIDES OF WAR

FRANK J. STROBEL

iUniverse LLC
Bloomington

THE DEVIL'S DISCIPLE
DIFFERENT SIDES OF WAR

iUniverse books may be ordered through booksellers or by contacting:

iUniverse LLC
1663 Liberty Drive
Bloomington, IN 47403
www.iuniverse.com
1-800-Authors (1-800-288-4677)

ISBN: 978-1-4759-7453-9 (sc)
ISBN: 978-1-4759-7455-3 (hc)
ISBN: 978-1-4759-7454-6 (e)

Printed in the United States of America

iUniverse rev. date: 10/10/2013

TABLE OF CONTENTS

This is a compilation of many of Frank Strobel's experiences while in the U. S. Military, particularly as a member of the 114th Assault Helicopter Company in 1970 while stationed at Vinh Long, Viet Nam.

This book shares many personal experiences Frank had while in the Army, including the conversations he had with other members of the unit with whom he flew in Viet Nam and provides a glimpse from the pilot's seat of a few of the missions he flew.

Frank And His Ship 69-15"085"

Aviation in itself is not inherently dangerous.
But, to an even greater degree than the Sea,
it is terribly unforgiving of any
carelessness, incapacity or neglect.

Author Unknown

DEDICATION

It's quite difficult to know how to make a dedication of this compilation of events that occurred mostly while preparing to fly and flying helicopters as a member of the US Army.

So many people encouraged me to write a book, how do I thank everyone? Shortly after returning from Viet Nam both my mother and my wife encouraged me to write down these events that were so profound in the making of the man I have matured to be. More than twenty-five years later, I was again encouraged by Jack Ehrhardt of the Erie's Veterans Hospital Outreach Program to do the same. Although I often thought of it, I just never put pen to paper.

In the year 2000, 30 years after leaving Viet Nam, I was introduced to an electronic message board that was dedicated to the gentlemen that I flew with in Viet Nam. Shortly after, I began to slowly write down my experiences one short blurb at a time and it has become a very cathartic task. I would like to dedicate this book to those who encouraged me and gave me the opportunity . . . to begin:

Christmas 1969 Mom and Dad, Frank and Lucy

My Mother   Thelma A. Strobel
My Wife   Lucille M. Strobel
My Friend   Jack Ehrhardt
and the group of brave men I served with in Viet Nam

One of the best quotes I ever read in my life I didn't see it until
I returned to the "THE WORLD". From where it came,
I don't know but it reads as follows:

"Life is not a journey to the grave
with the intention of arriving safely
in a pretty and well preserved body,
but rather to skid in broadside,
thoroughly used up, totally worn out,
and loudly proclaiming
—WOW—WHAT A RIDE!!!!!"

Author Unknown

That is exactly how I felt when I returned from Viet Nam
to "THE WORLD"!
. . . AKA the States, the Mainland, the Lower 48

. . . I'm still skidding!

PREFACE

When I returned from Viet Nam, I felt as if I had used up a great deal of what I can only call my personal "life force" in that year. That might sound melodramatic but I don't know of any other way to state it. I worked very hard that year, physically, mentally and emotionally. I don't know which of those three took most of that expended energy. I had experienced almost every emotion available to a man but most importantly to me, every one of those emotions I had felt, had an exclamation point following it. Every one of those emotions was experienced at such at a very high intensity. Nothing was experienced at "normal" speed. Everything I experienced just happened so incredibly fast.

While in Viet Nam when looking back at my emotions, there were monumental highs and abysmal lows and sometimes they occurred during the same experience. That itself took a great deal of my energy. When I left for Nam, I set three personal aims or goals for myself. First, I wanted simply to adjust solidly to the new situation into which I was being placed. I wanted to learn to hang on in a combat zone in order personally to "plant my feet firmly on the ground" in that new and strange circumstance. As the year progressed, I saw that there were a few individuals that never managed to get past that first step in their own lives. Second, I wanted to grab as much stability as I could in a mostly uncontrolled situation. That would probably be done by becoming an Aircraft Commander and being the "boss" of my own aircraft. Hopefully that would be achieved in five or six months. Finally, I wanted to garner as much control in a wartime situation as I was able, which would allow me better to protect myself as well as those who depended on me and my decisions. I would rather trust in my abilities and decision making than trust on someone else for my own safety.

When I left the United States, I met the first and only group of men in my life with whom I would ever completely bond. These were the members of the 114th Assault Helicopter Company. I had used 100% of the physical and emotional strength I had available to me while with them in Viet Nam. When I came home, I was tired, really tired. That in itself wasn't all bad; it was just a fact of life.

It took me time to recover once back in the States. All of my friends and family insisted that what I needed the most was to get actively back in the civilian world; to get a job and 'blend' back into society. I soon came to feel it <u>was</u> time to get in gear and do something for my future as a civilian. I now wish I had taken more time at that point in my life just to sit back and think a bit. At age 23, the Army no longer wanted me; there simply were too many helicopter pilots. I was still young but many of my friends had moved away from Erie, or were married with young families and understandably busy with their young careers. Back in Erie I felt alone. I never felt lonely in Viet Nam while a member of the 114th Assault Helicopter Company, maybe that was because I was simply so busy. "Why did I leave Viet Nam?" even surfaced in my mind.

One last thing before I start. I always felt that my stories were the same as those of 'umpteen' thousand others who served as helicopter pilots in Viet Nam and therefore my stories would be the same as theirs and interesting only to me and possibly my family. After speaking with members of the 114th over the internet for a few years and attending a number of reunions, I have found that many of my stories are a bit unique. For that reason I have spent much time and energy since then in transcribing them. You will notice that many of my "war" stories really don't have anything directly to do with actually fighting a war. It was just because of the war that the story arose. I could have written many more stories that were more closely related to fighting a war. I purposely didn't write about most of the nasty situations I encountered. I wanted to write something 'different'. I hope you enjoy them.

Frank J. Strobel
"Knight 27/Knight Hawk 6"

Three White Knights in Formation Over the Basaac River

INTRODUCTION

No one experience in my life has been a watershed for living the balance of my life. However, the experiences to which I was a witness and those of which that I was an integral part while in the military were and continue to be a dominant factor in my life. Although my military experiences were limited to a very small portion of my life, they continue to be a major part of my memories. This is probably due to the intensity and the regularity of those events that in many ways were counter to the ways in which I was brought up by my parents.

The events recorded here are not written in any strict chronological order. The stories are presented in very near the order I actually wrote them, closely linked to my first combat experience. That story is extremely high on the list in importance. It easily could be rated number one not only because of the specific events but the fact that they occurred at the very beginning of my tour. I added a few stories from basic training, flight school and my time in the Pennsylvania Army National Guard. Those stories are inserted in a 'general' chronological order.

I first began to transcribe my "war stories" when I found that the unit members with whom I had served in Viet Nam had formed an association to reconnect with each other. They also had set up a discussion group on the internet to aid that reconnection.

I received a phone call from George Young, a former unit Commanding Officer whom I had never met. He introduced me to the 114th Aviation Company Association. It had been over 25 years since I had any contact with anyone from the unit. The interesting thing for me was that, through the association, I have made many new friends with some of the men who served with the 114th long before I was assigned to the unit. Many of my "new friends" were part of the unit when it was originally formed in the early 1960's. Others served in the unit later and they were already 'back home' a long while by the time I arrived in Nam. To a man I have found them to be a great group. I'm very happy to have had the opportunity to know and to be a part of the organization.

The numbers at the top of each story or message refer to the number that was automatically assigned to it as it was posted by the email discussion group. It was an easy way to control what messages or stories were related to each other when placed in this listing. I included a few messages and replies I received after posting a particular story to that forum, because those replies/ memories enhanced the original subject and give another person's perspective on that story. Those replies appear in <u>Appendix 1</u>. Most postings were from other pilots and aircrew members who flew with the unit at different times during the Viet Nam War.

If there is no number then the story was not posted on the internet, it was written and then sent to Steve Stibbens for possible inclusion into the 114th Assault Helicopter Company's unit history book or specifically for this listing of stories and thoughts.

You will notice throughout this grouping of my stories, short statements. Many of these I heard while I was a part of Army Aviation both in and out of the 114th Assault Helicopter Company. I threw them in just to make me happy. Here is the first one . . .

ALL THINGS CONSIDERED . . . .
HELICOPTERS ARE COOL!

Many of my stories, those of others and the history of the unit are published in a beautiful book entitled:

"Knights of the Delta" ISBN: 0-97-42465-0-6

The easiest way to purchase this book is to locate our unit website on the internet and contact the Quartermaster.

MY FAVORITE POEM— HIGH FLIGHT

Oh! I have slipped the surly bonds of Earth
And danced the skies on laughter-silvered wings;
Sunward I've climbed and joined the tumbling mirth
Of sun-split clouds and done a hundred things
You have not dreamed of—wheeled and soared and swung
High in the sunlit silence. Hov'ring there,
I've chased the shouting wind along and flung
My eager craft through footless halls of air . . .
Up, up the long delirious, burning blue
I've topped the wind-swept heights with easy grace
Where never lark, nor even eagle flew -
And while with silent lifting mind I've trod
The high, untresspassed sanctity of space,
Put out my hand and touched the face of God.

Pilot Officer Gillespie Magee
No 412 squadron, RCAF
Killed 11 December 1941

This poem was printed on a card carried by me
in my wallet while flying in Viet Nam.
. . . And yes, I did have the poem memorized.

SETTING THE STAGE

I couldn't remove myself from the Viet Nam War but I could use my training and new skills for more than just what one would think in a combat zone. I didn't even know if or how it could be done. I wanted to help other soldiers as much as I could. I also wanted to meet the local people as much as I was able. It wasn't meeting government or military bigwigs that interested me but rather getting to know the 'real' people who lived in that country. This was a completely new people and new culture to me. I believe people are people and they all have the same basic wants and desires. There are some very bad people on this earth; but unless someone is brought up from birth to hate and know nothing different, I believe individual people are basically good.

Flying a helicopter offered me substantially different opportunities than most American soldiers would have available to them for personally meeting the Vietnamese people. Most Air Force bomber pilots didn't get close enough to the ground to see the affect their efforts had on individuals. Being a grunt or a leatherneck only let you see the country from the butt end of a rifle. Being a member of the 'blue water' Navy didn't get a person close enough, though the 'brown water' Navy did so.

I also knew that flying in a formation of helicopters, dropping large groups of armed soldiers in a Landing Zone would not accomplish one of my personal goals of controlling my personal situation. I had to create my own opportunities in preferably one, or if need be two ship missions, which was definitely not the norm in a typical assault helicopter company. I felt that was the only way I personally would have the chance to be directly exposed to the countryside and its people.

If properly managed I felt I could have unique opportunities to mingle with the people, even if those opportunities would be limited. I felt that children would be the key. I always loved playing with children; they were always an emotional release for me. Playing with children in a war? That might sound strange. Children are curious by nature and I found that whenever I landed somewhere near a hamlet, groups of children would suddenly appear. I enjoyed that. A few of the remote villages in which I would eventually land seemed to exist almost in the Stone Age, yet the kids would always be active and inquisitive. When we were not in a combat situation, the children would unfailingly be the first to my helicopter. They would always begin by standing at a distance and watching intently but as soon as they would hear the jet engine winding down, they would edge closer. At times we would have to usher them away from my 'machine of war' but luckily other times we could be more receptive. When encouraged only slightly they would be fearless, even though all the while in the background their parents would be trying to call them back into the village and their family's personal safety net.

Initially, I carried some American candy. I quickly found that many Vietnamese children did not like our candy because it was too sweet. They were fascinated by our 'bubble gum' though and that became my 'shtick'. I loved teaching them how to blow bubbles. Often I wouldn't even try to encourage them with Vietnamese candy. I tried to use a friendly face and a smile. I tried to use a little of my time and concern; to let them know I was a 'real' person. Later on, a can of C-rations might be shared. It always seemed to work for me. Probably the best example of getting close to some Vietnamese people is the story I wrote entitled, "The Old Man From Hong Ngu" It was not the only time I had that type of an experience but for me it was probably the best.

Life was just lived so fast over there. I wanted to live it and to enjoy it all but everything was just <u>soooo</u> fast! I would have enjoyed spending more personal time in some of those hamlets and villages. Most of those people did want to be friendly. I wanted to help them with their situations. It was just an impossible task. What a frustrating situation it often was.

I was lucky enough to speak directly to many people in some of those remote villages through interpreters I had on board from time to time. What I heard over and over was that as long as we were in their village everything was fine but once we left they were at the mercy of any Viet Cong in the area. It took only one informer in every five or six villages to call in a group of Viet Cong, from some distance away if need be, "to punish government supporters". Therefore, a very few people could control the entire population of an area. The other situation that would come up was the forced 'drafting' (actually kidnapping) of young men from the villages. Those people had no freedom of choice. They were being bullied and we could do nothing for them when we were physically not there and we could not be everywhere!

One thing you may notice while reading my stories is that I don't always remember names of the men who flew with me. I wrote too many stories and was unable to say who was flying with me. Yes, it is a fault of mine that I never totally understood when I began writing down my first stories. I worked with many good men and the situations were so intense that at the time I was sure I would remember those individuals. I then wouldn't fly with them again for a myriad of reasons and often I would never even see them again. Their memory was replaced by new and often more intense memories. I would remember situations but would often forget the names of the individuals who were there when it happened. Overlapping memories of situations can be frightening. Sometimes one memory merges with another. Those of which I am not 100% sure, I have kept from these pages. I don't exactly know why things happen or how the mind works but it happens and it happened to me. I apologize to those men whose names I have misplaced in my memory, because it was not intentional.

In my defense, albeit not a good one (yet the only one I have), the military in their infinite wisdom did something in the Viet Nam War that they had not done before and has not done since. Except for a unit's initial deployment to Viet Nam, the Defense Department did not replace units *'en masse'*. An individual unit flag and its assigned equipment stayed in the war zone but since every soldier only had a one year commitment to serve in Viet Nam, individual members were replaced as needed. That might be an over simplification but is essentially correct. In other wars, soldiers would train together and then would be sent overseas together as a team. When they went into combat, a long and strong relationship had already been molded and groomed with the unit's personnel. Even before entering dangerous situations, members already knew or at least had a good idea, on whom they could depend. In Viet Nam it was only known <u>after the fact</u>. That could be deadly. How can you trust an individual to protect you when you don't know how he will react in stressful situations? Every person is different.

From an accounting point of view, it may have made a great deal of sense but accountants don't face the muzzle of an enemy's weapon. It was soon evident that very cohesive units that had trained and bonded together, after a while lost that critical unity until the new personnel could learn to adapt to his new unit. It also required a unit's officers to be 'managers' first rather than soldiers. This wasn't a failing of the individual; it was a failing of the situation, the institution and the accountant's spreadsheet.

In fact, considering the constant personnel turnover, I feel the individual units with which I fought did remarkably well.

The fact that every soldier was required to spend only one year in Viet Nam, initially might seem to be a fine idea. When you realize, however, that quickly in units, everyone was soon on a different rotation, a completely different view appears. It was not uncommon to find that as soon as you became comfortable with someone, he would be gone. It happened so often, it was hard to count on many people.

It normally wasn't an individual's fault, if he had done his time over there he was entitled to go home but continually "breaking in" a new guy became very tiring. Just when someone became very competent in their job, he was gone. You quickly learned to make friends faster, sometimes within hours, all the while knowing you could lose them fast also. You tried to hold back on deep friendships until you knew whether or not you could depend on that person and if he was going to be around for awhile. Only after a person was found competent and dependable could a true friendship follow. Close friendship had to be earned. I only had one crew chief with whom I never got past that not-dependable/dependable period. I did not keep him around me very long. You quickly developed and learned to protect your own "inner circle". It was hard to break into that circle but once in . . . well, you were part of the family.

There were other reasons for people to leave besides going home. Some individuals would be transferred out of the flying platoon to another area of the company and would rarely be seen again because of their duties. Some were transferred completely out of the unit to other units that needed their specific skills. Others would become sick or wounded and yes, some were killed. All of those men had to be replaced. Each was usually replaced with a "newby", a new person that normally had to be trained from scratch. Yes, I was that newby once and I had to be trained too.

There were new faces all of the time. Sometimes I would fly with someone only once or twice and never see them again. At the time you wouldn't know that would be the situation. Sometimes a couple of weeks later, you would ask what happened to so and so? "Oh, he 'DEROSED' (went back home) last week" would be the answer. Obviously never seeing or hearing of him again would be the result. Soon the memory of his name was gone. I find that for me that, not surprisingly, most of my best name recollections are of those men I flew with the most.

Why didn't we know if someone was going home? It was felt to be unlucky to openly discuss your DEROS date with anyone. It was considered tempting fate. The general feeling was that most guys were hurt or died shortly after arriving for their one year tour or just before going back home. When you were a newby you were hurt or killed because you were inexperienced; when you were a "SHORT-TIMER" it was because you were careless or just plain unlucky. I don't know what statistics show but in my personal experience, it was true.

Compounding the problem further, is that you never knew who you were flying with on a particular mission. Although each Aircraft Commander usually flew his own assigned ship, once a day when assigning missions, the platoon leader would assign a co-pilot to each individual aircraft that was to fly a mission the following day. Yes, there were positives. The new pilots could fly with many different Aircraft Commanders allowing them to assess their skills and choose which ones would be best for them to adopt. For the Aircraft Commander, though, he was flying with different co-pilots every day. It was hard to remember everyone's individual skill level, unless he had done something outstanding or terribly stupid. Therefore, unless you knew them well, it was easier just to assume their skills were minimal. That was a very unsettling situation, especially when flying a special mission that requires a "step-up" in flight skills like Night Hunter-Killer.

Likewise, once a day the platoon sergeant would assign the enlisted crews that would fly with a particular aircraft. I often felt that they just assigned bodies and not skills for all flights. The only constant was that crew chiefs, like the Aircraft Commanders, usually flew with their own aircraft. The bottom line was that I often didn't know who my complete crew was for a particular mission until I arrived at the ship. Many times, I was unpleasantly surprised at what I found. Who do you depend on? It was unsettling and embarrassing to have to ask a crewmember his name when filling out the log book after a flight.

I was the Mission Commander for the Night Hunter-Killer Mission for most of my year in Viet Nam. I flew the C & C (Command & Control) ship, which entailed flying low and slow at night often between the trees, only a few feet from the ground. I was looking for and engaging with any enemy I would locate or who would locate me. Completing this mission as we did was not for the faint of heart. Though rare, I had a couple new gunners who were less than dazzling in their duties. I can understand that happening but a soldier should be gradually moved into a special or stressful situation and not dropped unprepared into it when possible so as to jeopardize the mission or its safety. It took a different type of person to fly that mission, whether he was in the front or a back seat. It took a person who was self-reliant and able to control his fear and most importantly not be "afraid of the dark"! When flying at night we were in what seemed to be a black box and it was often very difficult knowing up from down and differentiating the dark black mountains from the inky black clouds, let alone the good guys from the bad. Flying every night however, I grew to consider the night my friend. While it made it harder for me to find the enemy it also made it harder for them to find me.

I am sure that the crew rotation affected the execution of the mission. I tried not to let it happen but it did. It had to! There were many times that I wanted to do something but didn't know whether my co-pilot could handle the situation if something nasty occurred. At one point, I went to the commanding officer and asked that some things for the mission be handled differently for mission stability purposes. It was adjusted but that lasted only for a short while.

On a side note, I was proud of the fact that I did not use drugs of any kind while in Viet Nam. In a spirit of complete honesty though, it was not until about 10 years after returning from Viet Nam that I realized that I had actually been on a drug while I was over there. I wasn't aware of it at the time. <u>Adrenalin</u> was my drug of choice. It was not until I was home in the United States and I went into a depression that I knew something was wrong. (One thing that has always amazed me is that 72 hours after my last combat mission, I was home in Erie sitting with my family. There was no time to gradually come down from my adrenalin high.)

I didn't know why I was depressed. I now can recall taking a friend's Corvette one time and a motorcycle another time, out onto the newly paved nearby interstate highway late at night and driving each at its maximum speed. I now look back and see that I was just looking for that shot of adrenalin that I was no longer receiving on a daily basis in a helicopter in Viet Nam. I had no idea what I was actually doing until many years later. I just knew it felt good at the time.

In Viet Nam, I had received a thrill every time I started that jet engine. It might sound funny but as that piece of cold metal sprung into life I could feel it inside taking me with it. Anything that happened after that just added extra "shots" of adrenalin to my body. I came to depend on that but I didn't realize how much I depended on it. I knew that I was deeply afraid many, many times that year. I now see that a shot of adrenalin masked much of my fear, though only temporarily. I knew I liked the feeling, I had no idea how much I became dependant on that feeling.

I can remember after the engine instruments began to stabilize, closing my eyes for a few seconds and just feeling the life growing in that engine. What a beautiful sound it was. What a beautiful feeling it was. It may have been a naturally produced drug in my body but it was a drug none-the-less. It became normal to be "pumped up" with that drug. I wanted it and I needed it but I didn't realize that was the case until I looked back many years later. I guess maybe I **was** truly addicted!

MY TIME IN BASIC TRAINING

MY INDUCTION INTO THE ARMY

There were many things that contributed to getting me into the U. S. Army Flight School and thus my year in Viet Nam.

First of all I was a student in college and had a "2S" deferment that kept me out of the draft. Then sometime in 1967, I am not sure of even the month, the Army started drafting college students if their grades were not above 2.5 GPA. Mine was just below. One day, three bus loads of Gannon College students were "shipped" to Buffalo, New York, for their pre-induction physical. Guess what . . . I passed the physical.

I had figured that I would be going to Viet Nam but I had hoped to join the military after I received my degree. The following year (1968) I received a phone call from the secretary at the Erie draft board. We had known each other for a couple of years. She told me that my name had appeared on the new list of draftees and that she could delay my induction letter for a couple days but no longer, since it would have to be mailed. That would give me the opportunity either to move to Canada to avoid the draft or to enlist and possibly receive an assignment in a military occupational specialty in which I would want to be trained.

That day I went down to the Army recruiter and signed up for helicopter flight training school but I would have to go back to Buffalo to take and pass the Flight Aptitude Standardization Test (F.A.S.T. Test). The test was scheduled for a couple days later. I was told that I would have to pass the F.A.S.T. and a flight physical before I would be officially admitted to the flight training program.

Three days later I received my draft notice. My induction/draft would be superseded by the contract I signed with the recruiter but if I failed to get into flight school or if I failed to complete

1

flight school, the Army would have the option to place me wherever they needed me. With Viet Nam War raging, it was almost guaranteed that I would be in the Infantry! One thing that I knew was that if I went to Viet Nam for a year it would be a great deal easier sitting and flying above the mud than trudging through it!

I passed the F.A.S.T. and left for basic training at Fort Polk, Louisiana, the week after Thanksgiving in 1968.

BASIC TRAINING—
JUST THE BEGINNING OF IT ALL

After enlisting in the Army and passing the F.A.S.T. test; I was introduced to Army life at Fort Polk, Louisiana late in November 1968, North Fort Polk to be exact. To get to basic training, I flew out of Erie and into Shreveport, Louisiana and took a bus to Fort Polk. There at the airport in Shreveport, I learned my first good lesson, 'never dare anyone anything or bet anyone anything while in the Army'. You will LOSE!

I was sitting at a small four stool counter at the Shreveport Airport having breakfast. A kid sat down beside me who was also heading to basic training. While waiting for his breakfast to be served, a cockroach ran across the counter. "Swoosh" went his arm as he caught the quickly scurrying insect. He said, holding it's squiggling body between his thumb and index finger, "Give me five bucks if I eat 'im?", in his slow southern drawl. "Sure", I said, knowing he wouldn't.

Gulp! Crunch! It was gone and I was five dollars lighter as he crunched and chewed. That five dollar bill saved me a great deal of money throughout my stint in the Army. That was quite a bit of money to me at that moment. I knew then, that there would always be somebody who would be willing to do almost anything for a little money. I was not in the Army yet and had already learned something valuable that morning.

The first thing I learned from the induction cadre there was that if the world ever needed an enema, it would be inserted at Fort Polk. I never learned anything while I was at the Fort that changed my mind. Most of the basic training was done at "South Fort." Only two basic training companies were located at "North Fort" about seven miles away, which is where I was sent for Basic Training. All of the Advanced Infantry Training was conducted at North Fort.

I didn't know at the time what it meant for me but a group of the guys in my training company really didn't like it. We were miles away from the main Post Exchange (PX) and movie theater. The meager North Fort had little amenities to offer; maybe that was it. It really didn't make a difference to me since we didn't have 'base privileges' anyway.

I was assigned to Basic Training Company C-3-2 (Company C, 3rd Battalion, 2nd Training Brigade). It wasn't the most fun experience with which to start my military career but I did have a reasonably "good" time. At times I actually had fun. The first morning, I woke up and was officially welcomed into Basic Training. I stood in the company area in formation at 5:00 AM. They began teaching us all of basic Army things, e.g., how to get into formation, when, where and how to stand, who to call what, how to salute and a million other little things that would soon become automatic. You either did it or had a drill instructor "in your face". It wasn't anything difficult but I was amazed to see so many guys either not able or unwilling to follow simple instructions. Their failure made it easier on me since the drill instructors were constantly busy elsewhere.

A few mornings later when we were in formation our senior drill instructor, Sergeant Brewton, yelled out to the whole company "Anyone that knows how to drive a truck, fall out of formation and fall in, in front of me". I had driven trucks for United Parcel Delivery Service back in Erie, PA and before I knew it, even though I was in the last rank, I was the second guy to be standing in front of the formation. I don't even remember making the decision to go up front but there I was. I had been told by everyone I had met in the Army, "Don't volunteer for anything". Now there I was at the first opportunity, volunteering. All I thought of was that, if I was driving a truck, I was not walking or marching and that sounded good to me.

A total of six of us volunteered and he selected four to go down to South Fort to take their military drivers test. I was one of them. He said they needed four drivers to take turns driving vehicles for the training company, that way no one individual would miss a great deal of training. We were shipped down to the drivers testing area to take our test. There was an eye test, a written test and a driving test. Not surprising to me, we all passed the eye and written test. Then we went outside to take our driving "skills test".

We started with jeeps. One of the guys ran over an orange cone and then flattened a stop sign and he quickly flunked the driving test. We were down to three. We then drove a pick-up truck. The three of us who were left did fine. Now it was time for the "Deuce and a Half," the 2 ½ ton diesel engined large utility truck. I had never driven a truck that large or anything with a diesel engine or air brakes. I knew that they were different to start and shut down and you had to let the engine warm up before driving. Air brakes would be new to me but I didn't think they would be a major problem. At least I hoped they wouldn't be.

The first guy of the three of us who were left, was told to get into the truck. The staff sergeant was firing questions about the truck and driving situations at him rapid fire, I assumed just to pressure him a little. In his first turn he drove over an orange cone, a couple of turns later he did it again to another and then he missed a stop sign completely. He was done and he drove off the course without finishing it.

The second guy seemed to do okay but when he was done he again was being chewed out by the sergeant. I was the last one and instead of listening to him scream, I went over and climbed into the cab of the truck so I could familiarize myself with the dashboard.

I knew you had to turn on the electric and fuel separately on a diesel engine and I quickly tried to look over everything. I found the gas and turned it on. I soon found the electric and turned it on but there was no starter integrated in the switch. It must have a separate starter switch elsewhere but where? I looked everywhere and couldn't find it. I was flipping and turning everything, anything that would move and even tried several things that wouldn't move.

Then I remembered that a friend of mine from High School had a 1948 Jeepster and the starter was a spring loaded floor button that was mounted on top of the transmission under the dashboard. I quickly and almost desperately, reached my foot up under the dash and the engine sprang to life. This was completed just as the red faced sergeant climbed into the passenger seat of the truck. The first thing he said was, "It looks as if at least one of you guys knows what you are doing".

I kept quiet and just looked straight forward and he said, "Okay, don't just sit there. You can go". So I put it into gear and off we went. I drove around the track and had no major problems. To finish the course I had to back up the truck to the dock. I did so and as soon as I stopped he got out and I heard him say to the guys standing on the dock, "At least someone knows what they are doing." Meanwhile, I was trying to turn off the engine to the truck. I turned off the electricity but it kept running. What was I missing? Again, I felt a bit stupid.

Just as I remembered the fuel switch he opened the door and asked me "What are you waiting for?" I told him he didn't tell me to turn the truck off and get out yet so I didn't know if the test was over. He said that it was. I turned off the fuel switch and the engine became quiet. I heard him say to the other guys, "Finally today, there's one of you guys who knows how to listen for instructions."

Whew . . . I snuck by that one. Now I just hoped that I wouldn't hurt anyone while I was driving that large monster. Only two out of the four of us received a military license.

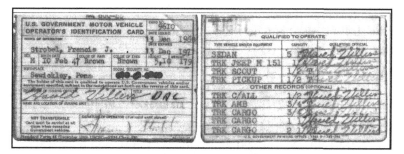

Frank's Military Driver's License

BASIC TRAINING—MY 'BASIC' ROUTINE WAS A BIT DIFFERENT FROM THE OTHERS

The drill instructors were very rigid in their time allocation. The daily routine for the trainees was:

0500: Rise.
0530: Physical Training (PT).
0630: Breakfast.
0700-1200: Morning training and transportation if needed.
1200: Lunch.
1230-1630: Afternoon training and transportation
    back to the company area if needed.
1700: Afternoon PT.
1800: Dinner.
1900-2000: Training and/or cleaning the barracks.
2000-2100: Free time.
2200: Lights out.

Since only two of us received our military driver licenses, I drove much more than I had expected. The other kid who passed his driver's test had a small accident and a couple of near ones, while driving some of the company staff around. Although he still drove a little, as time went on I did more and more of the driving. Most of the time, I drove a pickup truck or a ¾ ton truck with an olive green tarp. Occasionally I did drive the "deuce and a half" which was especially great when driving it cross country.

It wasn't all fun though. As I said, our basic training routine was to rise at 0500 and have lights out at 2200. When scheduled to drive, however, I had to get up an hour earlier so that I could sign out of the company orderly room and walk almost a mile to the motor pool. Upon arrival I first had to inspect the truck, report any existing damage and then sign for the vehicle. I had to sign back into the company area by 0530 for PT before breakfast. I soon found that the truck paperwork didn't always flow smoothly so I often missed a large part of that morning PT. I really, really felt bad about that but military rigors can be trying at times.

For the most part I drove the safety truck that would carry water, extra training staff and any basic trainee or two who may have been injured that day. We marched to the firing ranges, the gas chamber and had several 10-15 mile marches with packs. Unfortunately, I was unable to experience all of that. Well, **someone** had to drive the safety truck!

After training, I was required to take the truck back to the motor pool, wash it and have it inspected by someone from the motor pool staff. That was not a problem but it did take some time. It became time that I quickly learned to enjoy. I was by myself with no training staff around. It was just time to relax by myself with a quiet one mile walk back to the training company. By the time I signed back into the company, afternoon PT was over and the guys were finishing their dinner and were being moved out for their evening harassment before they had some free time on their bunk to relax and/or write a letter home.

I ate last and often had a nice quite dinner by myself. No one seemed to monitor how fast I returned to the company area after dropping off the truck, so I often walked back a bit slower than I could have. I figured that since I was getting up an hour earlier than anyone else . . . I deserved some free time. Well, didn't I?

Then, one day after returning to the company area, I was sitting on my bunk and Sergeant Brewton came into the barracks during our evening free time. He never did that in the evening. He usually spent his evenings and nights at home with his family. There were five other drill instructors that took over in the evenings. We all stood at attention at the end of our bunks facing the center of the room. Something was on his mind. He was yelling at almost everyone about just about anything then he walked in front of me and stopped.

SDS Roosevelt Brewton, Jr.
Senior Sergeant

He got right in my face and yelled at the top of his lungs, "What the hell did you do now, Strobel? The CO (Commanding Officer) wants to see you . . . NOW! GO . . . RUN!" And I did. I had to be in trouble for something. We never saw the CO. He didn't waste his time with the recruits. Maybe someone noticed my evening strolls back to the company area from the motor pool. I ran into the orderly room and the clerk just shook his head, looked down at the papers he was working on and told me to go into the CO's office. I was obviously in for it, for something.

I walked into his office and up to his desk and reported. Without looking up he said in a loud voice, "Strobel, what day is today?" I had no idea what one day was from the next. Every day was just like the next. I was just "going with the flow". He told me to look at his calendar. It was one of those one-day-at-a-time block calendars. I said "It's February 10th." Now, I realized that it was my birthday but that shouldn't make any difference to him. He pointed to a box on a table across the room and said "Take it, it's yours. Now get out of here." It was a white bakery box. It was a birthday cake. I was sure that it was not the norm for the CO to acknowledge a recruit's birthday, much less give him a cake,

My mother had called a bakery off the base and ordered a ½ sheet birthday cake for me. That was not an easy thing to do in 1969 rural Louisiana. My CO had to write a letter to my mom, telling her that it was delivered to me, which I am sure he didn't appreciate. I carried it back to the barracks, wondering what I was going to do with this huge cake. Sergeant Brewton was still in the barracks when I returned. He smiled and handed me his personal knife saying "This cake is to be gone by lights out and everything cleaned up".

No forks or plates but everyone received a piece of cake in their hands and everyone signed a thank you note to my mom. Mom always came through!

I got to know all of the training staff. Most had just returned from Viet Nam and were waiting for either a school assignment or discharge orders. They all had served in Viet Nam in the infantry; some had been wounded but were happy to share their very recent experience with me. I absorbed quite a bit of extra "training" while driving. Often the stories were interesting or funny but just as often, sobering. Sometimes the stories seemed embellished but I figured that they were entitled. A year later, after spending some time in Viet Nam, I realized that they were more than likely not exaggerated.

BASIC TRAINING—A VERY RAINY DAY/NIGHT

Early one very dark and rainy morning, I donned my poncho and signed out of the orderly room to get my truck for the day. I was not looking forward to the mile-long walk to the motor pool in the pouring rain. I knew that by the time I got to my truck I would be soaked and that would have me wet all day. Just as I stepped back out into the rain to begin my trek, Sgt. Brewton pulled into the company area for the beginning of his day. He looked at me and knew where I was going. He partially wound down his window and offered to give me a ride. I was shocked, I didn't expect it but I happily accepted and got in very quickly.

Now I have to tell you, I really liked Sgt. Brewton. The several times that I drove the safety truck and he rode with me, we had some very pleasant discussions. He actually treated me like a human being, which was not how a drill sergeant normally treated a trainee. During training he was a very gruff man but when we had our discussions I could easily see the nicer side of him.

We had a very short but dry ride to the motor pool. We were having a very lively discussion. I thought it was quite amusing that he drove past the entrance to the motor pool and had to turn around to drop me off.

It was very easy to see that day that he did his job very well, all the while caring about his men. There was no question during training he was **the** boss, yet that day I briefly saw a totally different side of him. As basic training ended, a couple weeks later, I was a bit sorry that I probably would not see him again but then again that's another story.

BASIC TRAINING—THE CONTRACT'S FINE PRINT . . . THE FLIGHT SCHOOL "GOTCHA"

About the second or third week of basic Training, those of us that had enlisted for flight training were sent to the Fort Polk base hospital to receive a flight physical. It was that day many found out why they waited until after we were already in the Army to have us physically qualify for flight training.

This is when the "Fine Print" of the enlistment contract kicked in. There was a bus load of between 40 and 50 fellow trainees who went to the hospital that day. Less than 50% passed the physical, most flunked because of their eyes. Entering flight school requires 20/20 eyesight with absolutely no waivers. Many of the men that I was in training with already had their dreams dashed and we really hadn't started flight school yet. There was a lot of grumbling that evening because it seems that a number of recruiters glossed over that part of the enlistment contract. That day the Army had many new infantrymen.

The following day those of us who passed the flight physical were officially told that we were accepted for primary flight training.

BASIC TRAINING—PHILIP FAULK, A FINE MAN

I have to tell you about one of the most courageous men I ever knew. He was in my basic training platoon. No, he wasn't a friend of mine. We never hung out together. I never saw him after basic but I will also never forget him.

Phil was a farmer from Iowa and was drafted into the Army. I have no idea how he passed his induction physical. I could only imagine that he should have flunked because he stood about 5'4" and he had to be as round as he was tall. He didn't really walk; it was more of a waddle. No one else was even near his size. When I saw him the first day I just asked myself, "How did he get in"? Throughout basic training the drill instructors harassed him relentlessly, usually during PT.

Part of our PT every morning and most evenings was a mile run in formation. After the first day they placed Phil in the last rank, so that, as he slowed down, the others could stay in formation and keep going. One of the drill instructors would always stay back yelling at him directly into his ear as to how out of shape he was, how worthless he was and why didn't he just quit. He never did.

While driving the safety truck, I would stay back with the last man, in this situation it was almost always Phil. How many times did I pick him up? Zero!

Other trainees would claim a twisted ankle or some such ailment and would climb into the back of the truck. Phil never did. How do I know he never did? I watched this man keep moving his feet while his body looked as though it was in convulsions. He would be throwing-up violently but he never stopped moving his feet.

How he continued to breath I will never know but his feet were always moving. During basic training, I had to drive him down to clothing issue on South Fort on two different occasions to get him new uniforms because he lost so much weight a belt could no longer hold up his pants.

How many pounds did he lose in basic training? I have no idea. He was still heavy at the end but he could do the mile without stopping.

I will never forget his strength and fortitude. If any man ever deserved a salute, it was Phil. I admired that man.

BASIC TRAINING—THE GAS CHAMBER

Oh, how I remember the day we went to the gas chamber for training. How could I forget? It was only about 3 miles away from our company area and I drove the safety truck. When we arrived, we were given the pre-chamber instructions and then I was told to park the truck at the far end of the lot, almost 100 yards from the entrance to the chamber.

Soon, my brother trainees were coming out of the exit door. All were coughing deeply, most were vomiting. Surely it was something I wanted to avoid putting my handsome young body through. I quietly but deliberately, walked back to my truck, opened its hood and stuck my head in it as if working on it, hoping to avoid that nasty gas. The guys were gradually filtering down to where I was and I saw their red watering eyes and wet faces, much of it from mucus they were wiping away from their faces with their handkerchiefs.

I realized now that all of the trainees had entered and the last were now exiting. I knew that I was now totally committed to my hastily devised ruse to avoid the chamber. I decided that I must look like the others, so I rubbed my face hard pressing my eyes deeply and as hard as I could stand it. I splashed copious amounts of water on my face from the back of the truck and lightly wiped it off, sure that unless someone inspected me closely, I would pass a quick review. We then stood formation and were quickly and superficially inspected. I passed. I then left the formation and started my truck.

As they were preparing to march back to the company area, one of the training staff hopped into the passenger seat of the truck. After a few seconds, he said, "Your nose isn't running. Did you go through the gas chamber?" I told him that it was really nasty stuff and I wouldn't want to have a heavy dose of that stuff. He Said,

"Yes but did you go through the gas chamber?" I told him, "No but I had been having a problem with the truck and . . . ."

He quickly took me out of the truck and back to the entrance of the gas chamber. As we arrived the last four of the training staff were leaving. He told them that "Strobel almost managed to beat the system and most importantly you". So they put their gas masks back on, told me to enter in about 10 seconds. They turned around and entered. I wasn't sure what they were preparing but I knew it wouldn't be good for me.

I went into the gas filled chamber and they took me through the training we were told to expect in the pre-chamber talk. They asked if I had any problem breathing with the gas mask on. I didn't. They said that the purpose of the training was to give me confidence in the equipment on which we depended actually worked. The next step was to take the mask off and say out loud my name, rank and serial number . . . which I did.

Then according to the pre-chamber training talk, I was to turn and go outside through the double doors. As I turned, I heard someone shout, "Wait!" All I could think of was, "Here it comes, whatever it is." There I stood, the only one in the gas filled room, without a gas mask on.

Ever so slowly, as I leaned through the suffocating, eye stinging gas towards the door, one of them said, "So you thought you could beat the system?" He then punched me, extremely hard in the stomach. The body's normal reaction is to take a deep breath, which I did, of concentrated CS Gas.

I felt myself immediately pass out. I don't know if I hit the floor but when I came around, I was told that two of the drill instructors carried me out of the chamber. By the time I had composed myself and drove the truck back, the formation had almost marched back to the company area.

BASIC TRAINING—"COOKIE" AND THE BIVOUAC

Our company had a cook and as his nickname implied, he ran the mess hall. He looked like he was in his early to mid-forties but it was obvious that he was an alcoholic. I never saw him actually drunk but then again I have seen many drunks in my life who could handle their job, just good enough to hang on. Well, that is what Cookie was doing, hanging on. He sported one simple chevron on his shoulder, so he obviously had recently been busted for something before I arrived there. My guess is that he had been "broken" (demoted) many times during his career.

Because I drove the truck so often, I was never assigned to work Kitchen Police (KP) duty in the mess hall. Normally everyone took their turn. I got to know Cookie because I would have to deliver the food he prepared for the trainees' lunch when they would be gone for the whole day.

The last week of basic training was spent on a five day bivouac about 5 miles away from our company area where a great deal of final training was done. It culminated on the last day with a 100 yard low crawl over a simulated combat zone with live bullets fired over the trainees' heads.

I was assigned to drive the water truck out the first morning, then the food truck the rest of the week. I really felt very, very bad because the other guys got to march, go camping for 5 days and walk guard duty each night. On the other hand I had to sleep by myself in my bunk each night between sheets back in the company area, so that I could drive the food out early in the morning. Boy was I depressed—not! I actually had a private room, although there were 30 beds in it.

The first day, Cookie drove out the food truck (a deuce and a half) and I drove out the water tanker (another deuce and a half) with 2,000 gallons (14,000 Pounds) of water. I had to follow Cookie, because after the first ½ mile, the last 4 ½ miles were over unmarked, winding dirt roads with scrub brush that all looked the same, everywhere. There were just enough trees to obscure any long range vision.

The first thing Cookie said to me was, "You had better follow me close because if you lose me and don't get the water to those guys; you will be in deep s—t. Don't you get lost out there!"

He drove nicely through North Fort Polk on the paved roads (where the MPs were) but as soon as he was on the dirt roads and out of sight of the post, he took off. All I could see was a cloud of talcum powder fine tan/red colored dust that spread 100 yards in each direction as if it were a puff of smoke. At first I was holding back but I felt I was losing him because of the swirling dust. It was the heaviest truck I had ever driven.

I tried to stay closer and soon could see him through the dust but only occasionally. Soon, I had caught up to him and every once in awhile as we rounded a tight turn, I could feel the back wheels of the truck slide sideways.

When we arrived at the bivouac area, we were just two trucks gently pulling into the area with our load. Wow, what a ride that was!

I was surprised. It ended up that I missed 90% of that week's training including the low crawl under the live ammunition fire. It ended up that I had to drive back for lunch and then dinner every day and after the last trip in each day, I stayed in the company area. It was quite boring.

I have yet to put up an army tent. No, I don't want to try now.

MY TIME IN FLIGHT SCHOOL

FLIGHT SCHOOL—THE BEGINNING, SURE THERE WERE NEW PRESSURES

In the early spring, of 1969, I began Flight School (formally known as the "Warrant Officer Rotary Wing Aviation Course", in Fort Wolters, Texas, (Class 69-37). I was assigned to the 4th Warrant Officer Candidate (WOC) Company, known as the "Gold Hats". Initially, our treatment was not much different than what we had experienced in basic training, except that the harassment was stepped up quite a bit.

On the first day we were ordered to stand in formation in the front of our company's building. The Tactical (TAC) Officers traveled up and down each rank as we stood at attention. Individually or sometimes in pairs or even groups, they began intimidating anyone that they felt would be susceptible to their antics. My approach to this was to pretend that I was like a duck, just to ignore any of their abuse and let their personal comments roll off my back. Actually, I felt that how they were harassing some of the guys was quite amusing as long as it wasn't me.

I truly wanted to smile but I controlled myself and held it back. It was obvious that they were taking the most time with the guys that either reacted to their confrontations with fear, or even worse with amusement by not taking it seriously or 'by smiling'. I just tried to do what they wanted done and answer their questions simply but directly. For the most part they left me alone. It worked for me but several of the students in formation quit flight school after that first confrontation. They must not have wanted to fly badly enough.

Our company area happened to be below one of the flight paths of helicopters leaving and returning to one of the two main heliports. Streams of helicopters were flying constantly overhead, approximately one every thirty seconds. As we stood at attention and looked straight ahead as required, one of the students in his eagerness was caught taking a glimpse at a helicopter that was flying overhead. That is what we were there for, so why not look? He was immediately verbally attacked by two TAC Officers, then three, then four. They were all screaming at him at the same time. Basically they were asking him why he wasn't looking straight ahead as he was ordered.

They didn't wait for an answer and asked him who was flying in the helicopter. The answer was an "Officer". "What do you do to any Officer when you see one?" they asked. "You salute him, Sir", was the reply. He was then removed from the formation and was faced towards the helicopter flight path at "Parade Rest". He then was ordered to come to "Attention" when he saw a helicopter approaching and to salute it as it flew over. After it passed he was to return to "Parade Rest". After our formation was dismissed he was ordered to stay outside the building for more than an hour in the Texas sun and to continue his unending endeavor every thirty seconds or so.

A quick lesson was learned by all. "Stay focused on your current task and under no circumstances do you lose your concentration. Don't be distracted by something that is not important to that current task no matter how intriguing it may be." That was a lesson that would be extremely valuable in flight school and just as important after graduation. The process of eliminating individuals who were unable to handle higher levels of stress had begun. We were quickly taught not to question or doubt anything presented. Every situation to which we were exposed had something to do with our training. It would be a concept that we needed to learn. That first day was a simple but quick and pointed example.

The first two weeks of flight school was "ground" school but the pressure the TAC officers placed on us back at the company area was unrelenting from the time we got up in the morning until lights out. Marching to class in formation became a time to relax.

The first week we were even required to eat "square" meals in a limited amount of time for no other reason than to add even a little more stress.

As the days progressed, time in the evening for study without any harassment gradually appeared. After two weeks when we actually began our flight training the evening active harassment by the TAC Officers lessened even more but did not cease. At least the TAC Officers didn't follow us out to the flight line. A few more students were gone now and we hadn't started to fly yet. We didn't even get base privileges until the week before we graduated from Primary Flight Training. After graduation we then left the Fort Wolters for the next installment of the flight training program at another base.

It really was surprising to me how quickly some of the guys washed out of the program. It seemed that everyday someone was gone. There was no other way to put it. All of a sudden they would be missing from class and when we got back to the company area everything, including their clothing, study materials and any equipment was gone. There was no margin for error for anyone. Any hint that the person even existed was erased. What you recognized first as you walked into the room that was initially shared with three or four others, was a rolled up mattress. It was quite sad that someone else's dream was over. You learned quickly not even to ask what happened. By graduation, I had gone from a room of four to a private room. It became somewhat lonely at times but I stayed encouraged because at least 'I' was still in the program.

I think what surprised me the most at the time was the pressure that all of the Warrant Officer Candidates were under. I did expect pressure but it was exacerbated by the short timeline we were allotted to master the academic portion of training as well as the actual flight skills portion required to become a military pilot. In addition, however, there was what I can only call artificial pressures that were added to the mix. These pressures were there merely to weed out even more students. We were left on our own to find effective coping mechanisms that worked for each of us. It was a very effective technique to measure an individual but a very exhaustive way to measure someone in a short time period.

I QUICKLY LEARNED THAT "GRAVITY" IS NOT A SUGGESTION, IT IS THE LAW!

During the third week of flight school, I began to fly. I was told by my instructor that teaching someone to hover was like teaching someone how to ride a unicycle while balancing that cycle on a beach ball. That may sound like an exaggeration but I can tell you that it definitely wasn't easy.

FLIGHT SCHOOL—HOVERING AND SOLOING

Everyone was required to solo between 7.5 and 10 flight hours and in order to solo a student had to be able to hover. Normally the first 5 or so flight training hours were allotted for hovering and basic flight knowledge and techniques to be used around an airport. Many classmates never got past that challenge. The pressure to perform was always there. That hovering 'thing' just wasn't that easy. Why there weren't any more helicopter crashes than actually occurred, I will never know.

About six weeks after I arrived in Viet Nam, I bumped into one of my former classmates who never managed to hover. He was now a truck mechanic with one stripe on his sleeve. When I saw him he was on his way to stand guard duty at the main gate. Though I often looked for him our paths never crossed again. I felt sad for him. Up to that point my last recollection of him had been a rolled up mattress.

The majority of our flight training was done at small remote airfields called stagefields. Each consisted of six paved parallel 100 yard long runways about 50 yards apart. The two in the center were reserved for the practice of auto-rotations (landing without power by using the free-spinning rotor blades to slow your descent.) The other four runways, two on each side, were used for general flight instruction.

'Rawhide' Stagefield

Each instructor was assigned two students. He flew the first flight training period of the day with one student and the second period with the other student. My first couple hours with my instructor (CW2 Mario Willars) trying to learn how to hover were a complete disaster. He hovered over to an "X" that was painted on one of the short stagefield runways. He sat the helicopter down and began to explain each of the controls to me, one by one. Then he pulled the helicopter into a 3 foot hover and again told me about the controls and showed me how they affected the machine.

While he let the helicopter hover, he allowed me use the pedals, turning the nose right then left. He retook control and at a 3' hover, showed me how the cyclic affected the aircraft and proceeded to let me use the cyclic. I carefully rocked the helicopter back and forth and to the right and left. He then retook control and again at a 3 foot hover, showed me how and then allowed me use the collective. I pulled power and then reduced it and we went up and down. What a simple process I thought. I can do this! I was an intelligent and well coordinated individual. I knew I would have little problem. He retook control again and had me do the same but this time with 2 of the three controls. I rotated through combinations of two. Then it was time for all three.

He retook control of the helicopter and again at a 3' hover, over the "X" he let me have all three controls plus the motorcycle grip to control the engine speed at the same time. Without wasting a moment, I was soon at an altitude of 50' still climbing and awkwardly moving backwards. I was way out of control. With no hope of regaining control, my instructor grabbed the controls and in a moment we were solidly back at a 3' hover over the "X". He wanted to know if I understood that I was supposed to keep it at a 3' hover. I said, "Yes but . . ." We did it over and over and each time I was doing no better. I was scaring the life out of myself! Even then, I had the utmost respect for the bravery of those primary flight instructors.

What soon became apparent was that every time any of the controls were moved the least bit, it changed the way the machine utilized the power it had available. The result was that every time any of the controls were adjusted in any way it required a compensating adjustment to all the other controls just to keep the machine "in balance". The more control movements that were made, the more compensating movements were required. It quickly became a never ending and increasingly difficult case of "chasing a dog's own tail" as it sped in a circle faster and faster. The key to the whole process was to refine the control movements so that smaller and smaller adjustments would have to be made thus easing the workload. That was a task easier said than done.

Finally on the third day with about 4.5 hours of flight time my flight instructor told me that he could not spend any more time exclusively on hovering, he had to start training on the traffic pattern. He flew one pattern around the stagefield, talking me through the process and then I was to do the second one. I was surprised that I did pretty well for my first time. When making my first approach, I was to return to that same painted "X" and to that same 3' hover.

My first approach was actually very good and I zeroed out my forward airspeed just at a 3' hover and right over the "X". I didn't say a word but I did keep it hovering. About 10 seconds later my instructor said, "See you can do it!" I happily said, "Yes." Then I promptly started climbing backwards out of control and he had to recover at about 50' in altitude. How embarrassing!

After that things began to fall in place rather quickly and I was making good and very fast progress. After another 1.5 flight hours, making a complete fool of myself became less of a regular thing.

At around 6.75 Hours of flight time, my instructor and I climbed aboard to begin flying the second training period of that day. I don't know what his other student did but he seemed to be in a very bad mood. I took off and flew around the stagefield and returned to a hover. He yelled at me through the intercom at the top of his voice the whole time. I knew I wasn't perfect but I didn't think I was really that bad.

I had to hover the hundred yards from where I had landed to where I was to take off again for another trip around the stagefield. I was hovering to the other end of the stagefield when CW2 Willars took out his swagger stick and began beating me over my helmet as he yelled at me. My helmet rang like a bell. Oh, what I would have given for a set of wheels on my skids so that I could have just rolled it to the other end of the runway. I was truly confused and quickly began losing my confidence. It seemed that every time he hit me the hovering helicopter jerked a little. The control tower quickly called down to my helicopter and asked if anything was wrong. My instructor told the tower not to worry. He was just beating the most stupid student he had ever had. That radio call was broadcast for everyone at the stagefield to hear. Damn, I was confused and embarrassed at the same time.

When I arrived at the other end of the ramp he told me to set down on the painted "X" we used for the take off marker. That was against the flight rules of the stagefield. Was this another test? He yelled, "SET IT DOWN!" So I did. He opened his door and started to climb out. I asked him where he was going because I was not permitted to move the helicopter without an instructor in it and I was sitting in a restricted area. He said "I'm getting out because you're going to solo now." I told him, "I'm not ready. You just told me . . ." He said, "You're ready. Remember three times around the stagefield, land it and get out, we will talk inside". He unplugged his helmet, closed the door and left me. I sat there for a few seconds, took a deep breath and then called the control tower for my clearance.

I was the second student in my class to solo. I was the second one that day.

That was the first day that the bus that was returning students back to the base stopped at the Holiday Inn in Mineral Wells, Texas. There were two crossed Huey rotor blades standing near the pool. When a student soloed, his classmates carried him under the blades and then tossed him into the pool for good luck. The water felt <u>reeeeaaal</u> good!

Frank Being Carried to His 'First Solo' Dunking

FLIGHT SCHOOL—A VERY CLOSE CALL ON MY FIRST SOLO FLIGHT TO A STAGEFIELD

The first time I flew solo off the main heliport was an exciting day for me. Three hundred helicopters all going one direction or another. I was by myself in the middle of this controlled mayhem.

I did a preflight inspection then started my helicopter and radioed for hover/taxi instructions for takeoff. I was able to take off without a hitch but before I got far from Downing Heliport, I heard a crack in my radio headset and my radio went dead. I decided to complete my flight to the stagefield and land with only 50 other helicopters around rather than fly back and fight the chaos of the three hundred helicopters at the main heliport without any communication. I flew the 20 miles to the stagefield, going over my lost radio procedures in my mind the whole way. Boy, did I feel lonely. When I arrived at the stagefield I began the procedures.

After watching the flow of traffic I entered on the downwind leg at 500' of altitude and a 45 degree angle while flashing my landing light. The tower flashed a green colored light gun at me acknowledging my problem and giving me permission to land. Wow, my first emergency procedure and all went smooth! I did make a mistake though. In my haste to get on the ground I did not look for the windsock.

What I didn't know was that the winds were in the process of changing direction and the tower was in the process of changing the traffic pattern direction but had decided to wait until I had landed. When I turned from the downwind leg to the base leg I had a quartering tail wind instead of a quartering headwind that would have naturally slowed me down during my approach. When I began turning final I only had a few hundred yards to touchdown. The visual clue I needed to watch for at that time was that the approach speed should look like a quick "walk" over the ground. I began to pull back on the cyclic to start slowing down and I reduced the power to begin my descent. I quickly realized that I wasn't slowing and I wasn't losing much altitude.

"Do something. It may be wrong but do something!"

While trying to analyze the situation I did the best I could, which was to continue the process. I kept pulling the cyclic back further and further into my stomach to put the nose of the helicopter higher in order to slow down. I reduced the power a little more but I still wasn't slowing at all. I didn't understand. What was I doing wrong?

What happened next took less than ten seconds. All of a sudden the bottom seemed to fall out of the helicopter. I was falling flat . . . skids down! I looked at my instruments and all my power settings were what they should be, except that my airspeed was absolutely <u>zero</u>. I was lower than five hundred feet off the ground, so I nosed over the chopper to gain some airspeed.

Now I was falling faster and I should be making my left turn to my final approach. My airspeed was still zero. I then decided I <u>was</u> going to crash and probably with little chance of survival. It would be better hitting skid first rather than nose first. At least there was some metal between me and the ground.

I had initiated my left turn to my final approach when I began to pull back my stick to level the ship before impact. I was below 150 feet in altitude when all of a sudden my airspeed jumped to 45 knots. That was way above what I needed to fly. I pulled in all the power the instruments would allow. Since I had already overshot my turn to the final leg of my approach I just continued my turn and slowly began to climb away from the stagefield. No, it's not over . . . .

As I began to climb out I saw that there were high tension power lines in front of me. All I could think about was that I just lived through the most horrific 10 seconds of my life and already there was another test before me. I pulled in more power than the engine instruments were marked to allow and pulled my stick back to climb up as straight up as I could. I still think I went between those electrical lines.

I circled around, redid my lost radio procedure and reentered the traffic pattern. When I turned my base leg I dove through it, thereby gaining speed. I wasn't going to repeat that experience. I landed and shut down the helicopter's engine.

I walked into the break room where the other half of the class who had not soloed yet were waiting for their turn to fly. A couple classmates tried to talk to me but I just brushed them off and sat in a far darkened corner of the small 'ready room' by myself. I heard one of the other students say "I don't know what happened but he is flushed white and won't talk to anyone".

An hour or so later my instructor came over to me and told me he was ready for his training time with me. I was going to get two periods of flying that day. I told him, "Thanks but no thanks. I'm done. I'm quitting flight school! I'm done and I'm just going to ride back to base on the bus." He said, "I don't understand. You are one of the most enthusiastic guys in the class. What happened?" I told him that I almost killed myself and it's just not worth that!" He said, "Let's walk. Tell me what happened."

We walked and talked for over an hour. All of a sudden we were at my helicopter. He told me to get in. I said "No, I'm going back on the bus." He said that I wasn't, "It left 15 minutes ago"! I had no way to get back to the base. Reluctantly, I said I would ride back in the helicopter but I would not touch the controls. I would do no more flying!

He took off and I sat there with my arms crossed, like a pouty little boy. As we flew towards Downing Heliport, he asked me again to tell him what happened. While I was talking he was setting up the same situation but this time from 2,000 feet above the ground. The bottom of the helicopter suddenly fell out . . . again! Talking me through the recovery as he performed it, he explained the situation the tower personnel faced with all the new pilots soloing. If they would have changed the traffic pattern at that moment, there would have been mad chaos. Then I showed up with no radio and they couldn't tell me about the changing wind conditions.

The important thing was that however I felt about the situation in an unknown emergency, however clumsily I recovered, I survived. I was able to think and react fast enough for the situation. That was something many guys can't do. He said that not only did I survive but I saved HIM a great deal of paperwork! Yes, he provided a little bit of much needed black humor.

Before heading west back to Downing Heliport we flew east towards Fort Worth, Texas and did a few "gun runs" on a train that was heading towards the town. It was the first time I was actually having fun flying.

Damn! He talked me back into flight school!

Thanks, Mario!

FLIGHT SCHOOL—MY FIRST FRIEND THAT CRASHED . . . AND BURNED

As primary flight training came closer to an end we were doing more dangerous training. It was a great deal harder but a great deal more fun also.

The last half of primary flight training consisted mostly of learning to land out in the middle of nowhere and then practicing and practicing some more. The government paid local ranchers to allow the training helicopters to use their land. There were three kinds of landing areas: white tire, blue tire and red tire. Those painted truck tires marked the landing areas.

White tire areas were the easiest and students were permitted to practice landings and take-offs at any time, with or without an instructor onboard. There was ample room all around for easy obstacle clearance.

At blue tire areas students were permitted to land and take off at any time with an instructor. They were a little tougher with either more obstructions or a harder approach. Once individually cleared by his instructor, a student pilot could land without an instructor onboard.

At red tire areas, which were the hardest, students were permitted to land and take off only with an instructor onboard. Either there were large nearby obstacles or they were located on cliffs or dangerous hills. I really remember one red tire area that was on the edge of a cliff. There was just enough room for the skids to fit. After landing, the tail boom of the helicopter was hanging completely over the 300 foot drop.

A White Tire Area

During solo periods we would practice landing at the white and cleared blue tire areas. During times an instructor was onboard we flew uncleared blue tire areas or red tire areas and sometimes even areas that weren't marked with that all important painted tire, though that was officially a no-no. When landing at any area while solo, we were required to slow the engine down to flight idle, friction down the controls, get out of the helicopter and walk at least 50 feet away. It was a way to make new pilots feel that they really had tamed that small mechanical beast. That simple act of walking away from it while it was still running did give me a strange sense of control. I don't know what it actually was but walking away from it in the middle of nowhere while it was still running and just waiting for me to come back to it, well . . . it was just 'neat'.

One day, I was preparing to take off during one of my solo periods and one of my fellow students came up to me. We weren't permitted to fly formation without an instructor but after leaving sight of the stagefield, we would often "join up" for a short formation flight around the area. We flew together for about 10 minutes then we headed off in our own directions to our practice tire areas.

Later I returned to the stagefield to refuel and pick up my instructor for a training period when, shortly after taking off, we received a radio call requesting us to keep our eyes out for my buddy. He was 30 minutes over due. I told my instructor where he was headed and 10 minutes later we spotted smoke and flew towards it. He had crashed . . . and burned. He had tried to crawl away from the rubble but was unable to do so. The fire finished the job. My instructor landed the aircraft in a way I could not view the results of the crash but I had seen everything before we touched down.

I had lost many friends in this flight school thing. Some were lost before flight school in basic training due to a failed physical. Many more were just suddenly gone from training one day with no warning but this was the first one who died. It was very sad that he had to die that way.

If I could lose a friend that quickly, then the only way to protect myself was to limit the number of close friends in this new profession of mine. It was another step in the hardening of my heart.

Frank's Primary Flight Graduation Photo

FLIGHT SCHOOL—THE FIRST HUEY CRASH I WITNESSED

After primary flight training was completed at Fort Wolters, Texas, 80% of my class went to Fort Rucker, Alabama and 20% of my class went to Fort Hunter-Stewart, Savannah, Georgia. Volunteers were requested for Savannah. I knew Savannah was a neat old Southern town. Fort Rucker, Alabama, was in a swamp. Naturally I volunteered and was sent to Savannah. There I go again, volunteering! It was getting to be a habit.

Our initial training in Savannah was in instruments. Then we had our Huey transition. During that transition, I witnessed my first Huey crash. It was a bit different from the aftermath of a couple crashes I saw at Ft. Wolters in the small TH-55 (Hughes 300).

It happened when I was making one of my first approaches with a B-model Huey. My instructor was in the left seat. I was a couple hundred yards behind another Huey about to touch down. He flared too deeply and put his tail rotor into the ground.

The Huey flipped onto its side and beat itself to death in front of me. The main rotor blades continued to beat the ground until the transmission tore itself from its mounts. Large amounts of mud and turf from the damp ground went flying in heavy chunks. It was the most horrific machine meltdown I had ever seen. Even through the vibrations from the Huey I was flying, I could feel every time the rotor blades hit the ground. I remember the massive amounts of dirt flying through the air. It was unsettling knowing that it was my first but more than likely not my last to witness.

My instructor took the controls; we watched the evolving mayhem and its aftermath from a very high hover. It was surreal, almost like watching a widescreen movie completely removed from the scene but no doubt I was there. I was watching it happen! It could have been a great disaster but only a machine was lost and no one was hurt. I guess because it was my first, if I close my eyes, I can see it happening all over again. If I had to explain it in only one word, it would have to be . . . <u>violent</u>.

FLIGHT SCHOOL GRADUATION—A 30 DAY LEAVE AND OFF TO VIET NAM

WORWAC Class 69-37
18 Nov 1969
Francis Strobel - 3rd Row 5th From The Right

Frank's Flight School Graduation Photo

After the graduation ceremony and before leaving Fort Hunter-Stewart in Savannah, Georgia, we were required to go to the dispensary. There we received <u>all</u> of our shots needed for overseas duty. We walked in a single line between medics with compressed-air injectors. I seem to recall we received three shots in each arm. A couple of the injections had multiple vaccines. At the time, we were told what they were all for, the only one that I particularly recall was "PLAGUE". Now <u>that</u> was unsettling! While on leave, I was sick with a fever for a week from receiving those shots all at once.

I packed my shiny green 1968 Ford Mustang and I headed back to Erie for my 30 day leave before departing for Viet Nam. It was a good but hard 30 days.

I had been away from home a great deal but for the first time I was faced with the real prospect of not coming back home again.

So without placing too much fear in my parents' lives, I tried to let them know how much I appreciated what they had done for me over the years. I did the same type of thing for my brothers and sisters and my friends. It was a long, busy and tiring 30 days. When December 26, 1969 arrived, the day I left for Viet Nam it was almost a relief. My last view of Erie was out of the airplane window, I waved to my Dad and Mom and my family, Lucy and to Bob and Pat Hayes and their family who were all standing there on the tarmac at the Erie, PA Airport waving.

Now maybe as I think about it, that was the hardest part!

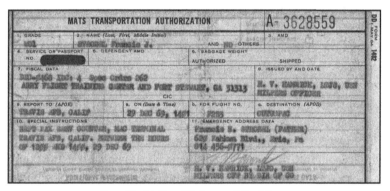

Frank's Airline Ticket to Viet Nam

3324 HOW'S YOUR MATH? . . . SISTER ANN STEPHANIE, MY FRIEND

In December of 1969, I was on my 30 day leave between graduating from flight school and leaving for my year long tour in Viet Nam. My sister Becky came home from Villa Maria High School, the all girl Catholic high school she was attending and told me that Sister Ann Stephanie asked how I was doing. Sister had been my 7th and 8th grade teacher at Our Lady's Christian Grade School. When informed that I was home on leave before departing for Viet Nam, she asked if I could stop by the school to see her before I left to go halfway around the world.

The following week, I dressed in my "greens", spit polished shoes and with my new Warrant Officer's Bars on my shoulders and my shiny new silver pilot's wings on my chest. I walked into the school shortly before 2:00 PM, which just happened to be during a class change. My chest was about as inflated as my waistline is 30 plus years later. The mass frenzy of girls laughing and talking while changing their classes immediately quieted to a hush and they stared at me as I walked past them down the hall. It quickly regained its volume and intensity as I left the hall and entered the school's office. By the time I reached Sister Ann Stephanie's classroom, the next class period had already begun.

I knocked on her classroom door and when she recognized me she quickly gave the girls some work and came out into the hall. She grabbed my right hand and said, "Francis Strobel, I need to talk to you." She always had been very strict in class and she was using her quick pointed voice that she used to use with me when I did something wrong. I was sure I had done nothing wrong recently and the stuff I did in 7th & 8th grade that she hadn't caught me with, well . . . . the statute of limitations surely had expired by that time. I didn't know what to expect as she walked me into the teachers' lounge still grasping my hand.

We sat across from one another at a small table as she grabbed my other hand. Then in a soft but stern woman's voice that took me completely off guard, looking at me directly in the eye she asked, "Francis, how's your math?"

How's my math?!?! That was not one of the questions I was expecting. I was expecting, "Is the Army treating you well?" or, "Was flight school difficult?" or, "What do you think about going to war? Are you afraid? Are you prepared?" That is what I had prepared answers for but "How's your math?" took me completely off guard. I knew my math wasn't perfect in 7th & 8th grade but I didn't think it was that bad! Was she going to give me another test? I am sure I stammered a little as I thought how to answer that question.

She then began to explain what her major concern was. "You know, Francis, as a pilot you will have to navigate and navigation requires extremely accurate math skills. I don't want you to make a mistake in your math and fly in the wrong direction. By doing so you could be in enemy territory and who knows what would happen." There was a true fear in her voice.

I explained that the Army gave me extensive training in map reading and navigation and I was very confident my math skills had developed enough to serve me well. We spoke for at least 20 minutes. Little did she know that as soon as we took off every day, we were already in enemy territory!

I will never forget the love and concern she showed to me that day. I left her that day with a tear in her eye and me with a very warm heart!

Frank Strobel
"Knight Hawk 6"

MY TIME IN VIETNAM

Just a reminder before I begin. *In the Preface I explained that in Appendix 1 there are comments from some of the other members of the internet discussion group on a few of my stories.*

The numbers at the top of each story or message refer to the number that was assigned to it as it was posted by the email message group forum internet address which is/was . . .

http:\\ groups.yahoo.com/group/114thAviationCompany.

It was an easy way to control what messages or stories were related to each other when placed in this listing. I included a few of the messages and replies that I received after posting a particular story to that forum, because those replies/memories enhanced the original subject and gave another person's perspective on that story. Most postings were from other pilots and aircrew members who flew during the Viet Nam War. If there is no number then the story was not posted on the internet.

1094 MY FIRST WAR STORY, AKA . . . MY FIRST TWO WEEKS IN VIET NAM

I'm somebody new to this forum. I have been monitoring this site with an automatic forwarding of all messages for months but I haven't seen many references to the men with whom I personally served during my tour in 1970. To help fill this gap I'm going to dive in with a war story about my first days with the Knights.

Frank on his way to Viet Nam

I left California on December 30, 1969 and arrived in Nam on a Flying Tigers Airline DC-8-63 late in the afternoon the following day. I was a 'real young' 22 year old. Most of my flight class (WORWAC 69-37) was on that plane. When we reached Saigon at 1600 hours, we were placed in a holding pattern for 35 minutes above Tan San Nhut airport because part of the airfield was being shelled. I remember talking with a lieutenant who was headed to the Air Cavalry (Air Cav) seated next to me. Both of us were shocked that this was happening in daylight in the capital city of the country.

After going through in-country processing, my flight class started getting split up. Who was going north and who south, who was going to the 101st Airborne or some other organization we never heard of before. To make a long story just a little shorter, after in-processing, eventually three of us were assigned to the same flight platoon, the 2nd Platoon (the White Knights) in the 114th Assault Helicopter Company in the Delta Region of IV Corps at Vinh Long. We looked at each other and marveled at our luck. Imagine us going through flight school together and then being assigned to not only the same unit but the same flight platoon. Things at that point suddenly became more comfortable. Gale Butcher, John Stevens and I knew that although there were many things we would have to adapt to in Nam, all three of us felt some little bit of security in this. A comfort level was achieved before we even arrived in the company area because we would be together in the White Knight Platoon. We teased Gale because the first evening we were in the unit, he walked into a small shelf in the hallway of our hooch that held a desk style phone. He cut himself slightly under his eye and we jokingly told him that he was after a Purple Heart already.

114th Aviation Company Shoulder Patch

Gale, John and I flew our in-country flight competency check rides together on January 4th or 5th and were to fly our first missions the following day. We talked with each other throughout an evening full of excitement and truthfully, a little trepidation. We spoke with some other "real live combat" pilots from our platoon and they graciously filled us in with some good information interspersed among many war stories. Some stories seemed wild to me but I was mesmerized knowing that the next morning I would begin my integration into their world. I was too excited to sleep well and was up a few hours before I was scheduled to fly that next morning.

My first day's mission was to fly people and supplies into the Moc Hoa area near the Cambodian border, north of Vinh Long. It was very uncomfortable wearing the very heavy bullet proof metal & ceramic breast plate. It was provided to aircrew to protect their chest from small caliber bullets. Little did I know that it would be with me every day for the next year. Everyone called it a "chicken plate". Chicken, in that you were afraid of being shot which I truly was.

I did my first high overhead approach that day to an outpost near the Cambodian border. The weather was great and no one shot at me. At least, I didn't know it if they did. What a day I had. I may have been a "Wobbly 1" (Warrant Officer, Grade 1) and "just" a co-pilot but my chest couldn't get any bigger without smashing my chicken plate from within.

We returned to Vinh Long about 1700 Hours and I couldn't wait to talk to John and Gale in order to exchange our first day's experiences. Shortly after we arrived back at our new home, I was told that Gale's Huey (Tail Number 66-16871) went down in the Mekong River. A day or so later his body, along with the rest of the crew's bodies, was recovered. Gale was officially declared dead January 8th. John Stevens and I looked at each other but I don't remember either of us vocalizing our feelings except our disbelief at the whole situation.

I remember going to the Vinh Long Chapel for the service. The four pairs of highly polished boots with the flight helmets on the altar was an extremely sobering sight to me. To this day when I hear taps, I think of him. My wife will confirm that I choke up and a tear or two always appears in my eyes every time I hear it played. I don't think the shock of his death so soon after our tour began has ever left me. My only consolation was that he died quickly and didn't suffer too much. But then again, how could I be so callous about one of my friends? This all was so new to me.

In my heart the only comfort I had was . . .
IT HURTS LESS TO DIE IN YOUR OWN UNIFORM
THAN IT IS TO DIE IN A HOSPITAL GOWN!

All of a sudden life and death became much more real to me. Not that I understood everything of which I was to be exposed. No, I didn't think Nam was going to be easy but his death on his first mission was very, very sad. I have often thought of how his family felt with him dying so suddenly in the first few days of his tour. I often thought of contacting them but never knew what I would say to them if I did.

Because Gale was so new to the 114th, none of the men in the unit knew him well enough to identify his body. I was flown to the morgue at Tan San Nhut Airport to identify him. It was the first but not the last time I would be in that unsettling room.

Naturally I kept being assigned new flight missions. I had very long days and no time off. I was kept so busy I hardly had a moment to think about Gale. His memory was still close and I felt guilty that I was too tired to mourn properly. Whenever I had a moment to myself I thought of him but those moments were few and far between. I didn't know if that was being done on purpose or if it's just the way things were in a war zone. I had never had a close friend die before and I was too busy to spend any time with "him". I look back on it now and it was probably a good thing for me. His death hit me harder than when my friend in flight school died but then Gale and I were much closer.

On January 13, 1970, I was assigned to my second combat mission and was introduced to my first Night Hunter-Killer mission. It was a single ship night mission in the Moc Hoa Area, so there was no backup for us if we got into trouble. I just assumed that was the way the mission was supposed to be done. We were flying the ship with the tail number '831' nicknamed "The Flying Coffin".

We flew one sortie with not much happening and returned to refuel and rearm. On our second sortie that night, we flew west out of Moc Hoa and over the Plain of Reeds. A couple minutes west of Cai Cai we began receiving .51 caliber anti-aircraft fire from three directions at once. The Viet Cong had set up their guns in a triangular formation a few hundred meters apart and no matter to which gun we returned fire, the other two had an unimpeded shot at us. Those tracers looked like medicine balls passing just in front of the left front side of the ship, the side I was sitting on!

I slinked down behind my armored seat with my eyes peeking over the sliding armored shoulder

"CHICKEN PLATES" ARE NOT SOMETHING YOU GET AT A RESTAURANT!

piece of the pilot's seat. I probably looked like Kilroy. We were steeply banking left as I remembered that my seat wasn't designed to stop a .51 caliber anti-aircraft round. I slowly sat upright. I was under fire for the first time.

I looked back in the crew compartment at our crew chief Jesse Sine who was directly behind me. He was standing with one foot outside on the helicopter's skid and his other leg was wrapped around the empty M-60 mount. There was nothing but his leg holding him in the helicopter. He was completely outside! Because of the helicopter's banking he was almost upside-down and he was holding his M-60 machine gun at arm's length letting its recoil support the gun. He was firing below the rotor disk and directly into one of the antiaircraft guns and HITTING IT REPEATEDLY!!!! His gun barrel quickly turned red hot. Damn, I was impressed! I never saw anything like it before or since. He was an immediate hero in my mind.

SP5 Jesse Sine and '831—The Flying Coffin'

I have always hoped he received some recognition for that! I have told that story many times and Jesse, if you are reading this, you have always been the "Star".

We were hit by those .51 caliber rounds numerous times as we turned east towards Cai Cai. No, I still wasn't flying the ship. I was the Peter Pilot (co-pilot) and was just along for the ride unless the Aircraft Commander was incapacitated somehow. The engine was hit and was rapidly losing power and we were losing altitude very quickly. My Aircraft Commander was able to extend our glide many hundreds of meters, possibly a click (kilometer) or so before we softly touched good old mother earth. It was a superb job of flying, especially with no lights in the middle of a very black night.

We quickly set up a perimeter around the ship and settled down, for what we didn't know. Was a click or so far enough away from those who brought us down? Was it enough to protect us? Was that enough space? I surely had no idea.

Everything was ghostly silent for about 10 minutes and it was going to be a long wait until dawn, the earliest we could expect any rescue. Jesse placed grenades around the ship to be used to destroy it if we were in imminent danger of being overrun. I remember looking over at my Aircraft Commander about 75 feet away from me and only seeing white eyeballs about 3 inches in diameter. Although he didn't say anything, he probably wanted me to close my eyes because they were twice the size of his and were probably visible at 100 meters. I started thinking about Gale and figured I had just come close to seeing him sooner than I really wanted to. It was just barely a week since he died.

All was very quiet and very <u>dark</u>! We were in a dry field. I tried to stay as close to the ground as I could. I could feel every small bump of dirt and each small pebble under me. I treated every one as a personal enemy, quietly sliding my body back and forth across the ground. I was trying to wear down the bump each of them created that held my body higher off the ground than need be. I was using the zipper of my Nomex flight suit as my own personal bulldozer as I slowly scraped that ground. Who ever thought that a metal zipper could be your best friend? You know you are scared when every 64th of an inch makes a difference in your mind.

A few minutes later we heard some rustling in a tree line about 50-75 feet away, north of the ship and then all quiet again. I was petrified and could hardly move. What was next? Then a loud whisper, "You guys okay?" I didn't say a thing, nor did anyone else! Then we heard it again, "You guys okay?" I looked at my Aircraft Commander, he didn't want to say anything either but after what seemed like an hour, he said in a loud whisper, "Yeah?!" The voice in the dark said, "Don't shoot, were coming in."

We had auto-rotated over a friendly unit Long Range Reconnaissance Patrol (LRRP) patrol. They saw us a hundred feet or so over their heads but we seemed to be very quiet. They thought that something was probably wrong and decided they would check us out. To this day, I consider it the luckiest day of my life.

What are the odds of us auto-rotating over a LRRP patrol in the middle of the night? With the infinite number of options that were available to them, they had they picked the same direction, the same path to patrol that we were forced to auto-rotate over. They secured our ship and contacted the American advisor at the South Vietnamese outpost at Cai Cai. The American at the outpost sent out a jeep to pick us up while we waited for a lift from "Road Service", the 114$^{th's}$ maintenance ship. Normally the stories you hear are about a patrol being rescued by a helicopter but this time it was the other way around. We were rescued by them. Just as easily it could have been a Viet Cong patrol that would have found us. No, more as likely as not, considering where we were, it should have been an enemy patrol.

The next day I was told that besides having the engine damaged by the anti-aircraft guns, one of the bullets hit the bottom of one of the "mixing levers", knocking off the safety wire and nut it was securing. That left only a loose pin holding our flight controls together. Those flight controls could have easily fallen apart and into many pieces. Had those controls failed, we would have lost all control of the helicopter and fallen into the blackness of the night. I would have been just another statistic.

The next day, sitting on the edge of my bunk, all I could think about was my first two weeks in Nam. How could <u>anyone</u> last 52 weeks? The odds were <u>not</u> in my favor. Now, those wild war stories that I heard my first few days in the 114th weren't as exaggerated as I had initially thought.

I quickly realized that I was flying with a great bunch of professional men and moreover, we were supported and protected by many others that I would never even meet. If you would ask anyone of them, they would say that they were just doing their job. I was honored to be associated with them all.

It was then that I made a vow to myself. If I could ever help a man on the ground, I would do everything in my power to do so!

Frank Strobel
"Knight Hawk 6"

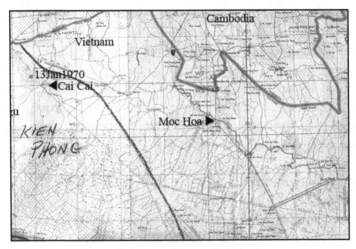

Map of the Moc Hoa—Cai Cai Area

Just short note: It was then that I found out that it was a company policy that an individual was not permitted to grow a mustache until their "cherry was broken" (their helicopter was hit by enemy fire.) I now qualified for this 'badge of honor'. So I began growing what was a very pitiful looking mustache but I kept it because I earned it! I have had it the rest of my life except for a short time in 1980 when shaving one morning while half asleep, I shaved half of it off. It was off for 2 months before I decided to grow it back. It was much easier the second time,

1259 MY SECOND WAR STORY, AKA . . . NIGHT VERTIGO

Things have been pretty quiet the last few days in this forum, so I thought I would write another "War Story". Here goes.

I was flying in Viet Nam about 7 weeks when I became an Aircraft Commander. I was very surprised when this happened since I had less than 200 flight hours since leaving flight school. My personal goal had been to make Aircraft Commander in my 5th or 6th month there. I figured that would be enough time for me to really get competent enough to do everything on my own and have the responsibility of an aircraft and its passengers in a combat zone. I had several of the older pilots tell me not to worry, that my skills were there. That didn't help my mind . . . completely. Now if something went wrong there was no one else to blame. It was all on my shoulders. I was assigned my first call sign, "White Knight 27." It was a great and proud day for me.

Frank's Aircraft Commander's Breast Patch

I was assigned "494" (four-niner-four) as my first ship. The first thing I did was go see her in her revetment. I had to spend some private time with her. Every pilot would say it a different way but a pilot must have a good relationship with his aircraft. I call it 'love'. Until that bond happens, a plane is just a pile of aluminum sheet metal and a few bolts. I believe that once there is a bond between a pilot and his plane great things can be expected in their relationship. That plane will work hard for its pilot. It will bring you back when it shouldn't. I spoke to every plane I ever flew. I wouldn't abuse it if it didn't abuse me.

My new ship, four-niner-four, was a "D" model Huey. It was old, not in years but it was obvious that she had an extremely hard life. The first thing I noticed was that almost every panel was painted a different shade of Army drab green. I softly touched every one of them. Obviously the paint job was a result of many repairs and replacements. It looked like a patchwork quilt. She had seen a lot of war but <u>she was mine, so she was fine!</u>

Note: I had been told that in flight school I would be taught how to keep a helicopter in the air and that in Viet Nam, I would be taught how to fly it. It wasn't until after I started flying in Viet Nam that I understood what that meant. In Nam, I flew a Huey in every possible type of scenario. It seemed that every flight was different and as a result I was able to learn many different techniques.

I had the opportunity to practice those techniques over and over, until they became second nature to me. That along with becoming totally familiar with the area of Viet Nam in which I was flying and the people with whom I would be working really made me feel like I had my feet on the ground. Did I know everything? Not by any means but I had a good solid base on which to build the additional knowledge I would need to be safe and competent. Before I was in Viet Nam 6 months, I felt as if I could make my Huey dance . . . just play the music! That is how comfortable I was at the controls.

The first few days with my ship I flew "Ash and Trash" missions. They were entered in our log books as Direct Combat Support (DCS) missions. In our off duty discussions we more lovingly knew them as the Mekong "Delta Cab Service". These were great missions for the new guy trying to get his feet on the ground with being completely in charge of the ship and no longer a co-pilot.

I remember the first day in the Aircraft Commander's seat. While standing on the skid and before actually climbing in and sitting down, I looked back at everybody getting ready to board and thinking, "Now everybody is depending on me to do things right. It was my responsibility to fly the aircraft, keep them safe and accomplish the mission."

Their lives are now in my hands. If something goes wrong I can no longer just point to the other pilot knowing that 'he' was in charge. From now on, it's all on me. A feeling of pride and a shiver of fear was with me as I left Vinh Long the first time on my own. Soon afterwards I flew a few combat insertions as my next step in my newfound independence. I was on my way.

A week or so later I was assigned my first night combat mission as the "Bug" ship, dropping flares from a couple thousand feet above the ground to light the way for a command and control pilot out of Soc Trang (The Tigers) flying the low ship. He was doing all the dangerous "dirty work". I figured I had the safe part of the mission. I was well out of small arms range and for the most part invisible to anyone on the ground. The only difference now was that it was at night.

Unfortunately there was a broken scud layer of clouds at around 2,000 feet and initially a heavy solid cloud layer a couple hundred feet or so above me. I was in a sandwich of clouds. I flew in and out of that upper layer on several occasions. I had little difficulty on the first couple of sorties, circling between the cloud layers while still keeping track of the low ship. I wasn't perfect in following the low ship but I think I was doing a pretty good job. On the third sortie that night, I followed "my boss" about five miles Southeast of Moc Hoa and began circling above him. The scud layer was filling in and I was having a tougher time following him. At one point, I was asked to stop dropping flares while he did "a little work".

I circled to the right in a standard rate turn for about 15 minutes, still between the two layers of clouds. It was now becoming a little boring. Nothing was happening. All of a sudden I felt a strong rush of air coming through my door's window and hitting my face. It was a little strange because the slip stream was obviously, not slipping past my chopper.

UP IS NOT ALWAYS WHERE YOU THINK IT IS!

I looked outside and everything looked fine, moreover everything felt fine. I then scanned my instruments a little closer. I was in about a 15 degree right (circling) turn but I was out of trim—no, way out of trim and nose low. My vertical speed indicator was showing that I was in more than a 500 feet per minute descent. I looked at my altimeter and I was rapidly passing through 1,000 feet. I was 1,000 feet below my intended altitude and yet I felt fine. I did not feel any type of descent and I felt as if I was in a very level, gentle turn. Then it hit me. I had vertigo.

Now watching my instruments, I started to correct my problem. I brought the cyclic slightly back and to the left. It felt completely wrong. Even though my instruments told me I had leveled out, I felt like I was climbing in a right hand turn. Now everything felt all wrong! I pulled in some more power and began a climb back to my intended altitude. Slowly my senses straightened around as I climbed out relying on my instruments. Making that correction was one of the hardest things I ever did in my life and it was something they try to drum into you over and over again during flight school instrument training.

"BELIEVE YOUR INSTRUMENTS, NOT YOUR BODY"

When I reached 2,000 feet and had myself reoriented to my mission, I said to my co-pilot, "Do you believe that. That was really close." He said to me, "What was close?"

Can you believe it? We almost died and neither of us would have known why. The rest of the crew members were also oblivious to the danger we just eluded. No one had any idea what we had just gone through. We would all have been standing together in front of St. Peter at the Pearly Gates wondering how we got there. I thank God I had my window open!

A valuable lesson was learned that was never forgotten.

No, I didn't tell them what had just happened.

Frank Strobel
"Knight Hawk 6"

Frank—New Aircraft Commander in Good Ol' '494'

This is just a random thought that needs to go somewhere . . .

One thing that took me off-guard was that several times during my first month at Vinh Long, the base was mortared at night. That made me very uneasy since the standing orders were that all pilots were to stay in their hooches during these attacks because they were not trained for ground combat. Pilots would just be in the way. This was true and I understood the orders.

I heard after one fight that several Viet Cong made it on base and were stopped about fifty yards from the 114th Officer hooches. What a feeling of hopelessness, uselessness and vulnerability to suffer a total inability to protect oneself.

Another night a couple mortar rounds hit about 25 yards from my room. This I did not like. I guess I took it personal. I didn't like sitting and waiting. Flying nights for me just had a plus side I hadn't expected.

1614 NUI BA DEN, AKA . . . MY FIRST "ARKLIGHT" SIGHTING

In January of 1970, I was just about as green a peter pilot as I could be and flying one of my first couple of night missions. I was sitting on the edge of my seat, never knowing what else was coming down the pike. It seemed that every time I flew with someone, at least one thing happened that would be an exclamation point in my mind. Everything was just so new to me. I never thought I was naive about the ways of the world but the ways of war were something different. I knew in my head we had the technological advantage during this war. My heart was no longer sure about the whole thing. I mean in the first two weeks I lost a flight school buddy and I was shot down in the middle of nowhere at night. I was doing a great deal of thinking. We were returning to refuel at Moc Hoa about midnight after a patrol west of Thuy Dong. I remember it being quite dark.

All of a sudden, as I looked past Moc Hoa, the Parrot's Beak, past Svey Rang in Cambodia and back into Viet Nam, there was a huge explosion! No, it was not one explosion. What I thought was one explosion quickly grew into a string of explosions. I remember saying out loud over the intercom, "What the hell is that?" I was told, "It's an arklight. It's a B-52 raid on Nui Ba Den. They're having a large battle up there on the mountain."

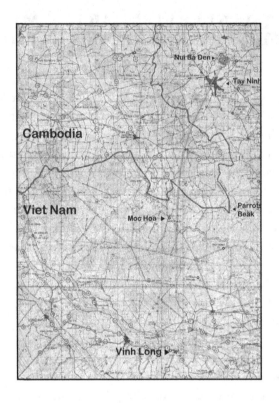

The string of explosions continued not only along the base of the mountain but some of the explosions were also climbing up the side. Each impact obviously had its own concussion. It was so real, so violent, I felt as if I should be feeling each of those concussions. Even though I was 60 or so miles away, I could see each of the jolts that had to have been felt by everyone anywhere near that battle.

In all of the movies I had seen in my life, I remember focusing on the flash of light associated with an explosionand I remember seeing the debris blowing out and away and finally falling back down to earth. They do not, however, show concussion in movies. Movie stuff? That was not what I was watching, as I intently watched the battle that night. I was witnessing more than just a bunch of bombs falling and "doing their thing." I could not see the debris falling in the night although I knew that it had to be there.

Yes, I saw the blinding flashes of light but I saw more than that. Even at that great distance at night, I was watching more than those great flashes. For the first time in my life, I felt that I could see <u>concussion</u>. Concussion has no shape. Concussion has no color. Concussion is not something really tangible. Concussion was only a word to me until that moment. I could see waves of concussion rolling out of each individual explosion until the cumulative effect of all of those individual explosions made the whole mountain appear to "roll".

Before it was over, I was briefly able to see the silhouette of the whole mountain. The area under attack seemed to expand to almost one-half of the Huey's windshield. It only lasted for a few seconds. Things quickly came back to normal. Everything was dark black and quiet. I do mean quiet. All I could hear was the steady whop, whop of the Huey's rotor blades.

No, I didn't hear a sound from all those bombs but it was all so vivid, so real, I am surprised that I couldn't hear it. My mind wanted to put sound to those explosions. It was too graphic not to have sound with it. There were no residual fires as I had expected to see; there was just the darkness. It was all over.

It wasn't over though for anyone near Nui Ba Den that night, on either side!

Frank Strobel
"Knight Hawk 6"

FOUR-NINER-FOUR—MY OVERLOADED "D" MODEL AS "TRAIL"

One day about a month after becoming an Aircraft Commander, I was flying troop insertions with "494". As I have said, she was a good ship but she <u>was</u> tired. She was beat. She had worked hard during her time in Viet Nam. I was flying the trail position of the formation. It was a position I had flown before. I liked it because if one of the other ships had any type of problem, it was my job to assist them. I was sort of the formation troubleshooter. I liked that extra responsibility. This day, though, I was the one who needed help.

IF EVERYTHING IS CLEAR AS A BELL, AND IF EVERYTHING IS GOING EXACTLY AS PLANNED . . . YOU ARE ABOUT TO BE SURPRISED!

It was a beautiful sunny morning and all the White Knight Slicks were sitting neatly in a row on a raised dirt road about 10 miles Southeast of Vinh Long. Soon the ARVN troops showed up and began loading onto our ships. Quickly everyone was loaded and the lead ship called for 'pulling pitch' (taking off). Just as everyone started to move, two additional ARVN soldiers ran up from behind my helicopter. It seems they had missed the chopper they were supposed to board. I radioed 'lead' and told him that I would load them and catch up. They all took off and I pulled pitch about ten seconds later but I didn't move! I was overloaded. Those two extra soldiers were just too much for 'old 494'.

My rotor and engine RPM began to fall as my rotor blades slapped deeply into the air. With those extra soldiers, I didn't have enough engine power to take off. So I used the engine boost and brought the engine up to 106% of normal operating power. That was the most we could coax out of the turbine engine. I began pulling pitch again and was able to get light on the skids but my rotor RPM began to fall again. If the rotor RPM fell far enough, not only would I not be able to take off but I would also lose my directional control and begin spinning and possibly flip over. I just couldn't break ground. I glanced up and the formation was now about a quarter mile away, a couple hundred feet in the air and slowly climbing.

I was very, very close to moving but just did not have quite enough power to go. I knew if I could get to about 18 knots I would hit translational lift, the natural flying efficiency of the helicopter would kick in. That would make things much easier but I had to get to 18 knots. The 'pucker factor' had definitely kicked in. Now I knew I was going to have to use all I had learned since being in Nam, just to get this thing up off the ground. I was going to be trying to fly at the absolute limits of this particular helicopter.

Although, the chopper was light on the skids and tipping forward at maximum power, it was still on the ground and wasn't moving. My final idea was rocking the cyclic stick lowly and gently left then right. That method would alternately take weight off one skid, then the other. It was a technique I had been told about called 'walking' the helicopter though I had never done it. I had never needed to use it. The helicopter was making great noise and vibrating heavily. Slowly it began walking down the road. It felt as if it was "stretching" left then right. It slowly began to move forward. It moved reluctantly at first but soon was at a walking pace.

Soon it began moving fast enough that I no longer had to walk it but the front of the skids were still scraping the ground. After several hundred meters on that dirt road I broke ground. I was only an inch or so over the road but I **was** flying! I could now use my power for airspeed or altitude but at this moment airspeed was most important. I kept the chopper just above the ground but in the next few hundred meters I was able to increase my airspeed to around ten knots. That was about half of what I needed to attain translational lift. I quickly looked up and the formation was almost a mile ahead of me now, ... but eyes back to the gauges.

The road was built on a twenty foot dike and the trees in front of me were getting close. I had to get off the road. I slid to my right, off the road and nosed over the Huey hoping to gain enough airspeed to hit translational lift. I did gain a few knots but was still a few short.

The chopper was now twenty feet lower than where I started and over water filled rice paddies. This was not somewhere I really wanted to set down . . . actually, crash. About a quarter mile later the helicopter finally hit translational lift and I could feel the aircraft shudder as the added lift kicked in. It was still way below treetop level and the engine exhaust gas temperature was climbing into the caution area of the gauge but things were looking up. I lowered the engine boost to 102% to help but was still able to slowly increase my speed.

I had to slide back and forth over the rice paddies several times to miss trees. Unfortunately, I was now coming to the end of the rice paddies and towards a full tree line. I had to use the airspeed that I had built up to do a cyclic climb (pull my stick back) to get higher than the trees. Once over the trees, I had slowed greatly but I was still over translational lift and flying. I think we took a few leaves. Whew!

The formation I was trying to catch up to was now about a mile and a half in front of me and about 1500 feet high. Me? I was still dodging tall tree tops. The formation had already crossed the Basaac River as I approached it. I had climbed to about 50 feet in altitude but after crossing the river bank I dove to just inches above the water and was able to increase my airspeed to 90 knots.

Finally I was not losing any ground to the formation. However the chopper was still only inches above the water. By the time I crossed the other river bank I was doing 110 knots and had climbed comfortably to about 50 feet above the trees. I was catching up to the formation as I watched them turn final for the Landing Zone. I caught up to them as they began their flare, slowing dropping my ship into the Landing Zone (LZ). It was a hot LZ (the enemy was firing their weapons) but that didn't seem to bother me as much as the take-off I endured just a few minutes earlier. My passengers were able to disembark at the same time their brothers did from the other choppers in the formation. All our guns were 'a blazing'.

The ARVN's were firing their M-16s from inside the helicopter as they were disembarking and with the M-60 machine guns from the Hueys firing, along with the radios and the normal helicopter noises, it made for quite a chaotic environment. I was trying to watch everything going on in my helicopter while thinking that if another chopper was shot down while hovering there I was still their cover, their help. My job wasn't over just yet.

I saw something that day in the LZ I had never seen before. I turned my head and watched an ARVN soldier jump out of the helicopter right in front right of me. He ran about thirty feet and then stepped on a booby trapped 105MM artillery shell. What a horrific sight! It blew him up into the air a great deal higher than the rotor blades of the helicopter from which he had just jumped. Flying through the air he looked like a rag doll. He then flopped onto and into the muddy ground. As fast as it happened it still seemed to be in slow motion. As the formation began to take off I quickly hovered over to the soldier. He was obviously dead. Had he been alive it probably would have been the fastest medical evacuation (med-i-vac) on record in the Viet Nam War.

We probably weren't in the LZ more than 15 seconds, yet all was in slow motion, it seemed like an hour.

I gave the controls to my co-pilot and he flew the chopper out of the LZ. After he climbed up a couple hundred feet or so, I rolled my seat back, stretched out my legs and closed my eyes. I didn't want to do that again!

Frank Strobel
"Knight Hawk 6"

HOW I INHERITED THE "NIGHT HUNTER-KILLER" MISSION . . . AND A BIT MORE

A number of the men in my association asked me how I got "stuck" with the Night Hunter-Killer mission. It's time that I come clean, so here goes.

Two weeks after making Aircraft Commander, they began being assigning me to nighttime as well as daytime combat missions. I enjoyed them all. Why not? It was all flying! During the day, I was flying troop insertions with the Knights. At night, I was flying the Bug ship for the Night Hunter-Killer Mission ship out of Moc Hoa. The Mission Commander was still from the 121st Assault Helicopter Company (The Tigers) out of Soc Trang. I didn't question why I was flying wing for him. I was too new to know that two ships from different companies didn't normally fly on two ship missions together. Shortly thereafter however, the Knights completely took over the Moc Hoa Night Hunter-Killer Mission.

At first I flew the Bug portion of the mission; they were assigning the more experienced pilots to the low flying Command and Control (C&C) ship. I was fine with that. I had been flying the mission for a couple of weeks and was beginning to feel pretty comfortable with my duties as an Aircraft Commander as well as the additional duties of flying Bug and dropping the flares accurately for them. I never flew in the low ship anymore. I didn't think too much about what the low C&C ship was going through. I was busy enough concentrating on accomplishing what I needed to do up top for him. Later around the Officer's billets, I found out just how frightened some of the guys were who were doing that flying.

After thinking about it I realized what was going on. No one liked flying nights, so the pilots were being rotated to share the load.

It seems simple but the pilots didn't like it for numerous reasons. The first and foremost reason was because they didn't do it very often and that in itself would just multiply the inherent dangers of flying combat at night. This was long before night vision goggles were developed. Different skills are needed to fly competently at night and to do the mission well. With the lack of continuous experience, the pilots would naturally cut corners on the general mission itself just to improve safety for all onboard. They would stay away from areas or situations that would stretch their skills too far. If something was going on they would be there but they just wouldn't look too hard for trouble that wasn't already in progress. I didn't blame any one of them for a moment.

With the mission being handled that way by the unit, an Aircraft Commander may not be rotated back into flying nights again for about two weeks. That may sound fair but it really was very dangerous. Being safe was an important goal at all times for everyone and I completely understood the unit's approach to the mission. By the time a pilot would start to become comfortable with night flying, he wouldn't fly the mission again for two weeks or more and would have to re-acclimate himself again the next time he was assigned. At night the terrain over which we were flying looked completely different. We couldn't use radio navigation and normal visual daytime navigation points were often unidentifiable. Flying nights was—well—just a different animal.

I made a comment one day to Lieutenant (LT) Osborne, our Platoon Leader, to the effect that if we continued flying those missions the way we were doing them, someone would be badly injured or killed accidentally. I explained all the details that I had been considering. He seemed to agree. A couple days later, he asked me to sit down with him for a couple minutes. He had been busy.

Evidently he had been getting flack from some of the other pilots and wanted to try to fix it. Whatever he decided would have to be approved by the Commanding Officer, so he would have to do a sales job.

We sat down and he began . . .

"How would you feel about taking over the Night Hunter-Killer mission, permanently as Mission Commander?" I was shocked. I wasn't prepared for that kind of question or a proposition for several reasons. I was still a relatively new Aircraft Commander and didn't have a great deal of experience to be completely taking over a combat mission.

Being my first assignment after graduating from flight school, I was a bit naive to the workings of the military. This was how I found out that in the Army, complaining in detail about a problem is a sure way of volunteering to correct it!

I felt the danger of the mission was definitely a legitimate reason to be concerned for myself. On the other hand if I accepted the job it might give me the ability to negotiate some perks. At least I hoped that might be the situation.

He then continued, "I've flown with you several times and your skills are there. You can do the job."

Obviously, the cream had started to flow!

I was the answer to a bothersome problem he had. If I wanted the job, this would probably be the only time it would be presented nicely. On the other hand, if they wanted to, they could just assign me to fly the mission and give me nothing. Hopefully, it was time to negotiate.

The 114th was just starting to receive the new Huey "H" Models to replace their older lower powered "D" models. We had just begun receiving about one replacement every week or two. With me being one of the the newest Aircraft Commanders, I would most likely be close to the last of the pilots to receive one. I wanted one of the new ships. I could ask for one.

The main reason I wanted a new ship was the fact that, although they were the same basic helicopter design of the "D" model that I was already flying, the "H" model had about 15% additional power and new radios, both voice and navigationand they would be working well. Together that would be a nice insurance policy to have at night far away from help.

LT Osborne continued, "Major Smith (the CO) agreed to allow me to give you a new callsign, "Night Hawk 6." That again was very shocking to me because the number "6" was always reserved for a unit's commander. Every commander with a callsign including the number "6" that I personally knew was a Commissioned Officer. It may seem like a small thing. I was a Warrant Officer, Grade 1 (the lowest rung on the Officer totem pole) and most Warrant Officers felt we were always treated like there was a class distinction. It felt like they had to "put up with us" and that was it. Adding a "6" was a good way just to jab at the egos of some of the Comissioned Offiers I knew. I knew many wouldn't like it. To me that alone was a plus; it simply would put a smile on my face. Oh, those little pleasures in life.

Another major factor that played a big part in my decision was how I felt about living my whole year in combat in Viet Nam. I truly didn't believe I would live out my year. I was fairly certain that I was going to die that year. I had made peace with myself and my God. It didn't matter to me if it was in daylight or at night. By taking this mission one of the other 114th pilots may not die. This was not altruism, it was just basic logic or so I thought at the time. Once you have made peace with yourself decisions like that are easy to make.

I wanted to know and so asked how the mission would be structured. He told me that as long as I performed the basic tasks requested by whomever I was assigned to on a particular night, he would not interfere. If I could not accomplish their requests I was to see him. What did that mean to me? It meant independence and a level of freedom I did not expect in Army, let alone in a combat zone. I was to find out later that it gave me much more independence than I ever could have imagined over there.

I asked to think about it overnight and indeed I did do a great deal of thinking. First, I realized that if I accepted and if everything worked, I would attain the third goal I had set for myself when I arrived in Viet Nam. If I didn't accept the proposal, I would be flying with most of the other men, doing formation take-offs and landings. That would mean mostly flying troop insertions, sitting in a field out in the middle of nowhere and waiting for something to happen the majority of each day. I would always be waiting for someone else's orders.

There was nothing wrong with that but doing that all day every day just wasn't for me. I could do it but would find it extremely boring.

Can you imagine being bored flying a jet powered helicopter in a combat zone? I have never been one to sit and wait.

In addition, I spent time thinking about the fact that by flying the Night Hunter-Killer mission, I would be on my own. That amount of freedom would come with a great amount of responsibility to protect a large number of outposts and the men in them. That could be overwhelming.

The last item on my mind was that my wing man and I would be out in the Area of Operations (AO) all alone at night. If either or both of us 'went down', help was not near. At best, it would be a minimum of 2-3 hours to get help out there if we went down for any reason. That is a very long time, especially if it was a combat related mishap. We would have to depend on each other; we would be completely on our own every night. The fact that help was not close by was not a comforting thought.

My Decision? To ask for the world and negotiate down from there. I met with LT Osborne the next morning and told him that I would accept the position if he could do a few things for me.

First, that I receive the next new "H" model that came into the company and I explained to him the reasons why.

Second, there needed to be a permanent crew that would fly the mission with me regularly. Crew cohesiveness would be extremely important because of the dangerous and stressful work. In addition as part of my crew there needed to be additional (5th) crewmember to handle the Xeon Light and the Starlight scope and to serve as an extra gunner when needed. Although every ship had an assigned pilot and crew chief who flew with it, no ship that flew combat in our company had a permanent crew.

My third request was for Pasqual Mantanona to be my crew chief. This suprised LT Osborne because "Pas" was not a school trained crew chief. He was trained as an Airfield Fireman. However, I had seen how Pas worked. He was a gunner at that point and wanted to be a crew chief, so he spent many extra hours every day working on any helicopter that needed work done. He was a quick learner and if he didn't know something he would always ask a knowledgeable person to get a correct answer. Besides, I had already been witness to his courage. I wanted him on my crew. He would also get a promotion and that would keep him happy. Just like your wife or girlfriend, you MUST have a happy Crew Chief.

Fourth, I wanted a slightly different call sign. I didn't want "Night Hawk 6", I wanted "Knight Hawk 6" because our helicopter company was called the "Knights of the Air". That I felt, would be easy to concede if I had to give something away during our negotiations.

He took my offer to Major Smith and came back an hour later and said . . .

Number 1—Is approved

Number 2—Is approved, except that we need to change your co-pilot for training purposesand

Number 3—He really didn't understand my choice but if I really wanted Specialist 4 (Spec-4) Mantanona, he was mine.

Number 4—This was a problem because it is so close to the CO's call sign (Knight 6) but surprisingly, it also was approved.

I was shocked. For all intents and purposes, I received everything I requested. That scared me! Then I thought, "Why didn't I ask for more?" It would have been nice to have ice cream for the crew every Friday!

That's the moment I became **"Knight Hawk 6"**.

The next day, I was told that "085" (serial number 69-15085) was mine. Together, the crew named this beautiful new ship "The Devil's Disciple". We thought the name was appropriate for the job we were doing at night. It was a new ship to the company with only 20 recorded flight hours. I had my own <u>new</u> Huey. It even smelled new and previously I had no idea what a new helicopter was supposed to smell like. What a special time I had walking out the ramp to her the first time and spending a couple hours, "just getting to know her". We talked together for quite awhile.

"085" and Her Newly Painted Nose Cover

That night was the first night I used my new call sign. I had flown to the Green Beret Camp (B-43) near That San in the Seven Mountains. I called my normal inbound radio call, stating 'Knight Hawk 6' was inbound and would be landing in five minutes. The radio operator called back and said, "Say again call sign." I repeated it, truly thinking nothing special out there of it at that moment, just that it was a new call sign to them. When I sat the helicopter down every Commissioned Officer and all of the Senior NCO's met me with bells on. With my call sign ending in "6" they expected a high ranking Commissioned Officer.

When they found out that it was just me, a lowly Warrant Officer Grade 1 . . . well, I am sure there was a great deal of grumbling as they filed back into their bunkers. I was sternly asked who gave me that call sign. I explained and never heard anything about it again. Unexpectedly, the ego jabbing had begun. Now I had to show them I could do the job.

I soon realized that my life in Viet Nam had completely changed!

I did enjoy flying my Night Hunter-Killer Mission. I liked being on my own. It was exciting and I enjoyed every minute of it . . . well almost. There was a great deal of combat at night supporting the troops on the ground and the outposts but being the only aircraft in the area at night, I also did numerous med-i-vacs. I guess that had to be expected . . . with combat come casualties. Several med-i-vacs were out in the middle of God's country with their buddies having to use "directional" battery powered hand held strobe lights while they were under very heavy fire. They substantially increased my blood pressure. If we weren't there though, at best a wounded man would have to wait until morning for a flight. We could have him to a medical facility in an hour and usually much sooner. That was a very important part of my satisfaction with the whole night mission scenario.

CLEANING UP NEVER ENDS BUT IT'S EVEN WORSE WHEN IT IS STICKY AND RED!

The missions were all very exhilarating and the fact that I was never sure if I would survive any individual mission made it even more so. That idea was always on my mind. Would the "Golden Bullet" arrive today? It was a dangerous mission and it was exciting but . . .

I found pluses and minuses in my new status as a Mission Commander. The first morning after returning to Vinh Long I stayed with "085" to do my post-flight inspection. I then helped clean up everything so that my new ship was ready for the coming night's mission. It only took about an hour and a half and I was fine with that. We had flown her quite hard. I then grabbed my helmet and all my maps. At that point the new Mission Commander happily strutted the ¼ mile down ramp 1 to Flight Operations.

Once in Operations, Captain Papapietro, the Operations Officer, asked me a great number of questions about my first night as Mission Commander. About twenty minutes later I turned to leave for the two minute walk to my bunk for some badly needed sleep and he said, "Where ya going"? I said, "I have to get some rack time. I have to take off in about 5 hours for tonight's mission. He said, "You haven't completed your After Action Report yet!" Personally, I had completed many reports but never that one.

New Helicopter, New Job, New Call Sign, New Title: Mission Commander

. . . NEW PAPERWORK!

The Mission Commander had to document the number of ships with him, where they went, who was supported, whyand what was done. I also had to list the resources used, everywhere we fired a bullet and what was hit and the results. That is a lot of information. In duplicate, so carbon paper was required. I sat down at a desk and began writing. I felt like a kid taking a test in high school. It took me about an hour. It wasn't handed back, so I assumed I passed.

Three hours of sleep later I got up for the next night's mission. Less dilly-dallying after the mission, though from then on. It was a lesson quickly learned.

After flying the mission for a couple weeks I realized that there was an extra unexpected perk. No one ever asked me any type of question as to, "Why I would fly so many hours, or why did I go here or there?"

Helicopter assets were always very closely guarded. Then over the next several weeks, I overheard numerous conversations at the Green Beret Camp, Bravo-43. They would ask many times, without success I may add, for a helicopter to move an individual or some supplies to one of their outposts or back. I told them that as a convenience, I would help when I could but would not be used as their main mode of transport.

I think it worked out well for the Green Berets. I would do something once or maybe twice a week for them. We would sometimes integrate these "missions" with our normal daily missions when possible and it didn't add more than an hour or so of extra flight time per week. They were careful in how they used me. Occasionally, a case of steaks would suddenly appear in my cargo compartment. That is how the White Knights were able to have their BBQ's in 1970.

White Knight Platoon BBQ

One thing that I didn't realize at the time was that I was getting used to the feeling of adrenalin in my system all of the time. It became important to me to have that feeling. This is something the ramifications of which I wouldn't appreciate until much later.

One particular routine that I definitely remember, though, was that every day as we left the officers' hooch for the flight line, we pilots would openly talk with each other. One saying to the other, "If you don't come back today, I would like your desk fan or I would like your stereo!" The other responding in kind, "It's yours" as he walked out. It was a bit of dark humor but we were serious because that was just the.environment we lived in.

As far as some of the flight rules we followed in 1970, I don't know where they came from or when they were implemented. You have to remember I was a Warrant Officer, not a real live Commissioned Officer. I have no idea if the 140 flight hour per rolling month limitation was just within our unit or not. I was told that it was the "law" so I followed it like every good Warrant Officer did with <u>all</u> the other rules and regulations. All I knew was that I loved flying, I was there to fly and I would have flown more hours had I been permitted.

The flying limitation was actually 120 logged flight hours in any 30 consecutive day period and after crossing that limit a pilot was required to get clearance from a flight surgeon to add an additional 20 flight hours for a total of 140 in that 30 day period. As far as I was aware, it applied to every aviator. After 140 hours, I understand that you could only fly additional hours in a combat emergency. I'm sure Miles knows the actual rules. After every flight we had to add the new day's hours to our tally board in our hooch remove the oldest posted hours and then re-compute the total hours. I know I was never turned down for a 20 hour extension but I was never authorized to go higher than that. Earlier in the war this rule didn't exist. This is just another example of a creeping increase in regulations as the war went on.

I had no flying rotation in my mission except the 140 hour rule. At times when a great deal of flying had been done, I would have several days off in a row, until my hours would return below 120. Sleeping? At first, I had a fairly difficult time of it because of the daytime noise around the base and the heat, except that I was usually pretty wiped out by the time I hit the sack.

Frank and His Room before Remodeling

I ended up remodeling my room. First I bought a used small window air conditioner from an officer returning to the States and then I added a small refrigerator. Next I built a bunker under my enclosed bed, complete with a light, books to read and a bottle of scotch.

I sold my room to two newly arrived lieutenants for $450 when I left Nam. If you think that is just a story, I have pictures to prove it.

Frank's Remodeled Room

Frank Strobel
"Knight Hawk 6"

A MAN HAS NOT LIVED UNTIL HE HAS ALMOST DIED . . . FOR THOSE WHO HAVE FOUGHT, LIFE HAS A FLAVOR THE PROTECTED WILL NEVER KNOW!!
. . . and I do believe this is true!

Just a footnote. This item was discussed at the 2000 reunion. The total hours I logged on "085" while in the company was over 2,000 as listed on the 114th Company's website That data was taken from the company records. If I read it correctly '085' had more in Company flight hours than any other helicopter. I am absolutely sure that was due to how hard we flew her at night when she was new with me and the Knights. She was a very good ship. She never failed me or left me wanting. Yes, when I left Nam it had quite a few bullet hole patches but that just gave her some character.

I ended my tour in Viet Nam with a two week "early out." An early return ticket back to the real world was given to me by President Nixon. In actuality, I flew just short of 12 months (1327 flight hours) in country. After I heard the details of the new early out policy, it cost me two cases of beer to a clerk in the battalion personnel office to do my paperwork on Sunday, December 20th. The following Friday was Christmas.

Reflecting on my new 'Mission Command' status, I realized . . .

I had set three goals for myself when I arrived in Viet Nam.

First, it was just a matter of hanging on in order to plant my feet on the ground.

Second, was to get as much stability as I could in a mostly uncontrollable situation.

Finally, grab as much control and personal freedom as I was able."

My personal feeling was that I had accomplished my first goal.

I felt I had accomplished my second goal when I was made an Aircraft Commander.

Now, with being Commander of the Night Hunter-Killer Mission; My three goals were accomplished <u>and it was only March!</u>

1583 MY FIRST NIGHT MEDICAL EVACUATION

Part 1

This incident took place very, very early in my tenure as an Aircraft Commander. I was flying Bug for a night mission with my flight lead from the 121st AHC Tigers out of Soc Trang. Flying west of Moc Hoa we had received fire on several occasions that night. Around 2:00 AM, as we were flying out of Moc Hoa having just refueled and restocked our flares, we received a 'May Day' call from one of the Navy's small river boats, a PBR. It had been under fire from an ambush along the canal and had been hit in the stern with a B-40 rocket. As we arrived on station we found that the stern was completely missing and one of the Navy crewmembers had a severe head wound. Some of those PBR's (the Model 2's) had a .50 caliber machine gun mounted at the stern. If this one was equipped with one, it was gone. Thanks to the liberal use of foam in its construction, the boat was in no danger of sinking.

With the extra Navy personnel on board and having just refueled and rearmed, my flight lead was very heavy and didn't feel that he would be able to safely complete the med-i-vac. He asked if I could do it.

As we reached the area we had no problem locating the fire fight. They were under heavy attack. The Mission Commander immediately started giving the boat crew air support while I lit up the area slightly away from the canal where most of the enemy fire was originating. Within 10 minutes the fighting dwindled by about 90 percent. Although there was still some sporadic firing, I was asked again, if I thought it was a "do-able" job. Up until that moment I had never done a med-i-vac, let alone one at night under fire.

As a new Aircraft Commander this was the first time I directly asked myself a question that I asked many times that year. "If I were the guy hurting on the ground; would I want me to try?" I always seemed to answer, "Yes!" I always felt that the way a person handled high stress situations defined them as an individual. Maybe this was my time. Wendell Jarrett was my left seat and newly arrived in Viet Nam; we both felt that we should at least attempt the evacuation and see if the incoming fire would be too much to handle or not. When your life is on the line, that is when you learn about yourself. Only at that moment in your life do you really know what you are made of!

The boat was floating in the center of a small canal that, in the dark, looked to be no wider than 75-100 feet, or not much wider than the Huey was long. My new concern was the trees hanging out over the water that were very difficult to see. Hitting one of those trees especially with my tail rotor, would be disastrous not only for those of us on the helicopter but also those below, on the crippled boat. We made our approach to the far center of the canal, just to the stern of the boat with my Huey perpendicular to the canal. My flight lead was spraying both sides of the canal with his M-60's to suppress any fire he could. I came to a hover with my skids touching the water.

Even in the darkness it was immediately obvious that my ship's cargo compartment was several feet above the exposed deck of the boat, making removal of the wounded seaman impossible. I started sinking my skids into the canal water, trying to get low enough to make the extraction do-able, yet at the same time watching my rotor disk to make sure it did not contact the top of the boat since they were overlapping. That would have been embarrassing! I was now low and close enough that my rotor wash was blowing the boat down the canal. Meanwhile, the fire fight was regaining its intensity. I began dragging my wet skids sideways down the canal slowly chasing the boat—sideways!

I finally got close enough that Pas Mantanona (a new gunner for me that night) was able to get hold of the wounded man but he was unable to drag him into the cargo compartment. Pas was very strong yet he didn't have enough strength and leverage to make that transfer. He climbed out of the helicopter, one foot on a slippery wet skid and one foot on the open damaged deck of the boat! My Crew Chief moved to the other side of the helicopter to help Pas, leaving no defensive gun on that side of the chopper. Soon the transfer was made.

The adrenalin was pumping hard and there was too much noise to hear much of anything through the intercom. I then saw something that made me smile but only for a second. I glanced over at my co-pilot Jarrett and he was firing his .38 caliber pistol out the window, laying down an intense barrage of fire with all six rounds his pistol carried. Obviously singlehandedly, he was making all the enemy fighters on that side of the ship cease fire and keep their heads down low!

I finally heard someone and I don't know who, in all that confusion, yell "GO GO GO"! I pulled as much power as the engine gauges would allow and then beeped in the maximum power available. We very slowly began to climb up and over the trees lining the canal. I knew we were draining a lot of heavy water from our belly as we gradually climbed out. With the water's weight the climb out was extremely slow and stressful on the ship. It was noticeably creaking as it reluctantly began to rise.

At about 300 feet AGL and about 60 knots of airspeed the Huey shuddered and the windshield in front of me smashed with cracks in the Plexiglas going in all directions. I remember calling my flight lead and telling him I was hit; actually I was probably screaming at him that I was hit. As I looked over my instrument panel, Jarrett told me that all the gauges looked normal. I was able to fly looking through the right corner of the windshield and out the pilot's side window.

We flew as quickly as possible to a hospital near Saigon and shut down the Huey to check the ship's damage. A medical team quickly tended to the seaman. Once the engine was shut down and my feet were on the ground someone said to me, "We made it!" It was then that I began to shake and had to lean against the nose of the ship to help myself remain standing. I took a deep breath and that oxygen felt <u>very</u> good. I needed that oxygen badly.

As we started inspecting the damage to our ship, Pas Mantanona came up to me and said, "Mr. Strobel, thanks for staying so close to that boat during the evacuation . . . I can't swim!" Oh, my! My heart skipped a beat, maybe two or three. Here was a guy with one foot on a wet slippery, hovering, vibrating Huey skid, one foot on the deck of a moving, damaged boat floating down a canal and physically transferring a wounded man in the dark of night while in a fire fight and he can't swim!

Had I not kept the correct distance from the damaged PBR he could have fallen into the canal between the two ships. I have no idea if we could have ever found him let alone rescued him in the dark. I was very impressed with this young man. I immediately knew he was the kind of person I wanted to have at my side. It was the first step in my getting to know the man who would eventually become my crew chief and a great friend. Although I didn't know at that moment, he later was to become the man whom I depended upon to "cover my six" when I took over the Night Hunter-Killer mission. How lucky it was that I met him.

We were shocked when we looked at the damaged windshield. It wasn't cracked like I thought. We had a bird strike. We hit a large dark colored bird, probably a hawk of some kind. Its entrails were splattered across the window and they spread in all directions. The lights from inside the aircraft highlighted those entrails and made it look as if it were cracks in the windshield. The rest of the bird bounced into the spinning rotor head, what a mess that was.

I have always wondered if that Navy seaman made it, I sure prayed he did.

I learned a great deal about myself that night. You never know if you can actually use what you learned when everyone is depending on you to perform, until a situation presents itself, especially the first time. I felt I used everything I had in me that night and I was exhausted. I had said a few silent prayers during the mission, or maybe they were just parts of prayers. The Man above must have been sitting on my shoulder too.

No permanent damage was done, except to my nerves. We returned to Moc Hoa about 0330 or 0400 hours and went inside for a mission debriefing and then received an updated briefing for a new mission. I don't know if it showed or not but inside I was shaking pretty good. The MACV team was not happy when I found out that everything was pretty quiet in the AO and I told them I was going home. I told them that I didn't think I would be much good for them the way I was feeling. So I "picked up my football" stuck it under my arm and I headed south, back to Vinh Long. That night as I was making my approach, the flickering flames along the main runway really looked good to me. They told me that I was home.

Just a quick note: The runway at Vinh Long did not have lights for use at night. The runway was lined on both sides with 55 gallon drums that were cut in half and filled with JP-4 (jet fuel) and lit to provide a little light. From a distance, the lights looked like they were flickering as they blew in the wind.

The next morning I was ordered by a flight surgeon at Vinh Long to start drinking scotch, or at least that has always been my interpretation of his orders. I have been drinking scotch ever since but that's another story.

Part 2, Another Story . . .

After getting to my bunk I didn't sleep. I had a bad case of the "what if's." I didn't feel very hot as the sun rose the next morning. I went to sick call to maybe get some Pepto Bismol to settle my stomach and something for my pounding head. The flight surgeon took my blood pressure and asked if I had had any stressful situations recently. I gave him a Readers Digest Condensed Version of the preceding night. He promptly grounded me and said, "Your blood pressure is up because of the stress of that situation. Normally, I don't prescribe alcohol but you need to relax. Get drunk tonight and come back to tomorrow morning's sick call and see me." I wasn't a drinker, if I had three beers a week I thought I was imbibing a great deal. I went to the Officers' Club that night with a couple of the guys from the White Knight platoon but there was a major problem. They had not received their shipment of alcohol and they were out of everything but scotch. I hated scotch. Over the entire evening, I had two drinks.

Early the next morning, I went to sick call so I could be returned to flight status. The Flight Surgeon took one look at me and said, "You didn't get drunk last night!" I told him that I felt much better; I had a couple drinks and a very relaxing evening. He said, "You didn't get drunk, I'm grounding you for another day. You know that if I have to ground you tomorrow (a third day), it is a mandatory 30 day medical grounding!" I wasn't sure if that was the case but I couldn't take the chance. I was in Viet Nam to fly. I was not going to get grounded out of my dream! I knew that the Army was not going to give me a 30 day vacation. If grounded, I would probably be assigned as Supply Officer, Mess Officer, Latrine Officer or Three Foot Stack of Paper to Complete in Triplicate Officer, or some such additional duty. That was not why I was there.

That night, I went back to the Officers' Club with a couple White Knights. They still had not received an alcohol delivery; they just had a great deal of scotch. Even though I didn't like the taste of scotch, I did it good that night. I really got blitzed! I don't even remember going back to my bunk. The next morning, Smitty and Tabacka got me out of bed for sick call. I was still gone. They started me up the gravel street towards the dispensary.

My right arm was over Smitty's shoulder, my left arm over Tabacka's. At one point, I was focusing, (Okay, maybe focusing is not the word!) down towards my feet. They weren't there. I remember asking, Smitty, "Where the H— are my feet?" as they dragged behind me. When we arrived at the dispensary the flight surgeon lifted my head up by the hair on my brow and said, "He can fly as soon as he's sober." He never even took my blood pressure.

That evening at 1600 hours I was flying my mission again. I was shocked, I had no hangover. I truly felt refreshed. Maybe this scotch stuff wasn't as bad as I thought. Actually, it is still my drink of choice.

Frank Strobel
"Knight Hawk 6"

2842 ROAD SERVICE—MOC HOA

One night during the monsoon season, we were forced to cut short one of our Night Hunter-Killer sorties near Moc Hoa by a low ceiling and an on and off driving rain. We landed and sat off to the west side of the runway waiting for the weather to break enough for us to resume our work. The rain was pounding down; we couldn't even open the doors to get some fresh air. The guys at the MACV compound at Moc Hoa were very frustrated by our lack of flying. They pointedly and sarcastically asked on several occasions within an hour, if we had any intention to return to the air. I explained the weather problem but to no avail; they still wanted us up flying. I didn't let their complaints worry me too much. If they had been pilots I am sure they would have never left the ground to begin with.

Although it didn't look promising after another hour or so, I cranked up to circle the airfield and check on the ceiling, the visibility and the turbulence. When I started my ship, Bug started his ship and called me on his radio. I told my Bug to stay at flight idle while I went up and took a look around. I wasn't too convinced that we would actually go back out in the A/O (Area of Operations). This way if I would return immediately, we wouldn't have two ships up at the same time in that weather mess.

I took off to the south and as I reached 300' AGL we started into the base of the clouds. Bug needed at least 2,000 feet to do his mission so obviously it would be a no-go. It was beginning to rain extremely hard again. I radioed back to my Bug and told him that I was returning to the airfield because of the rain, the lack of good visibility and a very low ceiling; besides, the lightning was tremendous. He radioed back and said that he could easily see my lights but he could see no lightening in the sky. I asked him if he was blind because it was in front of me, all across the horizon! He again said that he could see no lightning.

I then refocused and found that the "lightning" was <u>inside</u>! I had a fire in my overhead electrical panel and electricity was arcing all the way across the inside roof panel of the Huey. To me initially it looked like a huge fire, probably because it was only about 10 to 15 inches from my helmet and the fact that the outside sky was as black as pitch. I made a quick U-turn and landed downwind on the runway as our fire extinguisher was generously used on the problem. I couldn't get it on the ground fast enough!

At dawn with some light and the storm easing up, Bug returned to Vinh Long and while he was enroute, called Road Service (our company's helicopter repair team) for me. Road Service had us patched up and returning to Vinh Long by 11:00 AM.

Thank You, Road Service.

Frank Strobel
"Knight Hawk 6"

ATTACKS ON THE GREEN BERET CAMP—BRAVO 43

Part 1

The events in this story exposed to me for the first time just how powerful the word of the press is. More powerful than I ever knew. Their reporting can imprint things on a person's mind that takes actual visual proof to disprove. This story may seem a small example but none the less proves in my mind that power exists. It begins about 10 days before Easter 1970 at the Green Beret Camp of Bravo Team 43. It was near a South Vietnamese Army Base at Chi Lang.

It was dusk and I was flying out to the Base Camp for my normal evening briefing before I began my Night Hunter-Killer Mission. As usual I called them when I was about five minutes away to alert them of my arrival. That was normally the last time I talked with them until I was actually on the ground and in their briefing. This night was different. It seems, as they told me on the radio, that they had received some information alerting them to an attack that was expected on their base that night. I was asked to fly their base's perimeter to see if I saw something out of the ordinary. I gladly said I would.

I was in a slightly different situation that night onboard my helicopter. I was flying with a new co-pilot. That in itself was not a problem because it happened all the time but unfortunately he was brand spanking new! He had been in our unit only about a week and had flown a few ash and trash missions but nothing in the Seven Mountains Area of the Delta and he had flown no combat missions, let alone a night mission. He wasn't prepared to fly the Night Hunter-Killer Mission but it wasn't his fault. He was assigned to it! The first time I had ever seen him is when he showed up at "085's" revetment ready to fly. Naturally he was afraid; this was all new to him. I didn't blame him for a moment. I would have been very apprehensive too if I were in his shoes. I tried to talk to him on our flight out to Bravo 43 but there was nothing I could say that would adequately prepare him for what was to come.

As I approached Bravo 43 I told him what I was going to do. I slowly flew around the perimeter of the base and personally saw nothing out of the ordinary. I called that information back on my radio and then made my approach to their landing pad where Bug was already sitting. I shut down the helicopter and took my new copilot into the briefing room. The Major started. They expected the base to be hit at any moment so he was going to cut the briefing short so that we could get back up in the air. He then said, "So you didn't see anything around the base?" I said, "No. Things looked pretty quiet!" My Copilot then said, "I saw something."

I looked at him with a very surprised look on my face and said, "Why didn't you say something to me?" and then immediately, "What did you see"? "Well, I say someone crawling in the wire but he wasn't wearing black pajamas so I wasn't worried about it!" As he started that last statement the briefing had already come to an abrupt end as everyone started running to their duty stations. Everyone at the briefing knew that 'black pajamas' were not the uniform of the day for the Viet Cong. They wore normal everyday Vietnamese clothes that could blend into the surrounding population after an attack. I was up and running to my helicopter yelling over his statement to follow me. My new copilot quickly learned not to believe what was being broadcast in the press!

Bug and I both quick started our ships and took off through volleys of small arms fire! We gave B-43 cover fire through the next several hours, refueling and rearming at Chau Duc, which was only a 10 minute flight away.

In my copilot's defense he was new from the States and the media always referred to the Viet Cong as wearing black pajamas. That was his frame of reference. I guess I never even thought to brief him on that fact.

Part 2

One day I began my Night Hunter-Killer Mission with our normal briefing at the Base Camp B-43. The briefing wasn't even completed when all hell broke loose. The base was being hit from all sides. As we arrived at our helicopters our crew chiefs and gunners had already removed the machine guns from the helicopters and were using them to help defend the base. There was no possible way we could take off in the helicopters; the fire was much too heavy! Keeping us on the ground was obviously part of the Viet Cong's battle plan. There were three .51 caliber antiaircraft guns placed around the base. They must have known to hold off until we landed and were out of the picture.

I told the crews to fall back to the center of the base if they needed to but to stay in view of the helicopters. I told them to fire at the fuel tanks and burn the choppers if the Cong came over the wall. I went inside to talk to the base commanders and see if there was anything special they wanted done. They had already called their "A Team" at Can Tho. They had requested that another Night Hunter-Killer team from elsewhere in the Delta be released and reassigned to B-43 for the night. It took the other team about an hour and a half to arrive on station. It looked as if my crew were all going to be grunts for the night!

The commanders requested that my crews continue to defend the area they were already defending. The four machine guns from the two ships were doing a great job. Those machine guns were giving extra fire power badly needed on the east side of the base. They also wanted to know if any one of the crew was trained as a medic. The base medic could use some help. Unfortunately, my answer had to be no. I went over to where the medic was working and offered my help. It seems that when they were first hit, many soldiers were wounded before they could even prepare to fight. The Viet Cong's plan was working well. I did everything with the medic, from placing pressure on wounds and just holding the wounds together for him with my dirty hands, to giving a few shots of morphine with his quick instruction.

Shortly after midnight I went back outside to my crews. They were holding their own and the helicopters were still in one piece. I was a mess now with sticky blood all over me. I stayed out there for the next several hours with an M-16 rifle I had procured earlier. I fired more 5.56mm rounds that night that I did for the whole balance of my life.

Just before dawn I went back inside to see if there was anything else they needed. I was told that the Viet Cong now owned three of our own bunkers on the west side of the compound. They were firing at the defenders of the base from our own bunkers. That was not a confidence building scenario. I was asked if I could fire a 106 mm recoilless rifle.

I was trained as a pilot not a ground soldier. I said that I had absolutely no idea and that I didn't know one end from the other. That was not completely true but also not too far off. I had never even been near one that was fired. I was then asked if I could carry and then pass ammunition to a loader. I said that I could do that, so I was now drafted onto his team. That recoilless rifle was mounted on a jeep and in the next ten minutes he used it to blow up all three Viet Cong owned bunkers.

Dawn arrived and the fighting quickly stopped. The helicopters were flyable and we took them back to Vinh Long for a detailed inspection. A few days later I was presented with copies of some official black and white army photos of the dead Viet Cong and all of the weapons that were left behind as they melted back into the regular population.

The photos of the abandoned weapons were amazing. The photos of the enemy dead were shocking. The photos in general were very sobering.

There was so much going on that night in that fight that I didn't see. I would bet that there are many stories that could be told of that fight!

Frank Strobel
"Knight Hawk 6"

A Few of the Enemy Weapons Recovered in the Morning

Inspecting

A PROBLEM PAS HAD WITH THE NEW MINI-GUN

Soon after I took over as commander of the Night Hunter-Killer mission, I began tweaking the mission as well as the equipment needed to fly it. Particularly in the Seven Mountains area when flying for the Green Berets, we often tried new things. Obviously, I did what was requested of me but as I found myself more familiar with the area's needs at night and more aware of the individual outposts and their specific needs and wants, I became more efficient. This familiarity allowed more experimentation.

One piece of equipment that we quickly realized did not meet our needs was the single M-60 machine gun that was mounted on each side. The M-60 rate of fire of 600 rounds per minute was not sufficient to engage an enemy that often had multiple machine guns. Most of our flying was at a very low altitude, so individuals firing at us with AK-47's also came into play and they were all firing together at us. Additionally, in most engagements, all of the fighting was on one side of the helicopter so as the helicopter banked, only one of its machine guns could be used effectively.

In the Table of Organization and Equipment (TO&E), helicopters weren't authorized anything larger than a single M-60 on each side. The first idea to increase the firepower was to manufacture a bracket for each side and mount twin M-60's. My crew was able to scrounge up a couple extra M-60's. They worked well but this modification still did not provide us enough firepower even in a small firefight.

Next we mounted a .50 caliber machine gun out the left door but again it just didn't do what we needed. We were always engaging individual soldiers and their units and usually their small units had no trucks or other equipment that would require us to use a .50 caliber. The heavy .50 caliber's extra punch and its slower rate of fire were not needed aboard the ship. One day, Pas was talking with the Cobra Platoon Crew Chiefs over a beer and told them about our continuing plight. They told him that if he could find a couple basic mini-gun frames, even if the guns didn't work, they would rebuild them for us and keep us in replacement parts.

Where he obtained them I don't really know for sure but I didn't ask any questions. For me that was the beginning of the U.S. Army's "Don't Ask, Don't Tell" program. We had to rewire the electrical system of "085" to handle the guns. I expected flack from my platoon leader or the CO but I never heard a word. The Army doesn't allow guys to make permanent major changes to their ships. Then again, I didn't ask their permission, so they couldn't say no! Some things are better left unsaid. Soon the mini-guns were mounted out each side of the ship but for various reasons it took about a week before we could effectively use them in our work. None of the crew was school trained on the guns, so for the most part we resorted to on-the-job-training (OJT).

To us it was a new and strange combination of mechanical wizardry and electric motors. Once working, they would answer our main problem. As the days passed, we gradually worked out the kinks and everything began to run much smoother.

One fairly busy night, I received a radio call from the Green Berets at the camp for Bravo Team 43 and was asked to return between refueling and rearming for a special briefing. About an hour later, I landed on the PSP (heavy corrugated metal) landing pad. While I was in for the briefing, Pas was going to reload the ammunition for the mini-guns.

As Pas was preparing the guns for new ammunition, he slightly twisted the barrels, which was a big no-no. They were facing down towards the PSP at about a 70 Degree angle. The gun had not been cleared of ammunition as it should have been and there was one round in the chamber that snapped into place and the firing pin engaged the round. The bright flash from the gun powder that late at night blinded him for a moment. He could feel the intense heat as it burned a long yellow white flame slightly singeing the front of his Nomex flight suit. The bullet passed inches from his stomach, hit the PSP between his legs and ricocheted up behind him past his back into the night sky.

After the briefing, when I returned to my ship Pas was sitting on the edge of the helicopter's cargo compartment in the dark doing nothing. As I walked over, I called to him asking what the problem was. As I walked closer he stood up and looked at me.

Now, you have to understand that Pas is a native of Guam. He has a natural dark golden tone to his skin. When he looked up at me, he was as white as Casper, the Friendly Ghost! Pas told me what he did. He understood what he did and that he did it to himself but that was no consolation. Pas knew the guns should have been cleared before landing. He knew not to rotate those barrels on the ground and most definitely <u>not</u> when you are standing in front of them.

I didn't push him but it took about ten more minutes for him to regain his composure. Soon we were rearmed and back in the air.

He told me he would never make that mistake again. Somehow I just had to believe him. It didn't take much convincing. I guess that is part of OJT. I always thought that OJT was a great way to learn new skills. Now I was presented with the other side, the negatives.

Another powerful lesson was learned that night. It could have been a major personal disaster but thankfully it was not.

Maybe I should have called this story, "The Perils of Pasqual!"

Frank Strobel
"Knight Hawk 6"

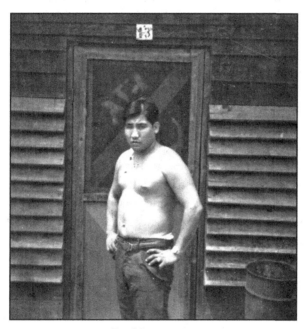

Pas Mantanona

FRANK J. STROBEL

AN EXPLOSION AT THE VINH
LONG AMMO DUMP

On 5 August 1970, there was a slight problem at the ammo dump. The morning it happened we had just come back from another Night Hunter-Killer mission. Most of the slicks and gunships were gone on their day's missions. I spent a short time helping the crew clean up '085' and walked in ramp 1 with my crew chief Pas to the hanger to get the needed supplies for a routine 25 hour inspection of our ship. I went on to Operations, spent an hour or so completing my after action report and then headed back to my bunk for some badly needed sleep.

Just as I reached my room and opened the door I heard and felt the rumble of a tremendous explosion, followed by a few smaller and possibly more distant ones. At first I thought it strange that we would be attacked on a clear beautiful bright morning. Of course most of the helicopters were gone; maybe that was the rationale for my surprise. Soon small debris began falling on the roof of my hooch. Flight gear in hand, I ran through the opening between the base chapel and battalion HQ and over to the "main drag" towards our maintenance hangar. I figured they would need someone up in the air as soon as possible. My ship's mini-guns were rearmed and ready to go. In an attack on the base they could be a very valuable air asset. I ran only a few yards and saw an unexpected sight.

A large group of men came running out from the area in the front of our maintenance hangar towards me. I quickly thought, "Oh my God, the VC are already inside the base and have taken over ramp 1. I knew there were few if any weapons in the hangar because the Vinh Long Base was so safe. For that reason alone it wasn't surprising to see the guys running for protection. Suddenly things seemed to go into slow motion. It almost looked like a "Keystone Kops" chase scene from an old silent movie. As a few of that group who were faster runners approached me, one yelled

"The ammo dump exploded and CS gas is blowing down ramp 1". Refocusing my sight on the corner of the hangar, I saw a large cloud of gas and smoke coming around the hangar. Now that put a whole different perspective on things!

If you are going through hell, just make sure you <u>keep</u> going!

I had recently been assigned as Company Chemical, Radiological and Biological (CBR) Officer and all I really knew about a gas mask was how to put one on. I was trying to teach myself what I could. There were several gas masks in my room and a manual titled something like, "Training Manual 1234567. All you ever wanted to know about gas masks but were afraid to ask!" I ran back to my room and grabbed several masks, put one on, put one on one of our mama sans (maids) and ran back towards the hangar. Luckily, the wind was strong enough that the CS threat lasted only a short time on the base. The cloud was blowing directly toward the orphanage and downtown Vinh Long but I never heard whether it caused any problems before it dispersed.

Debris On Ramp #1 And The New 'Cowboy' C-Model Hueys

I was very concerned about my ship, 085, since it was immediately alongside the ammo dump. I ran out ramp 1 towards her revetment for an initial inspection. Live and spent ammunition cartridges and numerous other types of ammunition, explosives and shrapnel littered the ramp. Everyone was yelling to be careful and not to touch or move anything until someone from Explosive Ordnance Disposal (EOD) checks and removes anything dangerous. As I went out the mostly empty ramp and its revetments, I thought how lucky we were that most of the choppers were gone. Halfway out the ramp, the parallel Red Knight revetments changed to the L-Shaped Cobra (AH-1G) revetments. I seem to recall that there was no major damage to Gold Knight or to the single remaining new AH-1G sitting in its revetment.

Further on, I caught sight of a couple of brand new "Cowboy", C-Model Huey gunships. They were on the south side of ramp 1 in L-Shaped revetments but the open sides of the L-Shapes faced the south and the west, giving no protection from the direction of the blast. Because of their orientation the revetments caused even more damage by catching some of the pressure and concussion of the blast and directing it to the far side of those ships and causing additional damage. The new C-Models had just been painted with the Cowboy's Logos and were being prepared to mount the guns and rocket launchers for the first time. They were trashed and never flew again.

Unfortunately, the Knights had just received a brand new OH-58 to be used for VIP's and special communications and it was sitting in the last L-Shaped revetment directly opposite the site of the explosion. It was mangled. As small as it was sitting behind the revetment, it was a mess. The shape and orientation of the revetment could not have been any better to protect the new ship; but since it was so close, it did little to save it from major damage.

It was so new that it didn't have any Knight markings on it and it was already trashed. If I remember correctly, we sent it back to the depot later that week in exchange for another. My ship, 085, was in the next revetment!

The 'Knights' New OH-58

"085" was in the first parallel revetment west of the L-Shaped revetment that the OH-58 was sitting in. I was very apprehensive as I reached it. She had been so good to me.

Yes, I expected the worst, since the parallel revetment had my ship's unprotected nose facing directly toward the center of the blast's point of origin. In effect the revetment did not protect "085" at all. There was no closer helicopter to the blast (no more than 25 yards) and "085" was without protection.

I quickly began my first once over of "085" as Pas got there. Thank God he wasn't working on the ship at the instant of the blast. He had been in the hangar getting some tools. I soon became amazed that even though it was so close and facing the direction of the blast there was no obvious damage. So many other aircraft further away from the blast were destroyed yet "085" looked good. The pressure of the explosion had hit the nose and streamlined past it just like a slipstream of air does when it is flying. I wonder what the airspeed indicator reading was as the blast hit the Pitot tube. It was covered with debris but had no significant visible damage.

After a very detailed inspection by our Maintenance Officer and me, we took her for a test flight. He ran her through his checks and then I then flew it the way I expected her to fly. We did two auto-rotations and she was cleared for the evening's mission. After landing and a small bit of preparation we were on our way to the Seven Mountains for a night of fun and frolic. So much for sleeping! "085" never failed me and I had a new respect for how she was designed and built.

The Cobra revetments were all empty except for the furthest one to the east. I found that it was far enough away that it had very minor damage but the trailer that was used by the Cobra platoon for spare parts and repairs was flattened like a pancake.

Why did the ammo dump blow? The story I heard at the time was that a soldier was given the job of "policing up" any trash inside the dump. He was assigned several female Vietnamese day workers to actually do the work. After all the debris was collected he piled it in the middle of the dump and burned it so that they wouldn't have to find some place to throw it. That was definitely a bad decision.

I understand that they only found one of his boots. The Vietnamese workers died instantly. At the 2000 reunion in Columbia, Missouri, I heard a slightly different explanation of the cause of the blast. It was something I hadn't heard while there in 1970 but the basic story is the same, so I'll stick with my version.

Vinh Long's Ammo Dump and "085's Revetment

CHAU DUC AND IT'S COFFEE HOUSE

When we would land at the Military Assistance Command Viet Nam (MACV) compound on the northwest side of Chau Duc, it was always very interesting. The thing for which we had to be careful when landing, though, was something we never expected. There was only one TV station in that southern area of South Viet Nam; it was in Saigon, all the way across the Delta. In order to receive the signal, homeowners had to mount a very tall antenna. They were at least 35 or 40 feet high and a few were even higher. Having to dodge them on short final to the MACV compound was not a task I had expected face in Viet Nam. Actually it was the only place in Viet Nam that I had that problem.

Why was it interesting there? Well, it was for a different reason every time.

It's not that I didn't feel good spending some time with the men who were stationed there. I would often fly the crew there after our Night Hunter-Killer mission just for the great breakfast that they served. The recreation room was very comfortable. The only reason I didn't spend any more time there is that I would have fallen asleep and would have had a hard time getting up again.

I loved spending time outside where the helicopter sat. As soon as my work was over or I had some stand down time I was out there. There always was a little down home entertainment for me. I never knew what would happen next. I was often playing with the children in the small space we used as the landing area. As always, when they could get near us, a large group of kids would appear and stay as long as we would allow them. I had a super time playing with those kids. It was also the only place while I was in Viet Nam that I witnessed a 'real live' dragon dance coming down the road. It was great to see the villagers out watching the parade.

I was able to see a little more of the local culture, first hand. I saw two kids about 9 or 10 years old pushing a 55 gallon drum that was mounted on its side atop a cart that was built over an old car axle. I had seen them push it a number of different days before I asked an interpreter what they were doing. He told me that they were going down to the Mekong River and filling it with water and selling it to homes in the town. They did it every day of the year, rain or shine. Age 10 and with no schooling, I wondered what did those two have to look forward to in the future.

There was a small coffee house across the 20 foot wide dirt street. The one story building was mostly a family home but with an integrated front porch and living room which was also about twenty feet wide and completely open directly to the street. Although it was open, it was one step up from there to the open living room. There were three or four tables with chairs in the front room/front porch.

We often went there during the day. On nights that were extremely slow, I would land after dark and get a cup of coffee. We were always very wary, waiting for some nasty guy to come down the street with an AK-47 or a bomb of some kind but thankfully it never happened. We were really defenseless when sitting there. I did this at night 8 or 9 different times but only about once a month. It was not often enough to set up a pattern for the Viet Cong to detect. I did not want to place us or that nice family that owned the coffee house in any more danger.

While our crew would stay with the ship, about 100 feet away, I would take my co-pilot with me, although neither of us spoke Vietnamese. The family always greeted us with great warmness.

The very friendly grandfather was always up and walking in the easily visible living room area. Although he was able to walk around, sometimes with a little assistance, he had a deep raspy cough which reminded us of tuberculosis.

The young woman in her mid-twenties usually served us. I always ordered *cafe su'* (pronounced "sure"). It was a dark, bitter coffee dripped into a demitasse clear glass cup that was 1/3 filled with sweet cream. After it was served, a quick stir with a spoon would make a wonderfully satisfying drink. I don't know how much caffeine was in it but after drinking it I didn't have to worry about going to sleep for quite a few hours. The kids would be all over us as we drank our coffee. It was somewhat surreal knowing that in as little as ten minutes we could actively be in a firefight just a couple miles away. Several guys asked if I came to Viet Nam for the kids or the war. I guess that was a fair question.

As I said, the kids would be all over us and we had a great time with them. One little girl that lived there was constantly around. I often saw her across the street near the helicopter. She loved to be all over me but not 'just' for me. She could see that I carried a pen and grease pencil in the arm pockets of my flight suit. She would play with me until I was distracted and then steal them. She was very good at it.

I lost a couple sets before I realized what had happened to them. Sometimes it would be several hours before I would reach for one that was no longer there. I could have been across the Delta, 80 miles away, by the time . . . *Okay, maybe I **was** a bit slow!* When I first thought that it could have been her, I doubted myself. I didn't think she could be so brazen, with such a playful nature and sweet smile. Boy was I wrong. I began to call her "Fast Fingers".

She also understood more English than I thought she knew. One day while she was sitting on my lap in my helicopter's cargo compartment. I caught her with her hand on my grease pencil, very slowly and gently pulling it out. I stopped her and pointed at her saying, "Your name, Fast Fingers!" She said, "No, my name . . . Mai!" I repeated myself. She soon was telling everyone, "My name . . . Fast Fingers". I'm sure she had no idea what her new name meant but she was proud of that new name.

I have some great photos of Chau Duc. I wish I could present them all.

The last day I was in Chau Duc in December 1970, I found Fast Fingers and gave her 2 pencils and 2 black US Army push 'n click pens. You would have thought I gave her a million dollars.

Frank and 'Fast Fingers"

NIGHTTIME FLARE DISORIENTATION

Some of the best tools for Night Hunter-Killer Missions were the U. S. Navy's canister flares. My wing man, Bug, would drop flares from about 2000-2500 feet above ground level (AGL) and prior to release, would set a timer. The timer insured that the magnesium flare would not ignite until safely away from the aircraft. When lit, they would burn for four minutes, falling under a large, white silk parachute. They would light up almost a "click" (1 kilometer) in diameter while at altitude and shine brighter than daylight.

We often used as many as 50 or 60 flares each night. On nights that we were in constant combat that number could increase dramatically to 100. Ideally, a flare would burn out while still a couple hundred feet in the air and if another flare was requested, it would be lit before the first flare was extinguished. It was not an easy task and took a disciplined pilot and crew to maintain a constant and even illumination of an area. I became very comfortable having Wendell Jarrett dropping flares for me. He had the touch.

I had to be careful since I spent a great deal of time below 200 feet, often just above ground level in the dark. There were several safety measures to keep in mind. First, realize that the bright light from the flares quickly and dramatically degraded your night vision. Second, be careful of the bright light and ink black shadows created by the flares. Areas lit by the flares were brighter than daylight, yet areas not exposed to the flare light, behind trees or hooches were as black as the blackest night.

There was no gradual transition from bright to gray to black. Third, be aware that as the flare drifted down, the shadows moved slowly but the lower it drifted and the closer it got to the objects on the ground that cast shadows, the faster the shadows would move.

Fourth, be mindful of the time each individual flare has burned and be aware of when it would extinguish, because then everything would be totally black again. Hopefully Bug would have another one burning first, if the mission in that area was to continue. Fifth, if a flare burned out before hitting the ground, to be aware of its exact location, so to avoid flying below it and entangling its parachute in the rotor system. That would be fatal! Sixth, if the flare continues to burn as it approached the ground, refocus on your flight instruments and begin a climb out away from any obstacles such as hooches, trees or even the mountains. All are most unforgiving.

As a flare floated closer to the ground the shadows moved in relation to any item on the ground. When a flare approached the top of a tree the speed of the shadow movement would grow exponentially. If the tree was at the base of one of the mountains near which we worked, the growing inky black shadow would climb the nearly vertical cliff face in mere seconds. This movement could instantly induce vertigo in a pilot! The flare would burn out leaving a pilot blind not knowing up from down. That would be a very dangerous situation in the best of circumstances, let alone in enemy territory. The enemy at that point, however, would be the least of a pilot's problems.

One night that is exactly what happened. I was snooping around between the bases of the Nui Cam and Nui Dai mountains in a small valley, an area we called "50 Cal. Alley" because of the enemy guns mounted on the summits. I was safe from those guns if I stayed close to the valley floor. I was looking for enemy activity reported to me from the outpost of Ba Xoai and lost track of the time while doing my work. I was about 10 feet off the ground when I realized the flare was approaching the top of the trees. I quickly did a "pedal turn" that faced the helicopter to the north and away from the mountains and pulled in as much power as the engine could handle. Totally blind to the outside world, I began an instrument take-off from between the trees in the valley. Very easily one of my rotor blades could have impacted a tree or a large branch. Slowly we climbed up to the safety of a little bit of altitude. The first few moments were quite scary. Five minutes later after wiping a few beads of sweat off my brow and regaining my bearings, my composure and my night vision, I went back to work.

MY "PERSONAL PROBLEM" WITH VINH LONG'S AMMO DUMP

I always had a good relationship with the guys that worked at Vinh Long's ammunition dump. They always treated us well. They would go that extra step for us, usually. The biggest problem I had was that they closed at 1630 hours. Yes, you read that right! At 1630 hours every day they locked the gates and a dog handler with his M-16 and his dog began to walk guard, inside and out. Can you believe that an ammunition dump at an airbase in a war zone held just daylight hours? Only if there was an attack on the base would it reopen. If Vinh Long came under fire at night, the dump could be accessed and needed supplies could be issued but that didn't help us leaving Vinh Long for our Night Hunter-Killer mission.

Pas was always very good at having what we needed at our ship when we were prepared to leave Vinh Long for the night. Well, usually he was. There was only one type of ammunition we had to get onboard before we left Vinh Long because it wasn't available at the places we visited. That was a case of 40mm CS gas rounds for the M-79 grenade launcher. It wasn't a major problem since we normally left for our mission at about 1600 hours. This particular day, Pas had been working all day on a maintenance problem and time just got away from him. He went to the nearby dump 5 minutes after they locked up for the day, so we were out of luck.

"Not so," I proclaimed loudly and somewhat angrily, "I'll get what we need!" I walked over to the nearby outside wall of the ammunition dump. I looked around to make sure the guard and his dog was not nearby and began my climb over the 12 foot high bunker wall. After reaching the top I surveyed the inside and then began my quick descent to the ground. My boots no sooner hit the dirt than I heard a deep snarling growl. I slowly turned around to see the handler and his dog. The dog was the biggest German shepherd I have ever seen. His head was as big as a Grizzly Bear's, in fact I am pretty sure that dog's mother, somewhere in her lineage, was a least related to Smoky the Bear.

Needless to say, I froze and didn't move a muscle. The guard with his M-16 pointed at me, asked me what I was doing in there. I wasn't worried about the M-16 as much as I was the dog. Shoot me but just don't let that dog loose, I thought. I would have made a nice appetizer before dinner for that monster dog. I quickly explained my plight but he was a good guard just doing his job and made me agree that my problem wasn't a life or death situation. He did permit me to quickly climb back over the wall empty handed.

Pas asked me, "Where is the case of M-79 rounds that you went after?" I just told him that the cupboard was bare.

Frank Strobel
"Knight Hawk 6"

FLYING LEFT SEAT ON THE NIGHT HUNTER KILLER MISSION

This story was in response to a discussion about the fact that in helicopters and according to our Company's Standard Operating Procedures (SOP) the pilot in command (Aircraft Commander) normally sat in the right seat while flying.

While flying nights and after becoming completely comfortable with it, I did something that several other Aircraft Commanders in my unit thought was strange. I started flying as Aircraft Commander from the left seat. It was our Company SOP that Aircraft Commanders flew the right seat. Unlike fixed-wing aircraft, the helicopter was designed for the Aircraft Commander to fly from the right seat. Most of the switches and all of the more easily readable flight instruments were mounted on the right side.

On the right side of the instrument panel are also the engine instruments, making them easier for the Aircraft Commander to monitor. The aircraft's starter and the "Christmas Tree", a panel of warning lights, are placed on the right side of the cockpit. On the other hand everything that is needed to actually fly is available to the left seat. It is definitely easier to read the instruments on the right side, especially the artificial horizon, which is about 50% larger than the one on the left and its markings are easier to read quickly. The package of flight instruments in front of the left seat were complete, adequate and worked fine but were somewhat smaller and the displays couldn't be read as easily.

My thought process was this. As the Aircraft Commander I had the most flight experience, especially flying at night. If I was in trouble and my co-pilot had to take over and bail me out of a dangerous situation, I wanted him to have the best instruments.

The co-pilot was usually the newer pilot. If I was in trouble, he could use all the help he could get. The least I could do was give him the best tools to get us out safely.

With my change over, I soon realized that there was another benefit to the left seat, which was a less obstructed view. The smaller instrument package on the left side required a smaller instrument panel in front of me. This extra room was designed to allow gun sights to be used from the left seat but I didn't use those sights at night. The left seat, however, now granted me much better visibility of the ground for the type of visual low level flying I was doing at night. It was a win-win situation for all.

TESTING THE NEW INFRARED
NIGHT VIEWING SYSTEM

During the summer of 1970 after flying the Night Hunter-Killer Mission for a couple months, I was asked to participate in a testing program. It was for a new infrared night vision system designed specifically for Hueys. The system was developed somewhere in Texas and was deemed far enough along in its testing to be brought to Viet Nam for a trial. The program at that time was "Top Secret" and luckily I had that clearance.

The reconfigured Huey was delivered to Saigon and then flown to the Delta for an operational test in actual combat. The helicopter wasn't even flown to a base in the Delta area. No one was to see it. I was to work with the testing program for the week. Initially I was given a set of coordinates to meet the test crew in a field out in the middle of God's country at dusk. I received a short briefing over the radio from the Green Berets on the way and then completed my flight to meet the men with whom I was to work.

I was instructed not to bring my Bug ship that week because this new test system didn't need flares to have its equipment function properly. Of course that would make me basically blind. I landed my Huey about 150 feet from where they were waiting for me. There were about a dozen people around the reconfigured Huey. I left my gunner to protect the helicopter and with my copilot and my crew chief in tow, I started walking over to the group of men near the helicopter. We were stopped cold about 50 feet away by two guards carrying 'stoners'. Stoners were belt fed 5.56mm machine guns. An Army Colonel came over and told me that only the two pilots could proceed.

The Colonel then asked me specifically about my crew chief, Pasqual Mantanona. Pas had darker skin than the rest of us but he was not black; his skin had more of a golden tone and he had a very round South Pacific type face. I told the Colonel that my crew chief was from Guam. I was immediately told that he could not approach the ship because, although he was an American citizen, he was not a naturally born one. I protested but quickly lost the argument. It was obviously non-negotiable. Even after all the things Pas and I had been through on Night Hunter-Killer missions the last few months, he couldn't even approach that helicopter. He returned to our ship.

The helicopter was a C-model Huey with mounted machine guns and 2.75 inch rocket pods. Additionally it had what looked like a 40mm gun turret mounted on the nose of the ship. I was briefed about the new equipment inside the chopper and its expected performance. In the cargo compartment was a console about three feet high, two feet wide and about a foot deep. It very closely resembled one of those x-ray machines shoe stores used back in the 1950's to make sure your shoes fit correctly.

The pilot's instrument panel was changed dramatically. All of the flight instruments were spread outwards from their normal position and a green phosphorous 10" TV monitor was placed in front of each pilot. Each screen had cross hairs permanently painted on it for the guns and rockets. The turret mounted on the nose of the ship did not carry a gun; it carried the infrared camera.

I was given no special instructions for the tests except that I was to fly my helicopter and lead the newly reconfigured copter over known enemy positions. They would evaluate the effectiveness of their equipment in locating the enemy.

The first thing I did was lead them up and over the top of Nui Cam. The Viet Cong owned the mountains at the time and didn't like us up there. I found some enemy activity almost immediately; however the test ship could not verify the location. I fired on the position to mark it with my tracers but they still couldn't confirm the location. The only thing I could think of doing was dropping one of my thermite grenades. I kept several onboard to burn the ship if we went down and couldn't secure it from the enemy.

I again flew over that location and dropped that extremely hot and burning grenade. For whatever reason, they were still not able to define the enemy position. I was getting very nervous repeatedly flying over the same enemy position on top of the mountain. From what I witnessed the initial use of the system looked like a failure. I was not privy to their analysis of the test. We left that area for another spot over a known enemy hamlet.

For the next several days we worked the area with what I considered mixed results. On the last night I flew with them I was permitted to fly one sortie as co-pilot. We mainly flew the valley area immediately north of Nui Cam and Nui Dai. One thing that blew my mind was that through the TV screen I was able to see an enemy soldier leaning against a tree smoking a cigarette. The tree didn't survive. In general though, watching a TV screen as we flew over the terrain made me dizzy.

I have never seen or heard of the system deployed anywhere, so I feel comfortable relating this experiment. The new style night vision goggles quickly made that system obsolete.

Frank Strobel
"Knight Hawk 6"

MY FIRST VIETNAMESE MEAL

I met a young Catholic girl named Mae Ling who was about 16 years of age. I met her while doing some volunteer work one day at the Catholic orphanage. The orphanage was run by Irish nuns and was immediately outside of the Main Base Gate at Vinh Long. About a month after meeting her, she invited me to downtown Vinh Long to meet her family on a Sunday afternoon. I thought it would be a neat cultural experience to spend an afternoon with a normal average Vietnamese family. It turned out to be a very interesting experience.

I took a Cycle-lo ride downtown. We had been warned to travel in groups for safety when going downtown but here I was, by myself. Before long I was wondering if I had made a really bad decision, since I was completely alone. It was in an area not frequented by American GI's.

I arrived at their home about 1400 hours. The map she drew me was very accurate and I found their home relatively easily. The home was on the south side of the main street of Vinh Long shortly before it bends to the North and rises over the Mekong River near the theater. I turned South on a small street (really a glorified alley) and walked about 150 yards, all the while the street seemed to get narrower and darker. I had become cautious when I turned into that smaller street but as it became smaller and darker in the middle of the day I began to seriously question if this was a smart idea to enter that part of the town. I turned East onto an even smaller street/walkway. It was really just five foot wide and only paved with packed mud and some stone. I then crossed a small foot bridge over an open drainage ditch. The only protection I had was a pistol on my belt. Those rounds would not last long if I was attacked. The poverty, even squalor, in the neighborhood was most apparent.

The homes were built directly abutting the walkway and although it was mid-day and sunny, the sunlight rapidly vanished. I definitely felt out of place walking down that small street and was getting some very strange looks as I passed many of the neighborhood people. Definitely, this was not an area that many Americans frequented. I started to think about possibly being attacked by the Viet Cong and never being found.

As a brave and fearless 23 year old American soldier, I was about to completely lose my courage and turn around and leave, when Mae Ling came out of her home and greeted me. I was committed! Besides, this was one of my personal goals, getting to know the Vietnamese people.

Her family was waiting there as I entered their home. I met her father, mother and two smaller brothers who were about six and eight years old. It was interesting. This was the first time I was so close to the Vietnamese culture on my own. I had been downtown before to the market but never to someone's home.

I didn't realize it until then but I was having dinner, not with the family, just with her father. All of a sudden, a flash hit me, "Was this some kind of an engagement party?" I didn't find out until much later that day, it was not. I learned later that I was considered an honored guest to the family and this was the way they showed their respect for me. At the time I did feel honored but I was still extremely concerned about their concept of a commitment. I didn't want to get up and walk out because I was unsure of what it meant to them. Maybe I should have consulted someone on Vietnamese culture before doing this on my own. It was a little late but then I realized that no one on base even knew I was off the base. I somewhat reluctantly decided to stay though I tried not to show my uneasiness. All my communication consisted of smiles, hand gestures and inflections in my voice while I spoke English since I only knew a few words of Vietnamese. The father knew no English.

The home was no wider than twenty feet. It opened up directly onto the walkway where Mae Ling had come to meet me. The whole front of the house opened up onto that walkway through lightly constructed, bamboo accordion style doors. When fully open, the first two rooms of the home were completely exposed to the traffic on the walkway.

It was about an eight inch step from the walkway into the first room which we would call a porch. It served as a family room for the house. It was the width of the house and about ten feet deep. There was about an eight inch step up into the second room. It was again the width of the house and about twelve feet deep. It looked as if it were the living room/dining room but later I found out that it was also the parents' bedroom. There were two back rooms. They were created by splitting the back half of the house vertically with a wall but one room was slightly larger than the other. The larger of the two was the children's bedroom; the smaller was the kitchen. I did not see how deep those rooms were.

The house was spartanly furnished. The only major piece of furniture was the table on which they served dinner. It was finished very nicely and was about fifteen inches tall. I later found out it was also the parents' bed.

One item that caught my eye was a small half-moon shaped shelf on the wall. On the shelf was an eight inch tall Madonna and Child and immediately next to it was a statue of Buddha. Each statue had a lit candle in front of it.

All of a sudden the children were gone and I was invited to sit down at the table. My gangly legs were a problem but I was able to place them out of the way. I wasn't sure what to expect but I quietly took a deep breath. Mae Ling's mother began to serve us. She first brought out a French beer, Export 45 to be exact. She then returned to the kitchen and brought out the first course, hard boiled eggs. On her knees and bowing, she presented the bowl to me.

I thought, "Hard boiled eggs! I can do this!" I took an egg and placed it on my plate. She then did the same to her husband. I picked up my egg and gently cracked it on my dish. Immediately, a great amount of green, slimy, sticky ooze flowed out over my fingers and onto my dish. I am sure I had a shocked look on my face.

Mae Ling's father began talking at 90 miles an hour as I tried to apologize for my mistake. His wife came back from the kitchen with a towel for my hands, a new dish and an egg to replace my first one. The father then showed me how to eat the egg. First, you poke a small hole in each end of the egg, gently suck out the fluid and then peel the egg. What remains is an embryo duck with very small pin feathers. After grabbing it by its beak, you raise it up and place it in your mouth biting off the beak, which is returned to the dish. I did it! Of course, I also used a great deal of that French beer to wash down the aftertaste. Don't ask me what it tasted like, I don't remember. That beer did its job.

It was then I noticed something else. They had not closed the front accordion doors to their home. There were at least twenty people watching us eat. They were standing two and three deep and talking amongst themselves very quietly on the walkway only fifteen feet away from the table. I don't know how I didn't see them before but I hadn't. I have no idea what they were saying but they were quite interested in what they were watching.

For the second course she carried out a small charcoal fired stove and placed it on the table. Then she brought out a dish of small cubed pieces of beef, Boc Choy (Chinese cabbage) and rice paper wraps, along with a "mayonnaise & pimento dip". After cooking the beef over the fire, a small pocket would be made with the rice paper wrap and filled with the Boc Choy and beef. It was folded tight into a little cocoon like an egg roll. Dipping it into the sauce was the last step before eating it.

I could do this! I did so generously passing my creation through the dip, only to learn too late that the "pimentos" were not pimentos but were extremely hot, 1/2" long red peppers. They were the hottest peppers I had ever eaten. My family never served any kind of hot spicy foods at home. I think I almost put out the charcoal fire with the tears that were literally squirting from my eyes. I was careful throughout the rest of the course to dip but leave the peppers. It was very tasty and I did enjoy it. Later I found out that the tender delicious beef wasn't beef at all; it was dog.

The third course was similar to the second except that instead of 'beef,' fish was served. It was cooked at the table's charcoal fired stove with some oil in a small pot. The sauce was a salty flavored fish sauce called Nuoc Mam. It was quite tasty.

The last course consisted of a small bowl of a clear broth soup. With a few very small pieces of chicken (I hope) and small leaves of Boc Choy and onion. It was light and very pleasant tasting.

There was no dessert.

By the time dinner was finished, there had to be at least thirty or forty people watching us. There was no room to walk down the dirt path past Mae Ling's home. I guess I was the talk of that quiet, dark neighborhood. I was feeling pretty good. I had my fill of that French beer as well as a very memorable dinner.

When dinner was completed, the rest of the family reappeared. They had been in their bedroom throughout the dinner, 10 feet away sitting quietly. I never heard a sound. I had just assumed they left, possibly to visit friend's house. I could not imagine that happening over here in the States.

Frank Strobel
"Knight Hawk 6"

2661 MY TOO CLOSE OF AN ENCOUNTER . . . WITH A RAT!

I spent another Sunday at Mae Ling's home. I played an hour or so with her two brothers. We mostly wrestled on the floor. On and off the boys were playing with a couple of small airplanes, flying them and landing them all around the room. I took a closer look at them and they were about three inches long and made of stamped "white" metal, the kind I had when I was a boy. They were American F-86 Sabre Jets. All but one of the tiny black rubber tires were missing. I got a bit of pleasure looking at the well worn USAF markings. I wondered where they got them.

Around 1500 hours Mae Ling asked me if I was hungry and since I always had a hollow leg when it came to food I said, "Yes, I am." She gave the older of the two boys a 20 Dong coin and away he went. About 15 minutes later he came back with a sandwich for me. I unwrapped it and saw that, inside the locally made rice bread "hoagie roll," there was what looked like a pulled beef BBQ filling. It reminded me of a sandwich I would buy back in Erie, Pennsylvania. I offered but no one wanted to share the sandwich, so I quickly began to eat as they all watched me. Over the next five minutes or so I ate half of the sandwich and made a comment that I regretted for days. I said, "This is very good. What is it?" My insides turned to mush as she happily said with a smile, "BBQ rat!"

Now, what was I to do?!?! I had already told her that it was very good and had already eaten half of the sandwich. I quickly tried to regain my composure and not wanting to insult them by not eating something that I had already "raved" about, I decided that . . . If I was going to catch some disease, I <u>had already caught it</u>!

So taking a deep breath, I finished the sandwich. The last half was much harder to swallow. I was worried about my health for about 24 hours but everything was fine. In the next few months I ate at their home several times. I ate some very strange and exotic foods in Viet Nam. They always agreed with my body but not so much with my mind.

My wife told me after she first heard this story that I had better never complain about her cooking!

Frank Strobel
"Knight Hawk 6"

1276 NIGHT FLARE MISSIONS VS THE NIGHT HUNTER-KILLER MISSION

The following story was written in response to a question presented to me.

If all you ever did was circle and drop flares until 0100 hours, I guess it could get a little boring. Who were you supporting on these missions? Who covered the job after 1 A.M.?

My Night Hunter-Killer missions were anything but boring. Normally, the two ships on the team were the only aircraft in an area at night. On rare occasions the Navy Sea Wolves helicopter team would show up to support a Seal mission but they never called us to let us know where they would be. When we saw their lights we just stayed away from that operational area. We usually had enough going on elsewhere.

As my mission gradually developed, it had four parts. First: If any unit in my AO was under attack or expecting action, my primary focus was to give them air support. Second: Patrol along the Cambodian border, looking for signs of the North Vietnamese Army (NVA) or Viet Cong crossing or attempting to cross. I was at bottom of the Ho Chi Minh Trail. Third: if nothing was going on, choose an area in the AO and try to start my own private "war". Fourth: If someone needed an immediate med-i-vac, we were at their service.

When in the Seven Mountains Area, my nightly base of operations was the Green Beret Camp of Bravo Team 43. After completing our nightly briefing, the mission was normally staying in their AO and being prepared to fly from dusk until shortly after dawn. More often than not we spent little time on the ground. It was usually one sortie, refuel and rearm at Chau Duc and go out again. When there was activity or expected contact the following day, we would arrive a little earlier. If we were in active combat, we would stay in the area until relieved. Many nights it was a constant cycle of fighting, rearming and refueling and going right back out. We often logged 12 or more flight hours per day. I had many disparaging comments from the hanger crew that all '085' did was get its 25 hour inspections, sometimes twice a week and sometimes more!

When entering the area we were always in radio contact with Border Control radar. It was located in small trailer at Chau Duc. We used them to vector us along the unmarked Cambodian Border at night since they were the only "professional" aircraft radio contact in the area. We also used them for flight following (tracking our location) on all our missions so that someone would know if we got into major trouble and couldn't radio anyone. After flying the mission for a couple of months, the radar operators wouldn't wait for us to contact them while we were inbound. When they would see two blips flying in formation in the late afternoon from the direction of Vinh Long, they would often welcome us into the area before we even contacted them. One of the radar operators even flew a mission with us just to see what we actually did at night. That is another story and quite amusing.

YES, IT DOES GET COLD AT NIGHT IN VIET NAM!

During our evening briefing the Green Berets at the B-43 base camp would let us know about any active areas or areas expected to become active. Their AO followed the Cambodian border in West IV Corps. It was at the extreme southern terminus of the Ho Chi Minh Trail so there was a great deal of activity. They usually had at least one patrol out every night, so we would get their call sign and frequency just in case they needed some help. I am sure those briefings although tedious at times, saved some lives. It was a fairly large area with many outposts, so there was usually something going on somewhere.

After being assigned the night mission permanently, we soon began to recognize the men's voices stationed at the various outposts. Often we would be flying past an outpost and over the FM Radio we would hear, "How is it going Knight Hawk?" or, "Good evening Knight Hawk!" I would always answer and ask if things were quiet or if they had any concerns. It was nice knowing that just our being there brought some comfort to them. Of course, pulling an all night radio watch when things were quiet was probably quite boring for them. I guess they enjoyed anything that would break up a monotonous watch, except being attacked of course.

Ba Xoai

I was invited to spend an "all-nighter" on the ground at the small outpost of Ba Xoai at the base of Nui Dai Mountain. At one point I was grounded for going over 140 combat flight hours in a 30 day period, so I made arrangements to join them. What an experience! After that night, I happily did their bidding any time they called me. I would not have wanted to be stationed there for my tour. It was the only time I saw, from the ground, a "Mad Minute" of firing everything they had just to slow down or discourage any enemy who might be attempting a surprise attack. A Mad Minute was unbelievable to watch from the air but the noise while on the ground was deafening.

In the morning as I was being picked up, they presented me with their unit patch. They said that although a number of pilots were invited and said that they would stay a night with them, I was the first to actually show up. I still cherish that patch and have it mounted in my shadow box at home. Those were some good men. They were out in the middle of nowhere at the base of the Nui Dai Mountain, which was owned by the enemy. Somehow from that point on, when they called for help I moved a little bit faster. I was now part of <u>their</u> family too.

BA Xoai Breast Patch

These Night Hunter-Killer missions were anything but boring. If they became boring, it would have been my fault!

Frank Strobel
"Knight Hawk 6"

1264 MORE ON THE KNIGHT NIGHT-HUNTER-KILLER MISSION

I had a tactical instrument ticket while in Viet Nam. It was the standard training for Warrant Officer Candidates at the time. The only instrument time I had is what was presented in flight school. When I took over the mission, I had "0" in-country instrument flying time. I didn't get rated for instruments until I returned to the world and joined the Pennsylvania Army National Guard.

The Night Hunter-Killer missions were set up with two UH-1s, one (the Bug) flying high, dropping flares for the one (C&C) flying low. There were no gun-ships as part of the team. The low ship normally flew from ground level to about 500 feet AGL, depending on the situation. Armaments were just the normal two M-60 machine guns. In addition to the crew, about 10% of the time on board the C&C Ship was one American and one Vietnamese advisor, who were there to make immediate tactical decisions if there was any question as to the validity of a target and sometimes one interpreter but only if needed.

The 'Knight' Night Hunter Killer Team—1970
Pvt. Law, CW2 Strobel, SP-5 Mantanona and SP-4 Smalley

For armament we were only authorized the standard two M-60 machine guns. We also carried a 1.2 million candle power Xeon spotlight that could switch between white and infra-red light and a Starlight Scope. It didn't take long to realize that two machine guns were not enough when we were out there alone and snooping around at night. We soon mounted twin M-60's on each side; we even tried mounting a .50 caliber out the door. Eventually we did graduate to a mini-gun out each door.

We were not authorized mini-guns on our TO&E but the Cobra platoon's crew chiefs told my crew chief, SGT Pas Mantanona, that if we could find the basic guns, they would supply all parts needed to get it working and keep it firing.

THANK YOU COBRA CREW CHIEFS!!!!!!!

That was the beginning of the Army's, "Don't ask—Don't Tell" policy. When I asked where he got the basic gun, Pas said, "Don't Ask, 'cus I won't tell"! So I didn't ask! . . . But I did hear it involved a late night crawl down the ramp of the Air Cavalry unit, across the runway!

'085's' Mini-gun Ammunition Setup

In the summer of '70, for a week or so, we tried having a Cobra AH-1G-model fly with us, as a third ship. That didn't work too well for two reasons. First, they had just converted the Cobras for testing purposes to the blue canopies, which were great in sunlight but did not work well at night. Second, often with two observers on board, there was just too much time spent waiting for decisions to be made before going after a target.

The Cobras got frustrated and I didn't blame them. It just didn't work.

One night though, North of Chau Duc between the rivers, I chased three Viet Cong into what I thought was a sugar cane field. I called in the Cobra and he blew the hell out of the field with many pairs of 2.5" High Explosive rockets. I went back down to check out the results and found out that it was not sugar cane but rather a corn field. Suddenly, all we could smell was "popped corn" . . . it smelled wonderful. The Cobra came back down with me and opened its canopy. Can you picture two choppers, in the middle of nowhere, hovering around in a completely black night just smelling the fresh aroma of popcorn? No one onboard had any butter or salt though. I am sure it drastically affected that poor farmer's harvest.

Frank Strobel
"Knight Hawk 6"

1271 NIGHT AIR TO AIR COMBAT . . . A UFO . . . OR WHAT?

Was there any Air to Air Combat? I almost experienced some!

With all of the night flying I did, I only had one instance of an unidentified aircraft near my AO.

I was flying along the north side of the Ven Te Canal just south of the Cambodian border a couple clicks west of Nui Dai and just west of the village of Vinh Gia. I was being guided by "Border Control" radar Cambodian border. I often used the radar operators to guide me directly along the border while I looked for indications of NVA or Viet Cong crossing the border at night. They had the border traced on their screen, so I was able to fly the exact border with the help of their vectoring.

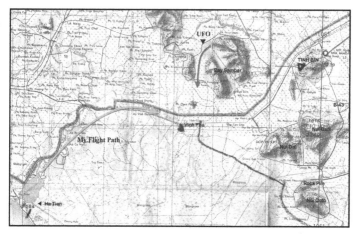

Both Flight Paths

I was at about 500 feet AGL and my Bug was following me but at a higher altitude at around 2,500 feet. Just north of the border area were a few small mountains inside Cambodia. The largest

141

mountain was called Bay Sambar. I saw a short flash of white light, which looked like an aircraft light several hundred feet higher than I was. It was coming towards us from the northwest side of the mountain. Its speed reminded me of a helicopter's. Suddenly its lights went out. I called my Bug and asked if they saw the lights from their ship. I think my Bug that night was flown by WO Wendell Jarrett. The night was a very clear one with a bright moon and millions of stars. To me, flying at night, I thought it was perfect weather.

He said, "Yes but the lights were at a lower altitude than his and were flying towards us." I called Border Control radar and they claimed that they had no blips north of the canal; his only blips on the screen were the two of us. In a climbing left turn to the north, I told Jarrett (Bug) that I was going to try to engage it with our mini-guns. It was quite a thrill, thinking that this could be happening!

Air to Air Combat—what a treat for a Huey driver!

We were about a click apart but no sooner had we started heading directly towards those lights, that whatever it was accelerated to what I considered at the time a fantastic speed. It returned back around to the north side of Bay Sambar. We lost sight of it and never regained it. Border Control radar insisted that they had no radar contacts except us.

Beware what you look for . . . You just might find it!!!!!

I have always wondered if the radar operator was giving me the whole scoop. To this day there is no question in my mind that an aircraft was there. I have often hoped that someday I would hear that the Navy, Air Force or the CIA or someone had aircraft flying "special missions" but have never heard a thing.

After seeing it accelerate the way it did as it disappeared, I was fortunate that I didn't get close enough to engage it. I have no idea what type of aircraft it was but the situation sure got the adrenaline flowing.

Maybe I should have called this story, "The Air to Air Combat that almost was."

Frank Strobel
"Knight Hawk 6"

1293 MY NIGHT FLYING HOURS

A response to a question I received from John Laughinghouse

No, I had nowhere near 90% night flying hours but probably around 25 or 30%. Flying to and from the AO was always in daylight and I often managed to complete one and sometimes two sorties before dark. It was a good feeling to get a sortie in while still dusk and visibility was not impaired, particularly when hostile action was expected in a specific area. I was able to get a better feeling of the lay of the land before everything was black. I never logged night flying hours while still dusk and often my last sortie in the morning was begun or finished as the sun was rising, so my hours would be split on those sorties. I ended with 1327 combat hours, with around 400 of them being night flying hours.

I did get between 40-50 instrument hours, most of those during the monsoon season, flying to and from Vinh Long to the Seven Mountains Area. It was good to have a new ship (085) that had dependable, working navigation radios. That was a very rare thing for that time. My ship was one of the few that had instruments that were accurate enough to fly (IFR) by instruments only. I tried to practice my instrument flying as often as I could.

Often, even on bright sunny days when flying into Can Tho airfield, I would call Can Tho Radio for a Ground Controlled Approach (GCA), that put me ahead of all C-123's and C-7A's who normally would take preference in the landing pattern. On one occasion, a C-123 pilot complained to the tower that he had to extend his downwind leg for a **helicopter**. He said "helicopter" in a very disparaging way! The tower told him that the helicopter was on a GCA and had priority in the pattern. He didn't say another word. I did it fairly often and became good friends with the controllers there. They were often bored to death at their screens in good weather. They would even try to "GCA

144

me" to a particular POL point (Petroleum, Oil and Lubricants) for refueling on the south side of the main runway just for fun. I assumed their trailer was close to the airfield and that they actually went outside to visually guide me to POL but I let them have their fun.

All that practice came to good use one night when I did a med-i-vac from Vinh Long to Can Tho during a full blown monsoon rain. Visibility was no further than my rotor blades. I did an IFR take off (Instrument Flight Rules) from the ground, headed west from Vinh Long's ramp #1. I flew to the Vinh Long Navigational Directional Beacon (NDB) and contacted Can Tho Radio enroute for a GCA. We were IFR from 10 feet off the ground until I saw the white runway numbers between my feet. We were bounced around pretty good by the weather. Because of the visibility the tower instructed me to just "sit on the numbers" once I landed at Can Tho since there was no one else in the air. Medical transport met us while we stayed at flight idle on the end of the runway. We sat there about 20 minutes until it was clear enough to hover to a pad. That flight was one of my personal thrills while in Viet Nam.

Frank J. Strobel
"Knight Hawk 6"

Note: After attending 6 unit reunions, I found no one who had nearly the number of night flying hours I had accumulated, nor did anyone know of anyone else who could even come near my night hours. Maybe I did have the most night flying hours.

1358 THE U.S. NAVY SEALS, AKA . . . KIDNAPPING THE VILLAGE CHIEF

While in Viet Nam, I flew several Navy SEAL insertions/missions but one in particular has always stood out in my memory. One evening, I had been given a mission sheet to fly for the Navy SEALs. Doing what, I didn't know but I was at their disposal for the day. While a "Peter Pilot" and new to Viet Nam, I had never flown a mission for the Navy except as cover for their hovercraft, which were stationed in the far northeast area of the Delta (southwest of Saigon). I had never been exposed to this group of men. This is a long time before the Seals were widely known. They were just beginning to solidify their reputation.

I had never even heard of the SEALs and asked one of the other Aircraft Commanders who they were. Obviously he also knew little about them. I was told that they were a sort of glorified "WWII style Underwater Demolition Team (UDT)". That was my complete introduction to the Seals. I had no idea why a UDT team would want an ARMY chopper in the middle of the Delta. There were the Navy's own Sea Wolves helicopter gunships and other CH-53 helicopters available to them while working the Delta area. The mission sheet had me meet them at dawn at an old unused airstrip southeast of Vinh Long near the coast. I was told the airstrip was originally built by the Japanese during WWII to protect the coastal area of Viet Nam from ships in the South China Sea.

It was a one ship mission and in the morning I flew over there as requested. On arriving, I circled the airstrip moments after dawn but I could see no activity. There was a small thatch roofed building near one end of the runway. I felt uneasy landing without any cover on the airfield but I made my approach anyway. I touched down about 50 meters from the building but still there was no hint of activity around anywhere that we could see. I told my Co-Pilot to keep the RPM at full speed and to leave if there were any shots fired while we were near or in the building. He was to head back to Vinh Long. My crew chief and I each grabbed a rifle and we walked cautiously towards the building. We each stood against the wall on either side of the front door and I hit the door once with my fist.

How our standing with our backs against those thin outside walls would protect us from anything I don't know but at the time it just seemed to be the right thing to do. The walls of the building were so flimsy they probably would not even slow down a bullet if fired from inside of them. Anyway, John Wayne always did that kind of thing, so it must have been the right thing to do!

From the inside an obviously American voice said, "Come on in!" We looked at each other and then opened the door. There were five young American men standing around a table with a large map spread out on the top. None of them were in military clothing. All wore cut off jeans and sneakers. One wore a Mickey Mouse t-shirt. One wore a burgundy University of Wisconsin sweat shirt with its sleeves roughly cut off. Two of them were carrying "Stoners". I had heard of that weapon but I had never actually seen one. (There may have been more but I only saw two.) A stoner was a redesigned AR-15 that used 5.56mm belt-fed ammunition. They were really cool. I only saw them a few times while in Viet Nam and usually with the Navy Seals.

I asked, "Are you guys the SEALS?" They replied, "Yes, we are". So we went in. After a few seconds I became comfortable with the setup and I sent Pas, my Crew Chief, back out to have the Huey shut down.

147

THE MISSION

Giving me the briefing, they told me that they wanted me to fly down to a known enemy village in the south central U-Minh Forest just North of Cai Nuoc. I was to land in the central square of that enemy village at <u>noon</u>, sit and wait for them! They would then go to the village chief's house and kidnap him. They would bring him out to the chopper and I would then simply transport them down to a Navy base further down the Ca Mau Peninsula near Nam Can. They briefed me in a very matter-of-fact way like they did this kind of thing every day.

Now I knew why they didn't have a <u>Navy</u> chopper do this . . . They didn't want a Navy pilot to <u>die</u>!

"You have the rest of your life to solve your personal problems. How long you live depends on how well you do your job now."

I looked at the Seal in charge and said, "Absolutely not!" The shocked look I was given by the whole team told me that no one had ever said "no" to them. Or, if so, it was very rare.

When I was becoming familiarized to the area by my Knight Aircraft Commanders, I was told to stay away from the U-Minh Forest. The Viet Cong owned the forest and we didn't even fly over it because if we went down there, we wouldn't survive the enemy long enough to get a rescue team into the area. True or not, throughout my tour I stayed away from it, choosing to fly around it whenever I had a choice. Remember this was a one ship mission, so I had no help or cover. I was not going to sit in the middle of a Viet Cong village at noon and <u>wait</u> for them.

I looked at the map and told them what I <u>would do</u>! I would fly them to the edge of the village where a small dirt road entered it, drop them off, then leave and return later to pick them up. They just needed to tell me how much time they would need to do their job. I would return, land in the center of the village and pick them up. I would land, count slowly to 10 and then leave promptly whether they were on board or not. If they weren't on board they would probably be dead anyway. I knew I didn't want to be <u>dead</u> myself. They huddled around the map for a few minutes and then agreed to my terms and told me they needed four minutes on the ground. All the while I'm thinking, "There's no way in hell that they are going to pull this thing off."

Well, I must have been to hell that day, since I flew them down to the village and dropped them off, took off for my short four minute circle and landed in the center of the village and then began counting. I saw no movement of any kind in the village as I touched down. I started to count out loud over the intercom for the crew to hear, "ONE . . . TWO . . ." by the time I counted to SEVEN the Seals were all onboard with the village chief in tow and I was taking off. To my knowledge not a bullet was fired. When I landed the team at the Navy base I got out, saluted the whole team and shook their hands. I told them, if that is how they handled business I would fly them whenever and wherever they wanted, just give me a call. I was then released to fly back home to Vinh Long. It was an early day for us.

What a day that was. I just couldn't imagine what I had just done. I landed twice on a clear sunny day at an enemy village in the U Minh Forest; the second time just sitting in its small village square. I guess I did have the easy part. I was just sitting the whole time. The Seals did all the work!

IMPRESSED? JUST A LITTLE!!!!!!!

For a guy who had never heard of the U.S. Navy Seals before, I received a quick and professional education.

After that first experience, I flew numerous missions with the Seals during my tour. Those missions were always very "interesting".

Frank Strobel
"Knight Hawk 6"

1393 THE OLD MAN FROM HONG NGU

I'm a little hesitant to publish this story for reasons you will soon see but what the hell, no one is going to file charges against me now!

While flying General Xi around one October day in 1970 I landed at Hong Ngu, one of the last villages up the East Bank of the Mekong River before entering Cambodia. After landing in a small grassy area, General Xi left for his meeting inside the village. It was a beautiful day and his meeting was to take a couple hours so we settled in for a quiet and comfortable afternoon under some shade trees.

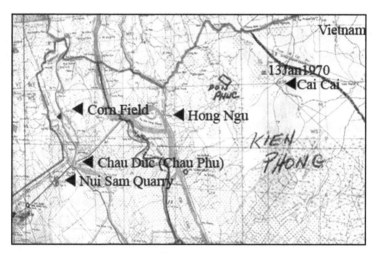

Map of Hong Ngu Area

As usually happened around these villages, about 20 children ages 5 to 14 came out to see the helicopter. For a while we were very cautious but after a half hour or so and seeing no visible problems, we started showing the kids the Huey but only a few at the time.

Some of the children were hesitant at first but they were very curious; even in their excitement there was no pushing or shoving. They were excited just to touch the outside skin of the helicopter. Oh, the wonder in their eyes! It was something they had probably seen many times flying high in the sky. When we allowed them, one or two at a time, they climbed into the cargo compartment. They were very courteous. Happily they seemed afraid to touch anything. Even though there was a language barrier, it was not hard see the absolute marvel they had for this machine.

KIDS ARE KIDS—EVERYWHERE IN THE WORLD!

A number of adults, mostly women of all ages, came through about 50 meters of small trees between the village and where we were, to watch our "Show 'n Tell" program for the kids. They seemed to enjoy watching their kids seeing something new and different. Although very interested, the adults stayed well away from us.

One young boy who was about 12, hit me on the arm the way kids do when they are playing tag and was very shocked when I started to chase him. He ran as I chased him, the other children squealed with glee. I was not just a stereotypical foreign soldier. I caught him several times and he, me. At one point he climbed up a small sapling that was just big enough to hold him. He was shocked to see me begin to climb it. As I climbed, the tree bent until I stepped off onto the ground and he was low enough for me to tag him. The adults as well as the other kids were laughing heartily at our game.

At that point, the group of adults started to split apart and a little old man came walking out to see what was going on. I could see someone giving him a quick update and he began to smile. He was obviously a respected village elder. He slowly walked over and greeted me in that old Vietnamese way of bowing. I greeted him and slowly gave him a "walk around tour," pointing out and explaining the different parts on the outside of the Huey. Even though I spoke almost no Vietnamese and he no English, he listened and watched most attentively. I opened the left side front door to show him the cockpit but he was very short and could see next to nothing. He was extremely interested in all he could see. The villagers had moved to within about 25 meters of the aircraft in total silence, just watching us very intently.

I invited the old man with gestures to climb into the left front seat and began to help his fragile body up. I walked around the front of the helicopter, climbed into the right seat and again began to explain in gestures and English about the controls and what they did and then the same about the instruments. On several occasions he pointed to something and spoke to me. I didn't understand him but tried to explain what I thought he was asking, mostly by hand gestures. I pulled the collective up and motioned with my hand how the aircraft would move vertically. I leaned over and placed his hand on the cyclic and motioned with my hand how the helicopter would respond and in which direction the ship would fly. He seemed to understand. The look in his eyes was indescribable. I did feel very good.

This is when I did something I never should have done. I had the crew chief strap him, put a helmet on him, untie the rotor blades of the ship and then clear the area. I did not allow any of my crew into the helicopter. If something bad happened, I didn't want anyone else onboard. As you probably have guessed, I started the Huey. To this day, I really don't know why but I guess it just seemed like the right thing to do.

I turned on the battery and the flashing warning lights and fire warning siren went off. He was obviously shocked but also somewhat excited and was surprised when he heard me speaking to him through the helmet intercom. I continued to talk to him in a soft comforting voice with some hand gestures and he relaxed a bit. As the different steps in the startup process progressed, I kept on talking to him and pointing to relative instruments and what they were doing. In a few moments we were at flight idle. I was talking to him all the while.

Now as a man settled into a normal lifestyle with a family, I'm sure the decisions I made that day would not be the same today. I couldn't tell you how many Army regulations I had already broken but I was going to break one more. Although I went through all the pros & cons in my mind about what I was doing, I wasn't deterred; I continued anyway.

After getting obstruction clearance from my crew, all who were still on the ground and giving my passenger instructions to keep his hands off everything (that, he did seem to understand), I pulled pitch and went to a hover, sliding a little backwards into a large open planted field. The excitement in his eyes was extraordinary. It gave me a thrill just to see it on his face! I did a slow hovering turn, keeping my tail rotor in one spot and moving the nose clockwise as if I was a hand on a clock. This was to keep the tail rotor clear of any obstruction. Once clear, I slowly slid over their fields and paddies as high as a 15 foot hover and as low as barely touching the ground. I went back and forth several times, then a peddle turn or two, all the while talking to him over the intercom.

I did go up to about 300 feet in the air to circle the village for him and then came back down and landed in the spot we had so recently left. As I shut down, my crew chief unbuckled the old man and helped him out of the Huey. Once I climbed out he came over to me, grabbed my right hand and spoke to me very rapidly in Vietnamese, bowing and re-bowing touching his face to the back of my hand.

He then turned around and walked over to the other villagers. They again opened up an area for him to walk through but this time as he entered the opening, they surrounded him all obviously asking him questions. Naturally, I assumed, about what it was like. In a few moments they were all back in the village and things were quiet again, except for a few of the children who stayed with the helicopter.

About 20 minutes later, General Xi came out to the aircraft. His meetings were done for the day. He then asked me what had gone on while he was in the village. After relating this story, he was quite amused. We got aboard and I started the Huey in preparation to leave. When I was ready to pull pitch I saw the old man, followed by a large group of people coming back out of the village. He was carrying a small wooden chest of some kind.

When I told the General that the villagers were coming out to give him a box, he said, "No, they aren't! You gave the old man something very important. It was something that neither he nor anyone else in that village would ever have had the opportunity to experience. He is probably bringing something in that chest that is very special to him. My guess is that he wants to give something of his, to you. The people in this village have next to nothing. The best thing you could do for him is to wave to him and just leave."

I did!

I will always wonder what was in that chest!

Frank Strobel
"Knight Hawk 6"

Frank Standing at the Base of Nui Cam, Background—Nui Coto

1407 WENDELL JARRETT &AND HIS DAD, AKA . . . VIEWING THE WAR FROM ABOVE

One night I was flying my Night Hunter-Killer mission west of Saigon and east of the Parrots Beak area. I was far east of Moc Hoa and the Plain of Reeds where I normally flew. Wendell Jarrett was flying my Bug and dropping flares as I needed. We refueled and rearmed a couple times at Moc Hoa. We had several small contacts before midnight but about 2:00 AM all hell broke loose. I had obviously ticked someone off!

Between our guns, the flares and the return fire we were receiving, it was like the 4th of July. That contact lasted over an hour until we had to return to Moc Hoa to refuel and rearm. When we returned to the area later, we couldn't irritate anyone enough to get the battle started again. The rest of the night was very quiet.

About two weeks later, Wendell received a letter from his father. His father was a pilot for Flying Tigers Airline and flew cargo into Viet Nam very often. No, that in itself wasn't very strange. What was interesting was that his father wrote to him about flying into Tan San Nhut airport two weeks earlier. He had been put into a holding pattern for about 30 minutes south of Saigon to await clearance for his approach. While in the holding pattern, he watched what he called "one hell of a battle" west of Saigon, about 2:00 AM.

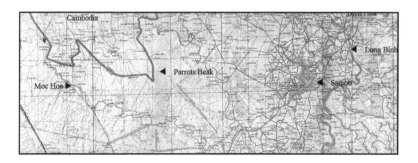

157

Wendell brought the letter over to my room and we looked at a map and calendar and confirmed that his father was watching <u>us</u>! Wendell said to me, "Can you believe that. How many guys can go to war with their living father high above, watching what was going on?" He was so excited that he could write his father with the news. We both had a warm feeling inside. It was almost like having a personal guardian angel watching over us.

Wendell was from Miami, Florida. On the two occasions I have visited Florida, I tried to look him up but both times was unsuccessful. Maybe someday we'll see each other again.

Frank Strobel
Knight Hawk 6

**Frank Strobel and Wendell Jarrett on top of Nui Cam
at the Entrance to a Viet Cong Tunnel**

1453 MOC HOA . . . IT'S A SMALL WORLD—DEE THOMAS AND DENNIS FENNESSY

Part 1

In the late spring of 1970 and after an ammunition dump explosion from a Viet Cong mortar attack, the airfield at Moc Hoa was reworked. The runway, their fueling area and the ammunition dump areas were all upgraded. Then a couple of new radio towers were built fairly close to the southwest end of the runway. Those towers were no problem in the daylight but at night they were a real hazard. I often said that, "If I ever found the moron who designed and placed those towers in that position I would 'shoot' him!" I couldn't tell you the years those towers took off my life during nighttime approaches for landings.

On many occasions making my approach to a landing at night, I would need to fly fairly close to the towers. Being in a combat area and not wishing to draw too much attention to them, there were no lights on either tower. Not wishing to draw any fire on my approach I would also keep my ship's lights off. Knowing that I was close to the towers, I would concentrate my efforts on avoiding the towers and their supporting cables. On clear nights there was no problem spotting the towers but on very dark and cloudy nights it was a matter of looking at the ink black crisscrossed metal of the towers against the charcoal black color of the clouds.

One night as I was making my approach, I was expecting the contrast between those dark colors to be almost nil. The lower I flew the more I was concentrating on seeing that minimal contrast. Just at the moment I was expecting to see the towers I looked to the right through the open window just inches from my eyes, I saw a <u>face</u> looking in at me. Actually, I didn't even recognize it as a face at that moment. My heart stopped beating. I didn't really recognize it as anything in particular, I just had the instant realization, that something was <u>really</u> close and <u>nothing</u> should be <u>real close</u>.

I was actually surprised that if something (one of the towers) was that close, why wasn't I at least entangled in one the cables? Either a tower or its cable would be deadly. Immediately, I pulled pitch and brought in as much power as the engine gauges would allow me, then I pulled little more. I definitely had the engine torque past the yellow caution area and into the bottom of the red zone. The Huey creaked and groaned, reluctantly stopped its descent and then it began slowly establishing a climb. I quickly scanned my instruments to see that all was okay for the moment and then finally looked back out my window.

What I saw was a very big shock. My crew chief that night was Sergeant Dee Thomas and without any kind of a restraint, he climbed outside the Huey. He side stepped forward on the skid until he got to my door. My window was open. His hands, holding the window opening at his three & nine O'clock positions, he pulled his face inside the window. When I turned my face to look out the window, our noses were within inches of each other. He was laughing heartily at his "practical joke".

Thank God that when I hastily pulled pitch, he had a good grip on a secure door and his feet didn't slip off the smooth metal skid. It took about an hour for my blood pressure to return to normal. I gradually, very gradually accepted the humor in his "joke". He did get me good.

Note: I had told my wife this story after returning to the "world". What I didn't know until several years later, was that my wife dismissed it as an exaggerated 'war' story. Who would actually climb outside (with or without a safety strap), especially at night?

One evening, my wife answered the phone and then asked me if I knew "Dee" Thomas? I said, "No!" Then she said "Dee Thomas who was a crew chief in Viet Nam." He was on the phone. Then I said, **"Oh, Dee Thomas. Sure I know, Dee!"**

I quickly answered. He and his wife were driving past Erie on the interstate when he remembered I lived here. They came over to our home. We offered dinner and Dee and I spent several hours talking about Viet Nam before they had to leave.

During our conversation we spoke of a number of situations from our time together. One he related was the one I just wrote about. Essentially, he told this same story without any prompting from me, confirming to my wife the truth in the story. He was with me when many "special" situations arose over there and he confirmed many of them that evening through our stories. She has never questioned my stories since.

Often the truth is stranger than fiction!

Believe it or not, there is actually a "Part 2" to this story.

Read on if you have a few moments.

Part 2

After returning to the "world", I finished college and began my working career in a management position at a local bank. One thing that I didn't give up was my flying. I couldn't afford to rent helicopters so I transitioned into fixed wing and flew a Cessna 150 or a Cessna 172 a few times a month just for fun. I flew out of a privately owned small dirt airstrip.

One afternoon in the summer of 1975 while I was flying, the weather began to deteriorate rapidly. I decided to land, reluctantly cutting short my flight by about an hour. I was beginning my shut down procedures when I received a call over the Unicom radio channel asking what the weather conditions were on the field. The airport in Erie had just shut down by a major storm, with lightening striking directly on the field.

I told him that the winds were variable but beginning to gust erratically. He decided to attempt a landing anyway. He made several approaches and "go-a-rounds" because of the winds. On his last approach, he forced his twin engine Cessna onto the dirt runway at a high rate of speed and bent a wing up pretty good making it un-flyable. The plane quickly left the runway and went around the end of a building. I raced to the plane expecting the worst. Upon reaching the plane, I realized that this guy had his whole family with him. Luckily no one was hurt. They were very lucky.

Being the only person at this private strip, I took them home to Erie with me. At my home they made arrangements for a hotel room and arrangements to continue their trip without the plane. While having a drink before dinner, he mentioned the military memorabilia on my walls and shelves. Our conversation instantly then moved to Viet Nam. It turned out that he was in Nam at the same time I was and he built new and repaired damaged airfields.

I said to him, "You know, it's a funny thing you should say that because there was one airfield that was rebuilt while I was there. It was a small airfield just east of the Plain Of Reeds, which had two towers built close to the southwest end of the runway. What a stupid place to put them! It was just another example of poor design and planning. They created a very dangerous situation for the pilots landing there".

Before I could continue, he said, "Oh, do you mean Moc Hoa?" He then explained to me that Moc Hoa was one of his projects and the ground where they were placed was the only area around the field that could support those towers.

Can you believe it! The guy who I wanted to 'shoot' so many times for placing the towers where they were built; the man I cursed <u>sooooo</u> many nights as I sweated profusely was sitting in **my** living room and drinking **my** scotch.

His name was Dennis Fennessy and was an attorney from Columbus, Ohio.

Small world, isn't it?

Frank Strobel
"Knight Hawk 6"

1472 THE NAVY SEALS, AKA . . . A MESS AT THE NAVY "MESS"

One day in the late spring of 1970 I flew a Navy Seal Team, on a single ship mission to insert them at the far southern tip of the Ca Mau Peninsula. It was the only time in Viet Nam I was involved with any US Troops, repelling on ropes down into the jungle from a hovering Huey. That day was actually 'treated' to several new experiences.

As I was transporting the Seal Team to the insertion location we watched three C-123's flying several hundred feet directly above us. They approached from the rear so we didn't see them until they flew over and past us. They were flying wing tip to wing tip spraying Agent Orange. By the time we realized what was happening it was too late to detour around the falling spray. As the droplets churned up by my rotor blades rolled through our door-less Huey, we discussed how we really didn't like. I said, (tongue in cheek) it was a good thing, as we were always told that it only affected the vegetation, not people. Before it was over, Agent Orange was dripping down the inside of my windshield, as we all breathed the mist.

After an interesting but uneventful insertion into a recently abandoned Viet Cong base, my crew and I were invited to eat in the new Navy "mess hall" at a brand new base they were building near Nam Cam. We had C-rations on board for lunch but a Navy mess hall sounded real nice for a change. I made my approach to a fairly large PSP landing pad but as soon as we touched down I was asked to move into a newly bulldozed and extremely muddy area to the side. They were expecting a CH-46 "Sea Knight" tandem rotor chopper very shortly. It was bringing in more Marines for base security and some supplies that were badly needed.

As we were tying the blade down and preparing to go to lunch, the CH-46 appeared overhead and stopped at a 50' hover. It seemed strange to do so since there was no sling load to prevent a direct approach to the pad. It hovered for a few seconds and then started rocking back and forth in the air. It was evident that the pilot was losing control. Meanwhile, we were only about 20 meters from the slightly raised pad looking straight up while standing in 15 inches of wet, sucking mud.

The Marine helicopter started settling towards the pad at a very high rate. It hit hard on it's back left landing wheel then bounced up about 10 feet and hit on it's right rear landing wheel and bounced again. We were in shock because we were so close and the ground was so very muddy and there was no way we could run away. Every step we took we sunk in eight or ten inches or more. As we pulled our feet up for another step we could hear the suction slowly release around our boots. If parts of that helicopter started flying off we were too close we knew we couldn't get out of the way.

The helicopter bounced up again and this time hit on its single nose wheel. The rotors on both rotor heads were flexing badly and I expected one of the blades to hit the helicopter's fuselage. A couple of seconds later the pilot was able to settle it onto the landing pad without any visible damage. That was a little too close for comfort. As the Marine passengers onboard very quickly embarked down the rear gate, we walked over to have lunch.

As we slogged through their new base, we could see that they were just beginning to get organized. There was nothing there except a few tents on wooden platforms and recently bulldozed mud. One thing that stood out though was the mess hall. It was a clean and white aluminum sided mobile home styled building. Yes, white! It was such a stark contrast to all of the mud. It was a fairly small modular building that must have been flown in and set in place on the ground. It was quite a sight compared to all the mess that surrounded it. I could see two doors one on each end of the building but there were no signs stating which was the entrance and which was the exit so we wiped our feet and went in the right door.

The place was immaculate on the inside. It even had music piped through it. There was a nice looking, 30" high white picket fence separating the small mess hall into two smaller seating areas. There was no place for a chow line so we just sat down to eye the place for a moment to see where everyone went to get their food trays. We needed to learn their process. Then a Navy seaman came out with 2 plates of food and placed them in front of two men a few feet away from us. We couldn't believe it. They were serving on china. They had beautiful flatware and nice but paper dinner napkins. It was just like a nice restaurant back in the "world".

The seaman, started towards us and then abruptly turned and walked away. He went back to the table he had just served. He spoke softly to one of the men seated there. The man got up and started over to our table. It was a Navy Captain (not an Army Captain O-4 but naturally a Navy O-6)and he didn't look happy. He asked if he could speak to me over in the corner by the door through which we had just entered.

He very politely but firmly informed me that we had entered the hall through the "Officer's" entrance and my crew chief and gunner would have to leave the building and enter via the other door. <u>My crew</u> had to go outside and back through the mud to enter through the other door, into a building they were already in. They were to eat on the "other side" of the short white picket fence. They could not step over the 30 inch "fence". All I could think of was Rosa Parks in Alabama. I guess I wouldn't make it in the Navy. Not wishing to enter a Navy brig via saying what I was thinking, I apologized (only slightly sarcastically) for my error. He went back to sit down to his lunch and I went back to my table.

When I was at our table I quietly asked my crew to get up, we were leaving. They looked very puzzled when I told them we were having cold C-rations for lunch. As we were exiting the building the Navy Captain got back up and just as I approached the door; he asked me where I was going? I told him that my crew was family; we fought together, we laughed and cried together and we slept together, we did everything together including eating. We had food on board my Huey, we would eat there.

With a puzzled look on his face he thought for a second then very politely asked me to get my crew to return. All of my crew could eat at the table we had been sitting at. As we sat down we noticed that the men on the other side of the "fence", had to get their own food on trays only the Officers used china. We had a very nice lunch served to us on that china, even though many eyes from both sides of the "fence" watched us closely the whole time. I guess that for a moment, I shook the establishment. Lunch was very nice that day, even though they didn't serve wine. I also found out why I probably wouldn't make it in the US Navy. I probably would have been keelhauled!

Frank Strobel
"Knight Hawk 6"

1484 CAMBODIA 1970—DAY 1, AKA . . . NIGHTTIME CONFUSION

We, the military, became our own worst enemy this particular day. In the spring of 1970 there was a big push into Cambodia. I was fairly excited at the prospect of being one of a hundred or so helicopters in IV Corps heading into Cambodia on a troop insertion. My excitement turned to fear and quickly to anger before we were all off the ground in Vinh Long.

All the helicopters cranked up to take off while it was still "O-dark-thirty". It seemed that all of Vinh Long was cranking and leaving at the same time. When ready, the Knights all hovered out onto the ramp and sat there waiting for a clearance for a formation departure. We were prepared to depart to the east **"in formation"** from ramp one.

The trouble was that the Air Force tower operator would only clear one ship for takeoff at a time from each ramp in rotation. We protested to the tower but were still refused a formation departure. At the same time the Cowboys were ready to depart north of the runway, likewise the Air Cav south of the runway. If this was a test, I think we failed!

Within a few minutes there was mass confusion, there were helicopters all over the sky, lights everywhere. There were no formations anywhere. Hueys were circling everywhere north of Vinh Long over the river. In the dark everyone looked the same. Knight Lead radioed, "I'm north of the river flashing my landing light. Form up on me." The only problem was that all Leads from all the units had the same idea and there were flashing landing lights everywhere you looked. No one had any idea where their Lead was. Within a couple of minutes I had two Hueys fly across my flight path in the dark night as they circled looking for something which they wouldn't be able to recognize if they found it. It was mass confusion in the sky and on both the tower's VHF radio frequency and our company's FM radio frequency. How there was not a mid-air collision, I don't know.

Finally, extremely frustrated I got on the Guard Channel (UHF 243. 0) and made a blind call, "Stop circling, head west and form up on someone, anyone ahead of you. Just be safe. We're all going to the same place. We'll sort it out when we get there in the daylight." I don't know if that is what everybody did but later as the sun came up, I found out that I formed up on a Cowboy aircraft and I rejoined the Knights after landing at Chau Duc Airfield. The Cowboy Lead didn't seem to mind.

The Air Force had placed a temporary tower at Chau Duc airfield the night before and although there were flights of helicopters all over the sky, things were slowly sorted out. I soon landed and found the rest of the Knights. As I was setting down I heard a blind call over the new Chau Duc tower frequency. "WE VNAF, WE LAND NOW!" There were still many flights of Hueys circling the airfield awaiting their turn to land. Everyone looked up because no one knew which flight was making a direct approach from their current position and without clearance. One flight then broke into about a 90 degree left turn and began their approach. When the tower spotted them, it made a general safety call about their location. Another danger narrowly avoided.

The actual incursion into Cambodia with our first troop insertion was much safer. I was flying Lead for the second flight of Knight aircraft entering Cambodia and we made our first troop insertion in a very uneventful way into a huge open plain with small areas of trees and scrub. We returned to Viet Nam and picked up our second group of troops. The only enemy I actually saw that day was during our second insertion.

I have a picture taken on short final to our landing zone, of some ARVN troops lifting up a woven mat of some kind that was floating in an irrigation or drainage ditch. There was a Viet Cong under it. Thankfully, the rest of the day was relatively quiet.

A Viet Cong Found Under the Mat

Frank Strobel
"Knight Hawk 6"

1484 CAMBODIA 1970—DAY 2, AKA . . . A 155 HOWITZER FLIES

In the spring of 1970 there was a big push into Cambodia. On the second day of the incursion, I was split from the Knights who were making additional troop insertions, to fly "Wingman" for a CH-54 Skycrane that was to sling load a 155mm howitzer into Cambodia to support the ARVN activity there. It was the first time I had even been near a Skycrane. I enjoyed climbing all over it doing a pre-flight inspection with its pilot and getting a good look at it.

When he was ready to depart, I watched him closely as the howitzer was being lifted off the ground. His rotor blades flexed tremendously into a deep saucer shape and then slowly the gun reluctantly let go of the ground. We climbed to cruise at 5,000 feet. My Huey was like a little gnat next to that huge behemoth. We were flying much higher than I had flown in a long time. About one click before we entered Cambodia the Skycrane suddenly started to climb like a proverbial "bat out of hell".

Frank and the Howitzer

I was shocked at his rate of climb and without thinking I said, "Where are you going?" He said, "Sorry, sonny. Cable broke, lost my load and I'm going home" and he was gone. That was the last I saw of him. As he started his call to me, I had already realized what had happened and spotted the howitzer on its quick trip to the ground. Do you have any idea how fast a 155mm howitzer can fall one mile? Well, I didn't stop to figure it out but I can tell you it was pretty fast.

When it hit the ground it made a crater about 50-60 feet across and at least 25 feet deep! Being the dry season the ground erupted like a huge bomb had landed there. Dust and dirt flew everywhere. Of course I guess for all intents and purposes it was a bomb, a very expensive one. The only thing visible was a small portion of one of the tires; the rest was deeply buried.

Thus ended my only encounter in Viet Nam with a Skycrane.

Frank Strobel
"Knight Hawk 6

1486 EXPENSIVE SPAGHETTI

One of the days I was flying insertions with the White Knights, I was again flying the trail position. Before we left for our second insertion which was only about three clicks away, we were already thinking of lunch at the base at Cao Lanh. Before our takeoff, we threw all of our canned C-ration "entrees" through the engine view port. I had spaghetti that day and the prospect of eating that gelled mass cold was not appetizing. C-Ration spaghetti when not warm looked like creamed red jell-o with pasta sealed inside. Letting those cans roll back and forth under the hot engine would heat all of our lunches very nicely and there would be no aftertaste of JP4 like they normally had.

As we returned to the assembly area, I was peeled off the formation to complete an emergency med-i-vac. I returned about an hour or so after we had originally expected to land. On short final my crew chief yelled through the intercom, "Mr. Strobel, our lunches!" With a med-i-vac in progress our lunches had been the last thing on our mind. I landed as quickly as possible. The can of pork was hot; the Pork 'n Beans were fine; but my spaghetti, well—had exploded!

A seam of the lid didn't open up and let the mess ooze out. The can blew up and it looked like shrapnel. It had exploded all over the engine compartment and the engine itself. Do you have any idea what exploded burnt spaghetti noodles looks like on an expensive, finely tuned jet engine? It was not a pretty sight.

For anyone reading this who doesn't understand the ramifications of this, the firebox of a jet engine is made of a very thin metal. The only reason it doesn't melt is that high speed air is forced along the inside of the firebox keeping the fire and extreme heat away from the inside of the engine compartment and thus away from the metal. Anything on the outside of the firebox, even a pencil mark, will draw excessive heat and burn a hole through the metal. Burnt spaghetti noodles will draw much more heat than a pencil mark and it can quickly ruin the expensive engine.

In maintenance terms, we "circle red X'd" the ship which allowed a one-time flight directly back to maintenance. I flew it directly back to Vinh Long for an engine change. I hoped the engine would last long enough to complete the flight. All the way back, I'm thinking, "How am I going to explain <u>this</u>?" There is no good or reasonable excuse for this mistake. I couldn't even concoct a story to even semi-reasonably explain this. Maybe if after landing at Vinh Long, I shot the engine a couple times with my .38 caliber pistol and told them about this "close call" I had with the Viet Cong. No, that wouldn't work!

So I did the hardest thing a young Warrant Officer in that situation, could do. I wrote it up for maintenance to understand exactly what had happened. It really hurt me writing, "Engine damaged by exploding can of spaghetti" but I did. I waited for hours, days and then weeks for Miles (Miles Hedrick, our Company Commander) to call me into his office. The longer I went without hearing from Miles the more I thought he was trying to think of something really "good" to do with me. It was torture. Even after leaving Nam for my next duty station, Fort Hunter-Stewart, Ga., I expected to have the paperwork catch up with me. It didn't. Thanks, Miles!

Frank Strobel
"Knight Hawk 6"

1508 CHAU DUC AKA . . . THE "BORDER CONTROL" RADAR OPERATOR FLIES

While flying the Night Hunter-Killer missions in the Seven Mountains Area, I would use "Border Control" radar to guide my flight along the Cambodian border and to do my standard day to day flight following. They had the border traced on their screen and could vector me within meters of the border. They were rarely busy at night and did a very good job for us. They could follow me on the screen almost everywhere I went in their area until I went below 200 feet AGL, which I often did. I some areas he could even "paint me" until I went well below 200 feet. One of them would call and tell me he lost me as I went down to do some "work". I would radio back that I'd call him when I was finished with my task. He could always track my Bug because he would normally stay between 2,000 and 2,500 feet AGL to drop flares. Sometimes though, when I thought I was being really crafty, I would leave my Bug circling in one area being painted on the radar while I went to another area below 50 feet AGL and off of radar to do my work untracked.

One night between missions, I invited myself into their trailer that contained their radar screens to meet them personally and have them show me their equipment's capabilities. When I was about to leave, one of the operators asked if he could fly with me sometime to "see what I do" when they lose me on the radar screen. I told him to let me know when he wanted to go. If he would tell me before I headed into the area, I'd pick him up. One evening soon after, he called me when I radioed "inbound," so I dropped into Chau Duc later that evening and picked him up.

175

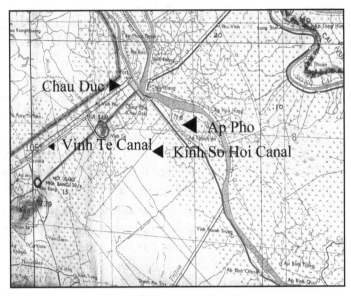

Map Of The Operation Area

We left Chau Duc airfield about 11:00 p.m. and flew southeast a short while to Ap Pho to find the small Kinh So Hoi Canal to follow. The canal left the river in a southwesterly direction. We started flying down the canal with no lights or flares at about 50 feet AGL. We had been briefed that there was to be <u>no</u> friendly units or civilian activity in the area because of printed fliers that had been posted for weeks prior in the small villages nearby. It wasn't a free fire area but no civilian was permitted to be out there. We flew less than a click and spotted three men standing in the total darkness about 20 meters from the canal. I pulled into a very tight left turn, put our one million candle power xeon light on them and asked my back seat ARVN military advisor (a Major) what he thought of them. I was told that "they looked okay; they were just friendly farmers." His American counterpart however, agreed with me, that the Major's opinion was **not** the case.

I told the American advisor to tell the ARVN Officer onboard that I wasn't leaving. I wanted him to check their ID. He protested because of the danger. I told him that if they were friendly farmers there was no danger! I called my Bug to come down to 500 feet to cover us since we were landing. By the way, I had forgotten about the fact that my radar operator passenger was even on board. I guess I was too busy.

We landed about 40' from the men with the xeon light still blinding them. My American and ARVN advisor left the Huey and checked the men's ID. The ARVN came back and stated that they were exactly what he had said and that we could not even detain them for questioning. How frustrating that was. There was no plausible reason for them to be there. We were not in a farmer's field. We were in heavy scrub far from anything farm related. We left them standing there as we took off. No, I didn't need to shoot them but as close to Chau Duc as we were, we easily could have detained them. I returned immediately to Chau Duc and made the ARVN advisor leave my ship. He had no desire to have me do my job so I wanted someone different on board. The ARVN Major was very shocked but both the American and the ARVN advisors left the ship. We shut down to see if we would get another advisor.

As they left the helicopter my radar operator passenger spoke up. He said, "Knight Hawk, is that what you do when I lose you on my radar?" I told him that it was not always that specific activity but the same type of thing. We usually look but don't necessarily find anyone but what we do often provokes a firefight. He said that when I landed, it was the first time while in Nam that he actually locked and loaded his M-16 rifle in fear for his life.

Not that they didn't before but after that incident I was treated very attentively by both of those radar operators. They would always ask what I found anytime I reappeared on their screen. I could not have designed a more involved personal flight following crew. They even were able to get an FM radio to listen to us as we worked in their local area. They too quickly became family.

Frank Strobel
"Knight Hawk 6"

1167 THE O'CLUB HOSTESSES, RE: BUFFIRILLA AND TI TI WA

After reading your notes on Bufarilla, the "O" Club waitress, they reminded me of the girls there during my time. There must have been a big change at the Officers' Club after you guys left. When I arrived in Viet Nam two of the girls at the club weren't too bad looking. I particularly remember one by the name of Ti Ti Wa! I'm sure many other guys remember her also; she would be hard to forget.

She stood about 4'10" tall and all of her parts were proportioned fine and all were exactly where they should be.

TiTi Wa was married to an ARVN Lieutenant. One weekend he came home to their apartment in downtown Vinh Long. It was his first weekend off in almost a year. The second night home they had gone to bed when they heard a great commotion in the stairwell. It was some local Viet Cong looking for her husband. They had a very small apartment and with no place to go, she talked him into getting under the mat on which they were sleeping and she then covered the mat with a blanket they were using. She opened the door just as they got to it and they burst into the apartment yelling all kinds of obscenities. She walked across the room and sat on the blanket/mat/husband.

After quickly looking throughout the small apartment they threatened her, trying to find out where he was. She told them that she hadn't seen her husband in a very long time. She was afraid for her safety but they soon left her apartment and surprisingly didn't touch her.

Portrait of Ti Ti Wa

Before he left to return to his unit, they agreed that he would not come back to Vinh Long until the end of the war. She was trying to set up contacts through her extended family in Saigon to set up a meeting with him there but as of the date when I left Nam, I didn't know if they were able to do it.

That is a very tough way to live your life.

Frank Strobel
"Knight Hawk 6"

1763 THAT SON AIRFIELD, AKA . . . THE FLAMIN' FUEL BLADDER

In the summer of 1970, the Viet Cong placed a 57mm recoilless rifle on the northeast corner of Nui Cam. Their announcement of the new weapon's location was made when they shot down a C-123 that was on an approach to land at the west end of the runway at That Son. Immediately, all aircraft were forbidden to land there. The only exceptions (I know you already guessed it) were helicopters. The Army, in its infinite wisdom, didn't want to risk having anyone disassembling the full fuel bladders; there were two of them and they were full of JP-4 fuel. Each bladder was composed of rubber and canvas and held several thousand gallons of liquid. The fear was that while emptying the bladders, the fuel handlers would become targets for the recoilless rifle which could possibly injure or kill the working crew. I guess they thought the enemy wouldn't shoot at helicopters.

At a briefing, I were encouraged to refuel from them as often as I was able to do so, thus emptying them as quickly as possible. As soon as they were empty, they would be removed.

Here were the rules we were to follow while refueling:

1. One aircraft at a time.
2. The Huey was to be grounded, remain at operating RPM and light on its skids.
3. Only one crew member was to exit the aircraft to complete the refueling, preferably the crew chief.
4. The second crew member, the gunner, would move over to the right side of the cargo compartment but stay onboard. While the crew chief refueled the ship, the gunner was to keep his helmet plugged in to listen to any changes in orders from the Aircraft Commander.

5. If any rounds were received, pitch was to be pulled immediately. The crewmember who was refueling the ship would drop the nozzle in place and jump onboard. We were then to be on our way, performing an expedited departure.

I assume that a non-aviation rated Officer developed that procedure.

Everything went along fine for about a week or so with no incidents. We were all very uneasy about the whole process and knew that the peace couldn't last. "Charlie" probably was waiting to shoot at a larger fixed-wing aircraft. One morning, however, Charlie must have finally resolved in his mind that no large aircraft would be using the runway again so he decided, "Let's shoot at Frank."

That morning, shortly after dawn we began refueling and things did change. Pas Mantanona was my crew chief and was to do the refueling; Frank Akana was my gunner. Pas had just begun refueling when we heard an explosion behind us. I pulled pitch and slowly at first, began to move to give Pas an opportunity to jump onboard. That was the fastest he ever moved.

"Never forget . . . incoming fire has the right of way."

We began climbing out to the east, accelerating as quickly as possible. We got to about 50 Feet AGL when a second tremendous explosion was felt. It rocked the Huey from behind. It was close enough to help our acceleration by pushing us forward. I climbed to 300 feet and made a left turn to head north. As I made the turn we had our first view of what had happened. The second impact was directly on top of the bladder we were using to refuel. The bright orange fire ball was as high as we were and was shaped like a mushroom—not the smoke just the fireball! Had the first round hit on that bladder we all probably would have been incinerated.

We all marveled at our luck. That was the last time I returned to That Son Airfield until after we controlled the mountain. Maybe that last bladder is still there but I never went back to check.

Frank Strobel
"Knight Hawk 6"

1861 MY BASIC TRAINING DRILL SERGEANT AKA . . . WOULD YA LIKE A LIFT?

Okay, here I go again. Maybe it's a bit long winded but this is one of my best memories of Viet Nam!

More than a year after finishing basic training, I was flying as Aircraft Commander for a "Swing Ship" mission southeast of Moc Hoa near Thuy Dong. We were still up on an FM channel for an outpost to which we had just recently dropped some supplies. We heard a very anxious call. "Is there any aircraft up on this net?" I didn't answer the call, figuring that there had to be someone else nearby. Then a minute or so later, we heard the caller again but now he had a somewhat more desperate voice. This time I answered.

A patrol had been ambushed and they were pinned down in the middle of a rice paddy. Except for a small dike they were crouching behind, they had no cover. I was surprised to realize that I was only a couple minutes away from their situation. I told them that I wasn't a gunship but if they could use a couple of M-60's, I would make myself available. They seemed very happy to accept my offer.

I made two firing passes with my M-60's into the tree line from which they were receiving fire to see how heavy the enemy fire was against them. It seemed not to be too bad now that I was there. I then made an approach to the patrol in the rice paddy.

The first to climb aboard was Sergeant Brewton, my Basic Training Drill Instructor. I looked back into the cargo compartment and he quickly glanced up at me as he was climbing aboard. After taking off and assessing that we were no worse for wear, I began to tell my Crew Chief to give the sergeant his helmet so I could talk to him but SGT Brewton had already borrowed my gunner's helmet.

The next thing I heard was, "Well, Strobel! You sure have come up in the world, haven't you?" I replied, "Yes I have, sergeant and aren't **you** glad?" I flew him back to his outpost and he bought lunch. We spent over an hour together hashing over 'old' times and some new ones before I continued on my mission.

Later that day as I was looking back, I realized that he managed to recognize me, even in an armored Huey seat with a flight helmet on my head, a tinted visor over my eyes and a mike boom across my lips. With all of the trainees that went through basic while he was a drill sergeant, he had remembered me. What a satisfying day I had, not only professionally but personally.

I will always have a salute reserved for him!

Frank Strobel
"Knight Hawk 6"

2193 JOHN STEVENS AKA . . . TINH BINH MEDICAL EVACUATION

No, John was not evacuated but it was the only time I saw him perform a medical evacuation. One night while flying Night Hawk for the Tinh Binh area along the Ven Te Canal, we had a very heavy night of fighting. John was flying my Bug. This night was just a short time before he transferred from the White Knight Platoon to the Cobra Gun Platoon. Although we normally spent most of our time in the Nui Cam-Nui Dai area, this night was a little different. Things were hot and heavy a little northeast at Tinh Binh from just after midnight until dawn.

We refueled and rearmed several times supporting the outpost. We were working around the Tinh Binh area all that night. Around 4:00 AM we were told that their Master Sergeant at the outpost had been hit and they were having trouble controlling the bleeding. I explained that things were too hot at the moment to help but, when things calmed down as they usually did at dawn, a medical evacuation would be out first priority. As expected, at dawn things did quiet down and we were on the radio preparing for the pickup. They did not want the extraction from their normal pad outside the compound. They wanted us to land inside.

There wasn't much room but with a vertical 50 foot hover between some trees to the ground, it could be done. With seven people on board I didn't want to try it, so John volunteered the Bug ship. As he hovered over the compound and began his descent, mortar rounds began falling in several places around the compound. He radioed and said that he was committed at that point and didn't feel that he could easily stop his descent and begin an ascent. We were both sweating bullets.

Speaking of bullets, I was out of them. We didn't have one left on board. I knew the general area where the mortar had been located for most of the night so I headed over to see if there was anything I could do. I figured that they had stopped firing at dawn to get out of the area but when they saw John hovering down into the compound, they knew that he was a sitting duck.

I found Charlie several hundred meters northeast of the compound next to a large pile of boulders firing the mortar. I began a dive at them from about 500 feet and told my crew when I got close, to throw anything at the mortar position but especially the brass cartridge casings that were littering the cargo compartment floor. I didn't stop my dive until Charlie started ducking his head.

"Shoot what's available, as long as it's available, then use anything else that is available."

Hands full of casings went out the doors as fast as they could scrape them up off the floor. Drawing their fire was the best thing I could do for John. Meanwhile, John was on the ground as another mortar round hit. I told him to get out of there as fast as he could. I don't know what I was thinking; I'm sure he wasn't dawdling.

He was beginning his ascent as I made my second dive. This time they watched us closely as the crew threw the brass casings out at them but they ducked only a little as we went by, only feet from their heads. On my third pass, I had the crew throw the empty 1500 round metal ammo boxes at the position; we had nothing else to throw.

Thank God that John called saying that he was up and out. The only thing I had left to throw was my seat. We spoke to each other throughout the mission and his voice never had a hint of strain in it.

Things quickly quieted down and I formed up on John as we left the area. I told him that I was tremendously impressed with his flying and his calm state of mind. Hovering in and out of that compound through the trees with mortars hitting all around called for very steady hands and a clear head. He showed his stuff that morning.

Again I remind myself of the quality of men with whom we served.

By the way, the men at that outpost later did cut down several of the trees in the compound, just in case we had to land inside again.

Frank Strobel
"Knight Hawk 6"

2204 CHAU DUC—THE SINKING SAMPAN

One evening, I was briefed on what was expected to be a great deal of overnight activity and infiltration along and across the Ven Te canal. Around 1:00 AM, I was not surprised to see a large sampan in an area of the canal near Ap Vinh Phu just southwest of Chau Duc. I had been asked to watch that area very closely.

The sampan was riding very low in the water and was camouflaged to look as if it were transporting bundles of twigs for use as firewood. It was carrying something heavy and riding much lower than bundles of twigs would have made it. I came to a hover along the bank of the canal with my landing light and spot light focused on the sampan and the two men who were on each end of it. I then brought my Bug down to 500' to give me cover fire if needed.

Through the intercom, I spoke with the American advisor sitting in the back and he agreed that no one was supposed to be on the canal. It was obvious that these guys were breaking a night curfew even as the South Vietnamese advisor onboard adamantly stated that they were friendly farmers just trying to go home for the night. They were heading however away from the towns of Chau Duc and Ap Vinh Phu. It was argued back and forth for several minutes, the American advisor finally stating that he could not get permission to shoot or even to bring the men in for questioning!

According to the Rules of Engagement (ROE), they were in the wrong place and "free game" but because of the South Vietnamese advisor, I was forbidden to proceed with our normal and appropriate response. Trying to find a way to do something proactive rather than reactive and without hurting anyone, I hovered over to the sampan. I moved to a position so that each of my M-60's had one of the men with the machine gun muzzle a foot from their noses. I slowly lowered my collective to "land" on the sampan. As the sampan began to sink, the two Viet Cong didn't blink an eye or flinch a muscle; they just stared at the muzzles of the M-60's.

The water quickly rose past their waist, to their chests and then to their necks. They still didn't move a muscle. I pulled pitch and we went on our way with skids-a dripping as their heads began to go below the water. I hope they knew how to swim . . . or not!

We may not have recovered any arms or captured any enemy that night but at least we temporarily slowed the movement of arms by one sampan.

"The two most important things to remember in any fight are:
1. always cheat, so that
2. you can always win."

We often felt that the South Vietnamese advisors that were assigned to fly with us were actually Viet Cong. What training we gave our enemies.

Frank Strobel
"Knight Hawk 6"

2208 RULES OF ENGAGEMENT

The Rules of Engagement (ROE), or their "interpretation", changed very often in 1970. That is why I made sure I knew what they were at our daily briefings. One of my biggest fears over there was the "interpretation" of the latest ROE that were professed. I would often get changes for the areas in which I was flying when I received my daily briefings from the Green Berets before the evening/night mission began. Even when we had so called "Free Fire Zones" we had rules and limitations.

NOTE: FREE FIRE ZONES WEREN'T REALLY FREE FIRE!

In the back of my mind in every mission was, "How would I be judged on what I did that night?" I knew that if I was wrong to the slightest degree as Mission Commander, it would be for me to defend but that wasn't all bad either. There do have to be controls; an armed Huey can do a great deal of damage in a short amount of time. I was however, not hopeful of a great deal of backing from the chain of command. I don't mean necessarily on the Company level; I'm referring to further up and sideways across the Chain of Command. Yes, I meant sideways.

By 1970, politics was a major portion of our daily life in Viet Nam. Too many things were happening, particularly back in the "world" with the protest movement and LT Calley's problem. Everybody was in the CYA mode and to a point, I didn't blame them. One mistake and a career was over . . . but you still had to fight a war. The problem comes in when the bottom guy on the ladder does his job and I was on the bottom.

My deepest concern was that the ROE could be interpreted differently after the fact. They could be interpreted in the light of the times after an incident would take place. While flying the Night Hunter-Killer missions, I knew that I was the Mission

Commander and if even one bullet was fired at or accidentally hit something that someone else felt was "out of bounds," I would be the one hung for it. Once, I did have to stand in front of the Commanding General of the 64th Aviation Group with my CO at my side! It was about action taken in a "Free Fire Zone". That was not a fun day though all did go well in the end.

It made me much more careful in picking my targets and also in the way I attacked those targets. That was not all bad since I would have never forgiven myself for hurting someone who was truly an innocent bystander but then so many of them were claimed to be innocent bystanders after-the-fact.

About 10% of the time I had two or three extra people on board. A Vietnamese Officer, an American Advisor and an interpreter for them but only if needed. While on board they would be the final authority on whether or not we should attack a particular target. It was a very frustrating situation in a war where skirmishes were often fast and fleeting.

Sometimes it would take what seemed like an eternity to have the pros and cons discussed in the back seat. All the while I had to concentrate on flying at night and keeping a good situational awareness of the battle field so that if permission was granted, I was still in a position to do something constructive.

Additionally, with five crew members, two or three advisors, the extra equipment and extra ammunition we carried and especially with a full fuel load, we were close to our gross weight limit. While flying at night we didn't have a great deal of extra resources to tap into in difficult circumstances. Sometimes I had to limit my fuel load to make allowances for other considerations but I didn't like that. I always watched my power use very closely. Monitoring those gauges was one of my co-pilot's major jobs while I was busy maneuvering during a fight. When I knew I was going into an already hot situation, I would often request no advisors. Many times my wish would be granted but sometimes not. When my requests were denied, I knew it was now their butts on the line; all I had to do was fly!

My personal Rules of Engagement were these:

1. If I had advisors onboard they had the final say on deadly force but
2. Anytime I was being shot at I would aggressively return fire.

They may seem fairly obvious, especially number two but they really weren't! Once a week on Monday evenings there would be a Company safety meeting to go over any problems or ROE changes. I was usually not there because I was out flying but I remember very vividly being at one meeting. USARV sent down new ROE. This is not a quote of the exact language but as close an approximation I can give after 30 years:

"Before firing any weapon, you must get clearance from:

1. Your Company Commander and
2. The American Advisor for the Province you are in and
3. The Vietnamese Military Commander in that Province, or the Province Chief."

Do you know how long that would take, even if you could get in contact with all three? I immediately became so infuriated that they would send us out in a war zone with those kinds of rules. We were no longer allowed even to defend ourselves. It was another major CYA move.

I stood up and asked, "You mean to tell me that if I am flying over the village of Long Thanh (it was a small village across the river from My Tho that often fired at us even in the middle of the day for just flying over it) and if I received fire and would lose my engine, my co-pilot was hit and my crew chief was dead, that I could not return fire until I went through this process?" The answer was a strong and definite "Yes!"

How could you send someone out to war with those kinds of rules? We were no longer able to defend ourselves. It was an obvious case of the brass attempting to "Cover Their A___s;" there wasn't even an attempt to disguise it!

In a situation where there is a flight of Hueys and their accompanying Cobras making a troop insertion during the day, the authority is probably there or easily contacted, if not "pre-approved". For someone like me, on a mission by myself, 80 miles away in the middle of the night with a short range FM radio, it would be impossible. I knew I was on my own; no one would help. That is what happened to me when I was forced to file a Serious Incident Report (SIR). I truly thought I was going to be hung out to dry. I wasn't but I was totally shocked that I wasn't.

That is when I came up with my personal theory of fighting a war. I would fly what I personally called "conservatively-aggressive". To lessen the ability of others to second guess my reasons for doing something, I would be as careful as possible before getting into a skirmish; but once in it, I would be as aggressive as I was able. I felt that the larger and hotter the fight the less of a chance I would be held accountable for something I did.

In small skirmishes, which most of them were, I flew low and as close to the enemy as I was able, adjusting my speed often and continuously maneuvering just to make myself a more difficult target. In larger skirmishes I would stand further off and, if it was too much for me to handle, I would call on the Air Force (OV-10's usually) or the Navy Sea Wolves Helicopter Fire Team if they happened to be in the area. At times, I was able to call in Air Force or Navy Bombers but I had to be very careful when doing that, since it could raise too many questions later. That was because Air

Force bomber assets were so expensive. Usually the Air Force and Navy bombers were up north and not where I was flying.

The theory worked well for me. Considering all of the fights I was in, I took relatively few severe hits. Since my Bug and I were the only Army helicopters in the area at night, protecting 25 or so outposts near the Cambodian border and at the end of the Ho Chi Minh Trail, we were in fights on a regular basis.

An interesting note . . . It was very difficult to work with the other services and needing them at night didn't help. We spoke (were trained in) different working languages, with different jargon. At times it was difficult to translate exactly what we needed into the jargon of the ship that carried the needed ordnance onboard. Several times I had to call off strikes because I could not confirm exactly where the rockets or bombs were going to be delivered. One night I called off an OV-10 that was carrying 5 inch rockets because I could not confirm that he could place the rockets where I needed them, which was between two small villages. That pilot was very angry with me but I wasn't going to take the responsibility when he couldn't confirm the target to my satisfaction. That was frustrating for all involved.

Frank Strobel
"Knight Hawk 6"

2387 MOC HOA, AKA . . . THE ADOPTION . . .

In the spring of 1970, when flying regularly out of Moc Hoa north of Vinh Long, we were always amazed at how the kids from the village would come through the coiled and stacked concertina wire surrounding the airfield. They had it down so pat that it didn't even slow them down. They took a few quick steps, shifted left then right and they were through. There always seemed to be a large group of them around and when I had a few moments I would play with them. The simple game of tag was a very popular game.

After a couple of weeks, I knew from which area they were coming, who the individual kids were and how they behaved. One day I realized that there was one kid who would stay inside the loops of wire and never came through with the others. She was a small girl about 9 years old and obviously very shy.

Frank and Children at Moc Hoa

Over the following days I purposely took notice of this same little girl. She was always watching our interaction with the others but still she stayed away. One day I had a Hershey chocolate bar and I walked over to the wire to give it to her. The closer I got to her the more she backed through the wire until she was on the other side but never taking her eyes off me. I motioned to her that the bar was for her. I set the chocolate on the loops of wire and walked back to the ship. Out of the corner of my eye I saw her quickly go through wire, retrieve the chocolate bar and retreat back through the wire running back towards the town.

The next few times I returned to Moc Hoa airfield, she came closer but never actually reached my Huey. Finally one day she came over to the ship with the other kids. She was still very shy and obviously untrusting. Gradually she would come over with the other kids whenever we would shut down our Huey. I even managed to share some of my C-rations with her. She loved peanut butter and crackers with a little bit of honey. Come to think of it, it's still one of my favorites.

Over a period of time, she would sit on the edge of the helicopter's cargo compartment beside me. She would even "scooch" pretty close to me while sitting in the cargo compartment. I even placed her in my Huey seat once. On occasion she would even put her hand in mine. Luan and I got to be a regular thing.

She rarely made a sound but it got so that wherever I was, she would be right next to me. One evening I landed about 2200 hours for a break between missions and out of the dark she quickly appeared. She stood directly beside me, leaning against me and she grabbed my hand. She just stood there gently squeezing my hand. I felt like a big brother or surrogate father. I grabbed an M-16 rifle, slung it over my shoulder and slowly started to take a walk with her down the whole length of the unlit and very dark runway. How incongruous it felt. She never released my hand.

Luan

Near the south end of the runway one of the American units had a small recreation club and when we got near I decided to go in. I thought I'd buy her a real American can of Coke. It was much different from the Coke sold on the Vietnamese economy.

We sat at the small bar. It was only big enough to accommodate two wooden stools. We quickly started to drink our soda pop and I had a conversation with the kid who was tending bar. We probably spoke for 15 minutes. Luan never spoke a word the whole time we were there. I'm sure that was a very strange environment for her. I did notice though that every minute or so, she would pick up her can then my can and quietly set them down. She was weighing them. I think she was just trying to finish her can of pop when I finished mine. When we were done, we slowly walked back up the dark runway and back to the ship. She grabbed my leg and hugged it very hard and then ran through the wire back to the town. I still wonder how those kids did that. We soon left to fly our next mission.

Our friendship blossomed and whenever I landed she quickly ran over. She must have been waiting and watching every Huey land to be there as often as she was when I would get out of my ship. One night after dark, I found out a little more than I really wanted to know. Two of the local girls who would offer their "services" to the American GI's, came over to the ship. Luan was about 10 steps behind them and now uncharacteristically, stayed back. One of the girls told me that Luan was their sister. My heart stopped beating for a second, or maybe 5 or 10 seconds. As sweet and innocent as she seemed to be and her sisters were prostitutes! Damn I felt sick but I didn't feel there was anything I could do about the situation. I thought about it so often after that night it almost haunted me.

My relationship with Luan, however fragile it might have been, continued over the next several weeks. My mission at that time was changed from Moc Hoa across the Delta to the Seven Mountains area and for about two weeks I didn't get back to Moc Hoa. One afternoon while preparing to go out on a night mission in the Sevens Mountains Area, I was asked to drop a package at Moc Hoa. I landed on the southeast end of the airfield near the rearming area and saw Luan running through the wire and across to the runway. She stopped short of the runway and just stared across it at my ship.

Frank And Luan

I hadn't planned to get out but I couldn't help myself. I rolled the engine down to flight idle and got out. No sooner had my boots touched the ground than she was dashing across the runway. She ran up to me and gave me the biggest hug around my waist I had had in a very long time. She had tears in her eyes and I'm positive a few appeared in mine. I knew I missed seeing her but I didn't think I missed her that much! At that time my ship didn't have any special markings that would distinguish it from any other Knight Huey flying into Moc Hoa. I'm sure it was a daily occurrence that at least one of the Knights was flying in that area. She must have been watching each and every one of them to have been there when I arrived. I spent about 10 minutes with her, gave her a couple cans of C-ration meat to take home, (my dinner that night) and then I was on my way again. That was the last time I saw her for several months. I was in and out of Moc Hoa several times but my main missions were in the Seven Mountains Area with the Green Berets.

If you remember my first story, I truly didn't think I would make it flying for a whole year Viet Nam. In the fall of 1970, the Night Hunter-Killer mission was reassigned, away from the Knights and to our sister company, the Cowboys. I was beginning to feel that I might actually make it a whole year and return back to the "world". In early November, I went to Moc Hoa and had a South Vietnamese Army translator find Luan's family house and I went to visit.

I spoke with her parents through the interpreter and over the following half hour or so I offered to adopt her and take her back with me to the States. I didn't know what the legal and military roadblocks would be but before I tackled anything else, I wanted to see if it was possible. I told them that she would be treated well, that she would be guaranteed a good upbringing and a complete education. Most importantly, she could come back to Viet Nam anytime she wanted.

We discussed it for a reasonably long time. Her parents were very polite but they did not want her to leave. I could understand them. I would have had great difficulty letting any of my three girls go halfway around the world, especially with someone I didn't know. Nevertheless, I had to try! I have never forgotten her. At Mass on Sundays to this day, I try to remember her in my prayers. She would probably be in her early 40's now. I pray she has had a good life.

I guess I should have called this story, "The Moc Hoa Adoption . . . that wasn't to be!"

Frank Strobel
"Knight Hawk 6"

PS. I just reread this story and made a few very small changes to my original version, through the tears in my eyes. Thank goodness that e-mail doesn't show water marks!

2422 PERSONNEL RADAR UNITS

The personnel detection radar units along with their operators
that were introduced later in the war were amazing. They were not
used widely and I don't recall what the Army's official name for
them was.

The individual units were about 18 inches long, three inches wide
with fins and were shaped like a small thin bomblets. At the end
of the fins was a small circular plate welded flat against them and
then 4 plastic-coated flexible antennas, formed to look like tall
grass about 15 inches long. They were battery powered and lasted
a couple weeks. I flew a mission to place them on one occasion.

While flying at 500 feet AGL, several units would be dropped
along a corridor that the enemy was expected to transverse. When
the radar units hit the ground they would bury themselves up to
the flat plate with only the antennas visible. The impact with the
ground turned them on. On three separate occasions at night, I
was contacted by the radar operators and given coordinates on
where to find the enemy.

On the first occasion, I was asked to find a moped that was going
down a small road or trail in the middle of the night near Moc
Hoa. I kept in contact with the radar operator and he would
tell me where the moped was as it passed by several of the radar
units. We never found the Cong but we did find the moped lying
alongside the road near a small wooded area. I briefly thought
about landing and picking up the moped for our use on ramp one
but with my luck there would have been a grenade with the pin
pulled underneath it. We shot up the wooded area and the moped.
I don't know if we hit anyone but I know the moped never ran
again. That Cong must have gone crazy trying to figure out how I
could be following him down a winding trail in the middle of the
night when neither of us had any lights on.

The second occasion was alongside the Ven Te canal. A few days before, I had assisted in the placing of four of these units along the canal just south of Tinh Binh. The radar operator called me and told me that there were four or five people walking down the road. One was either a child or a woman and they had recently left the canal.

I radioed back and said something very dubious like, "You're telling me that you can tell me how many individuals are there and what sex they are?" He replied that he often could tell by their speed, gait and how heavy they walked and could guess at the size of the individuals. I never found them but I did find where they left the canal and left wet marks on the road.

The third occasion was very near the location of the previous story but a couple days later. The operator told me that a large group, possibly as many as a hundred men or so, had crossed the canal.

While I was flying over to the area I radioed the outpost at Tinh Binh since the location was several hundred meters south of their position. When I arrived on station it was very dark and it was obvious that a number of people had come out of the canal but I could not locate anyone. There was a heavily wooded area a short way across the road, so I had Bug drop several flares over it. Then while flying over and hovering at about 150' above the ground, I began shining our 1.5 million candle power xeon light into the tree line. After circling for about five minutes I could see no signs of anything in the area and I wasn't able to draw any fire. The radar operator insisted that they hadn't moved too far away from the canal. The guys in the outpost were insisting that I shoot up the wooded area since they would be in deep trouble in a nighttime attack with a unit that size. On the south side of the wooded area, I came down to about a 15 foot hover, again shining the powerful light into the trees. You can imagine how bright that light lit up the area but again nothing. Again, they insisted that

I shoot up the area. So I told them that just so they would feel better, I would fire my mini-guns into the wooded area but only if they would agree to send out a patrol first thing the next morning and check the area. They agreed, so reluctantly I also agreed.

So at a 15 foot hover I let Pas Mantanona loose out the left door. Pas fired around 2,000 rounds straight into the woods, with the recoil of the mini-gun pushing my helicopter sideways. Wood and bark was flying everywhere with that gun firing at point blank range (about 50 meters). I could see that several of the smaller trees had leaned over as the bullets actually cut them down. I did a 180 degree peddle turn and let my door gunner do the same thing. To my knowledge, I didn't receive one round of return fire.

When completing my after action report the next morning in operations, I included the incident. Captain "P" asked me about it but I didn't think too much about it. It was just another almost insignificant incident, other than the number of rounds we expended. The next evening when I received my briefing from the Green Berets at B-43, I was told that they found over 70 bodies.

I never saw one person in the woods the night before. I had baited them for over 15 minutes before I began to fire on their position. It is obvious that they were good, well trained troops that I fired on that night. They had a mission and I wasn't it. It's probably lucky for me that they were on a mission. They did the right thing for them at the time and kept quiet. At least most of the time, it would have been the right thing for them to do. That night it wasn't. Did I kill everyone? Very probably not but I am sure we destroyed the integrity of that unit.

That memory is as vivid today in my mind as it was that night. I can still see the chunks of wood flying! Although in my dreams I usually see them in slow motion. That I could do that much damage and not even see that anyone was actually there blew my mind. To realize what those enemy soldiers were going through with that many bullets fired into that relatively small area of trees, well, it must have been hell.

Sometimes it would be nice to be an Air Force B-52 bomber pilot dropping bombs from the heights. They just locate the coordinates. They never see the bark flying. The bark flying and the trees laying over made it very personal even before knowing what I had done.

I wonder often at night, "What they were planning? Where were they heading?" I also wonder how those night missions would have been different if we had had the night vision goggles that are available today.

Frank Strobel
"Knight Hawk 6"

2428 NIGHT FLYING A BORING MISSION? AKA . . . "CSING" MYSELF

Those night missions were never boring. There were many times nothing was happening but that was when we could "enjoy" ourselves. That was when we had some of our own fun. We could let it all hang out. We could try something new. Every night at some point we flew our complete AO, just to let everyone, friend or foe know that we were around although we did not do it at a predetermined time. It just was fit into our mission early, in the middle or late (early in the morning) depending on what was going on. There were a few times we had a fight from the time we got out of our pre-mission briefing until we were relieved in the morning but that was rare.

The nights when things were quiet were the times we were able to try out new ideas or techniques. We could experiment. We would go to areas that we knew where there was usually something going on and try to provoke a fight. Sometimes we would go to an area where we rarely had anything going on, under the assumption that we may have missed something the other times we happened into that area. So we could snoop around a little closer and look for different signs of activity. At times we would find a sampan in the middle of nowhere. Knowing that it belonged to somebody we would do an intensive search in a relatively small radius around it and maybe see a small sign like trampled down vegetation. A friendly farmer would not leave a valuable sampan out in the middle of nowhere. Usually the sampan didn't survive.

Of course those were the times when we could get ourselves into the most trouble, like the night we "CS'd" (gassed) ourselves. Yes, I was that stupid. I have to admit it I made some really dumb mistakes while flying sometimes. We often flew with an M-79 grenade launcher and a case of CS gas grenades. We would shoot a couple of rounds into an area or building or a tunnel area trying to flush something out.

One night we were on the west side of Nui Dai in the Seven Mountains Area and thought we saw an indication that a couple of the trails had recently been used leading up the mountain. Yes, I could have sprayed the area with machine guns but that probably would have just been a waste of bullets. I decided to use an "area" weapon, something that we just had to get near the enemy to provoke a reaction. It was just something to irritate them and maybe start a fight. As I hovered about 300 feet off the ground at the base of the mountain, Pas Mantanona sat Indian style in the cargo compartment plinking round after round into the area of the trails.

After using half of a case of rounds, the gas started rolling back up the side of the mountain and rolled through our cargo compartment. I took a deep breath of it and realized what was happening and took a quick peddle turn to the west away from the mountain and started to climb out through my tear filled eyes. I was half on instruments and half VFR, while the other half of me was saying, "Now I remember why, when working around gas one of the pilots was required to have a gas mask on."

Yes, three halves!

So things were never boring. I was always able to put some excitement into the nights that were quiet.

Frank Strobel
"Knight Hawk 6"

2445 THE NIGHT AMBUSH

While flying the Night Hunter-Killer mission in the Seven Mountains Area, there were often times that I needed to talk to two different outposts at the same time. Often there was more than one skirmish going on at a time. I quickly decided that a second FM Radio was needed. I made an "informal wish" one morning to my crew chief, Pas Mantanona. Several days later it magically appeared on my radio console. He had a way of making things appear when requested.

One evening well after dark, I received a call from one of the patrols that I had been briefed about earlier in the evening. The patrol was supposed to set up an ambush along a road northwest of B-43 (That Son). It was on the road between the villages of Ta Moc and Tuey et Nap but just west of Ta Moc. The ambush worked rather well that night and they became embroiled in quite a heavy fire fight from directly across the elevated roadway. At that time we were just returning from refueling and rearming at Chau Duc.

From several clicks away we could see the fight far out in the night. There was a tremendous fight going on down there. I radioed back that we were on our way and would be there in just a few minutes. Bug left my wing and was climbing up to prepare to drop flares to light the enemy positions for us. Meanwhile, I took information on numbers and exact position of the "friendlies".

Suddenly, I received a frantic call on my second FM radio. It was a patrol that had been walking along the same road about one click west of my position when it was ambushed by a guerrilla unit. They were hit very hard and all hell had broken loose. It was not uncommon to have a couple fire fights going on at the same time and I thought it was going to be just another one of those nights.

As they were giving me the details on the second ambush, it became very obvious that I should be seeing the second fire fight in the distance but I could not locate it. I then noticed that all the tracers were red. The Viet Cong had green tracers. Was the Viet Cong using captured guns and ammunition? I radioed the second patrol to reconfirm the location details because I was unable to visually locate the action.

As I came on station of the first ambush, I was now listening on both FM Radios that was told that I have just arrived above both their locations. It was obvious that the second patrol was substantially farther along the road to the east than they had plotted on their tactical map. That was not a good thing to do but it was much easier to do at night than in the daylight.

I now had both patrols on different frequencies screaming at me the same frantic orders, ". . . to shoot the other side of the road". They were almost crazy yelling that I fire on the other. Both patrols were begging me to do something and saying ". . . don't just fly in circles up there!"

I tried to get both of them to cease fire but there was too much adrenalin and testosterone running down there that night. Neither side wanted to be the first one to stop. The muzzle flashes were constant on both sides of the road interspersed with an occasional M-79 round or hand grenade. It was a crazy scene for several minutes. Not wanting to give away their frequencies in the clear, I picked a frequency out of thin air and told both patrols I couldn't help until they changed their frequencies. After they were on the same frequency and spoke with each other for a few seconds their firing ceased.

It took less than 10 minutes from the start to the finish of this ordeal. Hundreds of rounds flew in each direction. Thank God, no one got hurt. It just showed you how fast situations can grow out of control and how important map reading really is day or night.

I'll bet someone down there reviewed his map reading course if not formally at least in their mind the following day.

Did I blame any of them? After committing to a fire fight, I know I would not want to be the first to stop fighting while still being fired at.

Frank Strobel
"Knight Hawk 6"

2447 VIETNAMIZATION

When I joined the Knights in early January 1970, the Vietnamization of the Delta was completed, in that there were no U. S. ground troops left there. I don't know when the 9th Division actually left Dong Tam but they were already gone when I arrived. I was told that all U. S. ground combat units had left the Delta and we were only there in support of the South Vietnamese. I was never involved in any operations that included large units of all American troops; I supported only the special operations of small Green Beret or Navy Seal units.

I do recall that during my tour we had to turn over several helicopters to the VNAF but I am not sure of the dates. There was some grumbling about that at the time on the flight line, since they had to be in perfect condition. If there was any type of problem with the helicopter the 114th had to keep it. In effect, the Americans could fly with inferior equipment but not the Vietnamese. The only other major situation I recall during 1970 was the VNAF pilots that were flying as co-pilot with the Knights for training; at the time I was still flying the Night-Hunter-Killer mission. I had one Vietnamese pilot fly with me once and to me it was a disaster. I was unhappily surprised that he spoke very little English, or refused to acknowledge that he knew any. He only reacted to hand gestures which is not healthy at night and in the dark.

I was so frustrated by morning that I refused to fly at night with a South Vietnamese pilot again. I thought I was going to get a great deal of flack over that decision and prepared myself for a confrontation with the front office but surprisingly received none.

Frank Strobel
"Knight Hawk 6"

2492 RUBBER DUCKY

From: Frank Strobel

Steve . . .

This probably doesn't qualify for "Popular" Delta music of 1970 but a favorite memory of mine was one afternoon during the 1970 monsoon season. The Knights were making a troop insertion into some very wet rice paddies. It was just a routine flight into a cold LZ. I was flying trail and we were listening to AFVN Radio. We were discharging our ARVN troops as the song "Rubber Ducky" started to play. Watching the Hueys bobbing their bellies barely in then out the water of the paddy and their rotor blades splashing water all over was a very funny sight. I never thought of a Huey as a duck before but I just had to sing along.

Frank Strobel
"Knight Hawk 6"

2624 THE WATERMELON PATCH AND A FEW BANANAS

One particularly hot afternoon during the dry season we were flying just east of Hong Ngu. My crew chief Pas noticed that far below he could see a watermelon patch. It wasn't hard to convince me that it was time to do a little harvesting. I made a high-overhead approach to the open field. As we got closer we could see that a family was gathering watermelons from that particular field. I carefully set the Huey down where we wouldn't damage any of the vines, Pas jumped out and gathered about a half dozen of the melons and tossed them in the cargo compartment.

Needless to say, the shocked family clung to each other in the far corner of the patch with the look of fear across their faces. I tried to smile and wave at them but that made no impression. They were probably swearing at me and I assume that they thought they were being robbed at gun point. It sure must have looked that way.

I asked Pas how much the melons were going for at the market in downtown Vinh Long. I gave him twice that amount in Vietnamese money and had him run it over to the father.

That is when the shocked look really hit their faces. They didn't expect to be paid! Their shocked looks turned into smiles and they were waving as I pulled pitch and took off. They got paid well for the melons and we did all the harvesting!

The melons were a little messy but our thirst was quenched with the sweet taste of fresh juicy fruit.

At dawn one day shortly after finishing a firefight a click or so to the west, we were heading back to Chau Duc to refuel and rearm. We were flying near the southeast base of Nui Coto when Pas spotted a banana tree. He immediately wanted to do a little harvesting. It was in an area with no villages or hamlets nearby. We could see no farmers' hooches either. I flew around and could see no evidence of enemy activity, so I landed near the tree.

Since I had no idea if anyone actually owned the tree I asked Pas to be judicious in his harvesting and said, "don't take too many!" He gathered enough bananas for each of us to have five or so. They were a little green but we ate them anyway. I had Pas to wedge a little Vietnamese money in the tree for our harvest but I don't know if anyone ever picked it up. Of course I may have paid a Viet Cong if he was the next one there to harvest those bananas.

Frank Strobel
"Knight Hawk 6"

2638 CARE PACKAGES, AKA . . . MONSOON FLOOD

Care packages were always greatly appreciated. Between my mother and Lucy (we were not married at the time), I rarely had a two week period without at least a small package from home. I was very surprised at how quickly "care" packages were delivered to Viet Nam. It was not uncommon to have a package delivered within three or four days of the time it was postmarked in Erie, Pennsylvania. On several occasions I would get a letter telling me a package was on the way the day <u>after</u> I received the package that was mailed at the same time. The military was obviously trying to keep us happy.

Lucy would send me canned jars of homemade spaghetti sauce and meatballs. It was a wonderful treat. She would pack it with popped corn to cushion it. I never had a jar break in shipping. There were lots of chocolate chip cookies too. One time a large box arrived inside a clear plastic bag. It looked as if a mortar shell hit it. The sauce jar was fine but everything else was crumbs. The one pound box of spaghetti was intermixed with crumbles of cookies and popcorn and whatever else was packed loose in that box. The longest piece of spaghetti was about 2 inches long. Since all the chocolate chips had melted into the mixture of cookie crumbs and noodle pieces, I had to wash each piece of noodle individually and then lay them all out to dry. They still tasted great though.

214

The first jar of canned homemade spaghetti sauce with meatballs I received was placed on a small shelf in the room that I had built for myself. I had it for a few days and was offered $50 for it. I ate it about an hour later. If it was worth $50, I wasn't about to have it sitting out on an open shelf. In fact, I have a picture of Marvin Tabaka and me eating that spaghetti out of an electric skillet.

My mother would send me a great deal of different foods that she would never buy for the family at home. Our family had 10 kids. Prepackaged and instant or prepared food was nowhere in our family diet, or should I say "pocketbook". When I received a box of instant potatoes or a can of Underwood Deviled Ham, I knew it was something that was carefully and lovingly considered before the money was taken out of the family food budget. Those items were treasured by me for several reasons.

My mother was given a recipe for baking a cake in a three pound coffee can. That was when coffee came in the large cans that actually contained three pounds. Of course she would send a can of icing along . . . it was surprisingly good and fresh but wouldn't last too long. All of my roommates and crew did share our good fortune with each other. Those back home treated me well. I often had enough stateside food to fill a footlocker. In fact, that is where I kept it until the monsoon season.

One night during my first monsoon deluge, the area began to show water beginning to seep over the grass. I went to bed confident in knowing that the water would not rise enough to overflow the 18" cement ledge into our hooch. Wrongooooo!

I had to get up at 5:00 AM for my day's mission. My wind up Baby Ben alarm clock woke me up on time and I promptly hopped out of my bed and into knee deep cold water. Then I was really awake. I climbed up onto my make-shift desk and turned my light on (didn't want to get electrocuted) only to see my footlocker floating with the lid partially opened from the pressure of expanded food boxes. Two boxes of formerly dry breakfast cereal were acting as water wings inside the locker. The unopened box of instant potatoes had exploded, allowing clumps of reconstituted mashed potatoes float throughout my room. All labels had left the cans to which they were originally attached and were floating independently on the surface of the water. The contents of any can that couldn't be identified by its shape, was now a mystery. My box of graham crackers was almost bursting at its seams and was threatening to become a grenade looking for a place to do its life's work.

I just figured that I would bail out my room when I got back from my mission. I carried my clothes to my helicopter before I dressed. From that moment on, all food was stored on a high shelf. One other thing my mother sent me was an electric percolator and a one pound can of "Electra-perk" brand coffee every week or so but that's another story!!!

Bailing Out The Hooch

Frank Strobel
"Knight Hawk 6"

Note: During the monsoon season we still had to walk to our helicopters through the flooded areas. Dressed only in our underwear and carrying all our other clothing, we went through flight operations to receive our daily mission briefing. We then went through the U.S. Air Force weather station for our weather briefing. Then we walked the quarter mile before eventually climbing into our helicopter's, cargo compartment and getting dressed for the day's mission. Flying the day in a dry flight suit was very nice.

Lt. Smith And WO Keefer On Their Way To "Work"

ELECTRA-PERC COFFEE

My mother always came through. I never became a lover of Army coffee. I missed a good cup of coffee in the morning since Army coffee never agreed with me. I drank it occasionally and always had heartburn afterwards.

I must have mentioned it in one of my letters home, because about my seventh month over there I received a package from home that contained a new coffee percolator and a one pound can of "Electra-Perc" Coffee. If I recall correctly, that coffee was the most expensive brand on the market at the time. It was a large purchase for my mother and father to make and then send overseas to me. Inside the package was also a one quart thermos with two cups, one nested inside the other. I made the coffee sparingly and I didn't normally use the thermos while flying the Night Hunter-Killer missions.

Once I was no longer flying the night missions, I began flying a much safer VIP mission. I flew General Xi and his American counterpart to meetings all around the Delta and Saigon areas. Often we would fly high cover or the C & C ship for offensive fights in the mountains of the western Delta area. Often we drop off General Xi at meetings at the Quarry at Nui Sam.

Frank on the Pier at Nui Sam Quarry

I began to develop a routine. When I awoke in the morning, I would brew a pot of coffee while I showered and prepared to fly. I would then pour it in my thermos and take it with me to my helicopter. At some point in the morning when flying between meetings, I would give the controls to my copilot. I would roll back my seat and stretch out, pull out my thermos and have a "high flying" coffee break. After several days of doing this in a row, I heard Colonel Connant through the intercom, "Frank, is that coffee I smell?" I said, "Yes Sir." Then he said, "No, I mean real American coffee." I said, "Yep."

Then he began, "Would you happen to have another cup onboard?" I said, "Yep but it is smaller than mine." I just wasn't going to give the coffee to him; it was too precious to me. He was going to have to ask. He then broke down and said, "Could you spare a cup?" I said, "Absolutely!" and I reached under my seat to grab the other cup I had. I passed it back to him with my thermos. He commented that it was the best coffee he had since arriving in Viet Nam. That quickly became a daily ritual. When he could he would "requisition" a box of doughnuts for the crew and enjoy my coffee with them.

Thanks, Mom and Dad.

Frank Strobel
"Knight Hawk 6"

2712 TRAN AND HIS HUEY RIDE

During my last couple of months of my tour, I often flew South Vietnamese General Xi of the Vietnamese Ninth Infantry Division and his Senior Advisor, Colonel Connant, to different locations for meetings with local civilian and military leaders.

One of the areas that he regularly visited was a compound near the Nui Sam Rock Quarry at the Village of Vinh Te, one-half click or so south-southwest of Chau Duc. We would land and remain near the area on a short pier from which the local canal barges would load gravel while he attended his meetings. Often we would be there for several hours waiting in the unrelenting sun through the hot summer afternoon.

The families of these barge owners were loading gravel from the quarry for road repair. Whole families lived onboard the barges. Usually, while we were waiting, we would be surrounded by the children of those barge families. One young boy named Tran, who was about 11 or 12 years old, would always appear and would often offer to get us a drink of water or to run some other errand for which we would "pay" him. That pay would usually be in the form of "C" rations. That may not sound like much but a can of meat would flavor a large bowl of rice for a whole family. If we were relaxing in the cargo compartment trying to stay cool as the summer sun beat down on us, he would even try to fan us to keep us cool. Over several weeks of seeing him on a daily basis, we became quite friendly. When we would prepare to leave with the General, the other kids would quickly leave but he would stay close to wave good-bye. I could see in his eyes the wonder of us flying.

One day while I was lying on the shady cargo compartment floor almost asleep, he grabbed one of my gray hairs (Yes, quite a few were growing in at age 23!) out of my head exclaiming, "Chung Wi" at his find! I chased and teased him about pulling it.

One very hot sunny day when the local kids were swimming in the quarry water, I stripped down to my white jockey shorts and joined them. Main highway 2 was just beyond the tail boom of my Huey. Though quite dirty, the water felt wonderful.

Frank Swimming From The Pier At Nui Sam Quarry

Another afternoon during a long wait, I decided to fly the short distance to Chau Duc airfield to refuel before the General returned. Knowing it was against regulations, I still told my crew to help Tran in and to strap him in the center of the bench seat.

I then instructed them to sit immediately on either side of him just in case he became afraid during our short time in the air since we had no doors on that ship. We strapped him in, started the Huey and then lifted off for our short five minute ride. I don't think we climbed above 500 feet. He was very excited and his eyes were wide open. He couldn't look at things fast enough as he tried to take everything in. We landed at the POL (refueling) area at the Chau Duc Airfield and after they all got out, my crew chief began the refueling process.

When we took off again I climbed to about 1500 feet. By the time I got to altitude, it was time to begin my approach back to the rock quarry. When I looked back at Tran he was staring at a huge white cumulus cloud; its base was at about 1700 feet. It was the only cloud in the bright blue sky and was only about a half click away, so I flew over to it. I circled the cloud only about 100 feet away from it. Tran's eyes couldn't have gotten any wider. He stared at the cloud as hard as he could. I had the feeling that he really didn't understand what a cloud was made of, that he didn't think that it was "fog only a bit little higher".

I flew away from the cloud and then turned, flying directly towards the cloud. You could see that he was somewhat concerned and as we got closer that concern seemed to turn to fear as he waited for the impact. He looked shocked as we entered the cloud. He looked like he had expected that flying into the cloud was like flying into a wall. We soon saw him reaching out his hand repeatedly opening and closing his fist, trying to "feel" the cloud. Then instantly we popped back out into the beautiful blue sky. It was easy to see that it took his breath away.

Making a small turn, I immediately began my descent and approach back to the quarry. I then made a low flying, circling flight around the barges. He was waving to everyone. When we landed he was greeted by all of the other kids from the area as well as his parents and many other adults. I guess news of his leaving in a helicopter traveled fast. All were happily waving their arms to him as he was helped out of the chopper. He ran over to them. You could see everyone talking at once. As I was shutting down the helicopter, the whole group surrounded him. It looked as though everyone was talking at the same time. They had to be asking him many questions about his experience. Then slowly as a group, they returned to the barges. I know we made him king for a day!

Frank Strobel
"Knight Hawk 6"

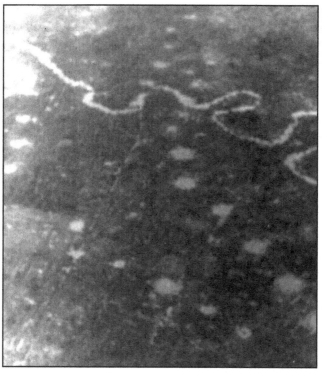

My First Remembered View Of Nam In A Huey

2944 PAS MANTANONA, AKA . . .
THE ONE THAT GOT AWAY

Once we had had a very long and very active week. Our Night Hunter-Killer missions were usually 12-16 hour missions but that week we had several 18 hour days (time away from Vinh Long) in a row. That left little time for sleeping and recuperating from the previous mission. Besides, the helicopter needed its daily maintenance. We put "085" in its revetment and began to clean it in preparation for an intermediate inspection and then prepared for our next mission later that day. I spent about 30 minutes with the crew cleaning the ship and then left them so I could complete my after action report for the previous night. We were all very tired. Pas Mantanona, my crew chief walked with me into the hanger to get the "rolling" steps to inspect the tail rotor. We were both half asleep. I had to do my reports 'cause "Pop" (CPT Papapietro) didn't let me go to bed until I finished all my paperwork.

I returned to the ship sometime after 3:00 PM to start my preflight inspection. Pas saw me walking up the flight line and met me about three revetments before I reached "085". He started to apologize immediately, talking very fast and was taking responsibility for something that really was not all his fault.

As we reached "085" he had already explained that just after he finished inspecting the tail rotor a "Cowboy" Huey hovered past and blew over the rolling steps. The rotor wash lifted the steps off the ground, picked up "085's" tail slightly and jammed the steps under the tail boom. It took about 30 minutes to retrieve the steps before they could even see the extent of the damage. The accident tore a gash in the skin about 8" long. Pas stayed with the ship all day while it was inspected and the sheet metal crew repaired it. He then primed the patch and as soon as the paint was dry he painted it olive drab. The work was completed just before I arrived at the ship. He apologized that the paint wasn't completely dry.

He showed me the repair and to be quite honest, it was such a good job, I probably would not have even noticed it. He then explained what he had gone through to get it repaired and that he had not left the ship all day. He had no sleep or rest at all and it was time to head back out.

The first several sorties that night went by very uneventfully. Around 0100 hours I found a lone Viet Cong with an AK-47 in hand running through a rice paddy a couple hundred meters northwest of Ba Xoai. Through the intercom I quickly briefed my crew on the target. I banked the ship to give Pas's machine gun a good firing angle and yelled, "FIRE"! Nothing happened. I came around, repeated my order and nothing happened again. As I prepared for a third try I yelled back to Pas, "What the H— was the matter?" Was his gun jammed? Again, there was no response. I turned around to look at him and he was leaning against the back fire wall, sound asleep.

I looked back out at the Cong just as he was getting out of the last rice paddy and was beginning to run towards the woods. I did not bank in the other direction as I normally would have for my gunner to engage the target. That Cong was sooooo lucky. I just figured God had a plan for him. We soon departed the area.

I wonder if he had any idea how lucky he was. That Viet Cong was saved by a set of rolling steps that were accidentally blown over by a hovering Huey.

We woke Pas up later. He was so sound asleep he was in another world. I never said a word to him about it.

Frank Strobel
"Knight Hawk 6"

3053 THE WHITE KNIGHT PUPPY—SAM

For a couple months in the spring of 1970 the White Knights had a mascot. It was a puppy named Sam. He flew every day with me and seemed to enjoy flying as much as being on the ground. When we had passengers onboard he stayed under one of the seats in the "well" area of the chopper. When there were no packs on board, he had free reign of the cargo compartment. We would watch him as he would walk over to the open cargo door and as soon as he could feel a little air movement from the slip stream on his nose he would know not to go any closer to the open door.

One day while he was standing next to the open cargo door I initiated a high overhead approach. He never moved a paw. He shifted his weight a little to keep his balance and watched intently straight down as we approached the ground. There was nothing between Sam's nose and the ground except 1000 feet of air. We only experienced one problem with Sam while he was with us.

Frank and Sam

One day we were flying out of Moc Hoa and a gruff old "E-9" (Sergeant Major) approached the ship and looked at Sam and yelled at the top of his lungs, "Who authorized a damn dog to be on this Army Chopper?" Sam yelped and ran under one of the pilot's seat and curled up for a nap. A few minutes after departing Moc Hoa he got up and started walking around sniffing the supplies we were carrying. It was his usual job. He slowly worked his way around until he got close to our unhappy pack. He lifted his leg and p—ed on the spit polished boots, then made a hasty retreat hiding somewhere he couldn't be seen or reached.

We could hear the Sergeant Major's roar behind us even without our intercom. When it happened I turned around to see this E-9's face turn a deep crimson color. Needless to say the small streak of uric acid immediately stripped the shining polish down to the basic leather. Many hours of work polishing those boots were lost. If he had been able to find and reach Sam I'm sure he would have immediately transferred Sam from the 114th Assault Helicopter Company to the 101st Airborne Division. After that incident we restricted Sam a great deal more when passengers were on board.

Frank Strobel
"Knight Hawk 6"

THE NIGHT I THOUGHT I LOST PAS

Back while flying Night Hunter-Killer missions I often thought, "How clever we were!" Now 30 years later after talking with some of the Knights that served earlier in the war, I find that we were just doing what was 'done before'. I had no doubt when we beefed up our M-60's to almost 900 rounds per minute that it had been done many times before. When we rewired and rigged "085" with two door mounted mini-guns however, each with two rows of ammo boxes under the bench seat in the cargo compartment, I was sure we were jury rigging geniuses. With our setup the heavy weight of the ammunition was sitting squarely on the center of gravity, which meant that and we could still install and use the seats. Well, what more could the Army want than guys that could "make anything work". Then I heard 30 years later that we were just "Johnny-come-latelies".

When I came to the Knights in January of 1970 there were no "fat little gunships" (UH-1 C Models); they were all the slim & sleek AH-1G's, so I never saw another setup like the one we had.

When we traded in our two sets of twin M-60's for 2 mini-guns, I was very happy at the additional firepower. There was a learning curve though, since we were not trained on the use of the mini-gun; after some pointers from the Cobra crew chiefs it was all OJT. We had several experiences during that time, a couple of which are worth passing on.

I vividly remember one night after a quick rearming of the mini-guns, we had a near disaster. We were in a hurry so that we could get back to the war we were conducting in the Plain of Reeds, west of Moc Hoa. It started when one of the rounds of linked 7.62 mm ammunition was incorrectly fed into the feeder-de-linker of Pas's mini-gun.

When the misaligned round hit the rotating gun barrels, they cut directly through the bullet's casing and then it did the same for every round thereafter. The motorized feeder-de-linker continued to feed the rounds to the gun at the rate of 2,000 per minute. The gun powder from the first round and every round that followed, quickly ignited in the open air as it was blown inside the flying helicopter. The motor didn't stop; it kept driving those rounds resulting in a tremendous amount of gunpowder blowing around the cargo compartment and feeding that flash fire. The motor just continued to run. It was as much of a continuous explosion as it was a fire. Between the noise of the helicopter, the noise of the explosively burning gun powder and the instantaneous change from a black night to flashbulb bright light, all was chaos.

I tried to look around into the cargo compartment but it was like looking into the sun. It actually pained my once night vision adjusted eyes. The fire was within inches of me and it looked as if Pas was completely covered in what seemed to be a never-ending flash explosion. I did see the guns barrels fly apart as the gun itself exploded!

I thought he was engulfed in flames and there was nothing I could do since I was flying. I couldn't just leave my job. I can remember thinking, "I can't lose Pas!"

By that time, Pas and I had been through too much together. Everything being in slow motion, my first thought was that Pas was burning inside that ball of flame.

With the explosive noise and the bright light, I initially thought we had been hit by a B-40 rocket. We should have been too high for that though. The doors were open; the air rushed through the cargo compartment and was blowing the flashing fire throughout the helicopter. The burning gunpowder ignited a couple small fires but luckily they were quickly extinguished by my gunner.

For a short moment I was not even sure if we were still flying, controlled flying I should say, or were we falling and I was just too disoriented to realize anything. I was blinded by the flash and couldn't read my instruments. Even before my eyes readjusted back to night vision, we began taking inventory. I couldn't believe his mini-gun blew apart with the barrels flying in all directions.

When all was over, there was no major physical damage other than the mini-gun itself. More importantly there were no serious injuries. Pas was obviously shaken but was fine. The air blowing through the cargo compartment kept the fire off of Pas, though it was extremely close to him. Everyone on the crew lost several years of their life that night. We were all very lucky.

I turned the ship around and returned to Moc Hoa for a complete inventory. Pas told me later that, although he released the firing button, the gun continued on its intended mission, unimpeded. In the blinding flash, he had to disconnect the quick release electric power cable we had installed as an extra safety measure before the gun would stop firing.

Frank Strobel
"Knight Hawk 6"

3746 A NIGHT FIGHT WEST OF BA XOAI

There are some things that people do in war when they are caught up in anger and revenge with the rush of adrenalin and testosterone surging through their body. I have told very few people this story in the last 30 years. If I say I have recounted it to five people before now that would be an exaggeration. I have always looked back at that night and what went on the following morning and wondered how I could have done it. Usually I had good control of my emotions. I was always proud of the fact that, whatever the situation, I didn't lose my cool, at least not until a particular situation was over. I may not have enjoyed some situations but I was always able to handle them. This particular night I lost more than my cool; I lost control.

It started as most night missions with a briefing from the Green Berets at the Bravo 43 Camp near That Son. They had intelligence that the Cong were expected to be attacking several outposts that night but they were not sure which ones. The last words in the briefing were, "Be prepared for anything tonight!"

On my first two tanks of fuel we flew the whole area we normally covered just to let everyone know on both sides that we were there and should be addressed in any equation. As usual we received several radio calls from Americans that were in many of the small ARVN outposts/compounds as we flew over their area. All seemed happy we were there. We refueled the third time at Chau Duc around 2200 hours.

As we were returning to the Nui Cam area, we received a frantic call from an American at a small outpost a short way west of Ba Xoai. I immediately recognized the voice of the American on the radio. Although I had never met him personally, I had a picture of him in my mind. It's funny how your mind will create a picture of someone just from the sound of their voice after you have talked to them very often.

He was quite frantic. It seems that all hell had broken loose in an area that had been peacefully quiet just a few minutes earlier. I told him we were only five minutes away, that he could fire a couple more mortar flares if needed to but to stop after that because we would be there. He did so. Bug and I nosed our Hueys over and beat feet. Bug began to climb to altitude. We could see the tracers going both directions, green from our enemy inbound and friendly red colored outbound. It was obvious which side was where. Every few seconds we could see mortar and rocket explosions, lighting up the area like flash bulbs, then total darkness again in that immediate area. Mortar fired flares were everywhere. It was almost surreal as we got closer to the fight. All of the explosions and tracer rounds were easily visible but up in the air I could not hear a sound, just the whop, whop, whop of my rotor blades. If you could forget what was actually happening down there to people you knew, the sight was almost beautiful. Such incongruity there is in war.

He finished giving us our quick tactical update as we got on-station. They ceased firing their mortar rounds and flares. As Bug's first flare ignited, I began my side of the fight. Bug's flares were many, many times brighter than the mortar flares they had been firing. They illuminated many Viet Cong out in the open rice paddies that previously had been hiding in the dark. I had both my crew chief and gunner begin firing. My third crew member who normally used my starlight scope and xeon light began firing his M-16 and when he was out of ammo, began 'plinking' M-79 grenades into the fight. The firing was intense and the calls from the outpost were, "keep it up as long as you can!" They were under considerable pressure.

Trying to take some of the pressure off the compound, I began flying in lower and tighter circles, pulling as much pitch as possible to make my rotor blades "pop" as loudly as I could. Maybe by making all the noise I could, in addition to the ammunition we were expending would, if not disrupt the attack, possibly slow it a little by distracting the attackers. At times I was flying as low as 25 feet. I was just high enough to keep my rotor blades away from the trees and shrubs. That was extremely low in a firefight at night!

Before long as I scanned my instruments, I saw that our fuel was getting low. Our low fuel warning light wasn't on but I felt it should have been. I was stunned that I had actually used my fuel load up that fast. No, I thought things were happening so fast and furious I must have lost track of the time. I had Bug drop three flares in rapid succession and told him to "Di Di Mau" (go quick) back to Chau Duc to refuel and reload himself with another load of flares.

We made a couple more quick passes; I used up our remaining ammo and headed away from the fight. My heart ached that I had to leave my contact alone in that fight. Now my low fuel warning light did come on! Chau Duc was an easy 15 minutes away and I quickly prayed that we had enough fuel to get back to the refueling area. There was supposed to be 20 minutes of fuel onboard when the fuel low warning light came on but I was always told not to trust that estimate completely.

NEVER GET INTO A FIGHT WITH ANYONE THAT HAS MORE AMMUNITION THAN YOU!

As I approached the refueling area at Chau Duc, Bug was just finishing. I told him to throw on a few extra flares and get back to the fight ASAP and to drop a few flares even if I wasn't there. It might just take their mind off the outpost for a minute or two while they looked for me. As soon as I refueled and rearmed I headed back out. As I neared That Son I saw that Bug had started dropping flares over the fight. A few more minutes and I was back on station. Oh, what a night it was turning out to be!

The fight continued fast and furious all night. At one point I was asked to back off a click or so, in order for them to listen to the movement of the Viet Cong. That was the only time that happened to me while in Viet Nam but to a point, it made sense. The whole night was the same, refuel, rearm and return to the fight, time after time. I don't remember how many times we did that routine that night. No other outposts were requesting support or I would have had to call the Navy Sea Wolves or call back to Vinh Long and wake up a few buddies. It was a very hard fought night and as morning approached we were all exhausted. Although we saw many tracers come our direction, amazingly, we took **no** hits! Saint Jude was on my side.

About 0500 hours, just before the sun began to rise, I received a call from the American's ARVN counterpart that my radio buddy had been shot. He was being attended to but would not be back to the "mike." My heart went into my throat again. I wished them good luck and went on with the fight. Shortly, as the sun began to rise the fighting quickly ceased. The Cong didn't get into the outpost we were defending but I still felt an overwhelming emptiness inside due to a lack of success. I guess I just couldn't help him enough.

As the sun began to illuminate the rice paddies, we could see Viet Cong walking back towards the village just to the south of the base of Nui Dai. Of course none of them had a rifle. They had to have already stashed them somewhere in the paddies. As I began to give orders to my crew chief and gunner to start picking them off, I heard in my ears, "Don't Fire" from the American advisor that had flown with me all night. I had forgotten that anyone else was even back there. He and his ARVN (a Major) counterpart had been quiet all night.

I was told that the ARVN advisor said that all of the people on the ground were friendly farmers, they had no weapons. Incredulously I yelled through my microphone, "WALKING BACK <u>INTO</u> THE VILLAGE, FROM IN THE MIDDLE OF NOWHERE— AT DAWN! HOW CAN THAT BE?" I held off fire while we argued but the ARVN would not budge. If I fired now I could be brought up on charges.

Again I knew, one more time, we had a **Viet Cong onboard as an all night "advisor"!** What training we gave those Cong. Anger was not the word I would use to explain my feelings. Furious would not even approach how I felt as I watched all those "friendly farmers" walk back to their village. Which one of them shot my radio buddy? Watching from above I was unable to do anything.

I flew down to several of them, hovering at about 10 feet AGL hoping someone somewhere would shoot at me. They didn't even look at me. They ignored me as if I wasn't there. I moved my helicopter even closer. I was right beside them hovering two feet above the ground and my rotor wash almost pushed them into the dry rice paddies! They just leaned into the rotor wash and kept walking towards the village purposefully not looking at me. It was as if I didn't exist. They were having such a hard time walking because I was blowing them off those rice paddy dikes. We argued a little more but my "advisor" wouldn't change his answer.

If a large armed helicopter was hovering next to you, wouldn't you at least look at it?

I was very upset with what was happening, I argued with myself and tried to reason with myself but I kept losing the argument.

"This would not do!" Finally, as the last "farmer" was walking through the last paddy approaching a small wooded area near the village, I knew what I had to do—personally.

I landed my Huey at the intersection of two rice paddy dikes. I told my crew to stay on board, stay light on the skids and leave if any fighting ensued. Grabbing a bandoleer of shells, I chased that last Viet Cong into the woods carrying my 12 gauge sawed-off shotgun. (I always had that shotgun on board just in case we were shot down.) On entering the woods, time slowed down for me and I carefully began my search hoping not to trip any booby traps. I had entered it only seconds after he entered it and it was very quiet except for the Huey in the background. I knew that he wasn't far away.

Amazing myself, I actually found him hiding behind some very large leafed foliage. As I slowly pushed the leaves away with the barrel of my shotgun, his face was less than a foot away. He froze! So did I. He knew I was going to shoot. I looked at him; he couldn't have been more than 15 years old. My heart sank at that moment but I motioned with my shotgun barrel that he should get up. My finger was on the trigger and if there was anything odd happening, I definitely would shoot. As he got up, I found out why he was the slowest getting back to the village. He only had a pair of shorts and a shirt on and had been shot in the right buttocks.

That wound was a good confirmation to me that he was out there in the war that night, since I had not been permitted to fire after dawn arrived. I dropped him off at the Green Beret Camp (B-43) a few minutes later for interrogation and told the Green Berets that I would not fly with that "ARVN-Advisor-Viet Cong" again. I would not permit him on my ship. I had done that one other time at Chau Duc and had never even seen the other man again. I soon headed home to Vinh Long.

That night has stayed with me all these years. Just rereading this story has my adrenalin flowing 30 years later. I can see the intense fighting, the radio calls and the Viet Cong, one even inside my ship! One was supposedly friendly, the other, a prisoner. The following day when I returned for another day's pre-mission briefing, I was given a souvenir. It was an "NVA postage stamp" that my prisoner had been carrying. To this day, whenever I view that stamp in a shadow box on my wall at home, memories flash back and the adrenalin begins to flow once again.

It's amazing how a little adrenalin (and probably some testosterone) can be your best friend and your worst enemy all at the same time. When mixed with some raw emotions, it could be deadly. I thank God it wasn't deadly for me that night.

Frank Strobel
"Knight Hawk 6"

3756 SLICK DRIVERS

I received some general questions about my situation from some members of the 114th Association.

If you guys have any questions about it, I did not fly a gunship. I <u>was</u> a slick driver . . . D & H model Hueys all year! Many times, though, I would have liked to have a few rockets available.

I have been asked how I slept during the day at Vinh Long. As far as sleeping with the crazy hours of the night mission, when my head hit the pillow, I was usually gone. On a few occasions I did take a few shots of Johnny Walker Red but those nights, I mean mornings, were not the norm. Now I can't vouch for the deepness of the sleep I had on some of those occasions. At times Vinh Long in the daytime was very noisy.

I was there to fly and would never turn down a flight. I was always approaching the upper limits of the 120/140 flight hour rule. I often was grounded for a day or two each month because of too much flight time. Once I was grounded for five days in a row. That was unheard of! That was when others took over and flew the night missions for me. I always felt that 140 hours in a 30 day month wasn't much. I could easily have flown another 30 or 40 hours more per month but 140 was the max, except in the case of a combat emergency.

I know we often had tongue-in-cheek complaints from the hanger because we would need 25/50/75/100 hour inspections quite often. We often needed them twice a week and sometimes more. Flying nights, it was almost the norm to have 10 or 12 flight hours per day. I maxed out at 18 logged flight hours in one 24 hour period but I didn't remember the last few of them. We all had long days.

Many nights were slower than others but there was usually something I could find to do, even if it was just harassing known Viet Cong and North Vietnamese areas. I started a lot of fights just firing at random in those areas. It was always nice to know "085" could get me away from a fight just as fast as it could get me into one, if the odds were not in my favor.

Frank Strobel
"Knight Hawk 6"

THANKSGIVING DINNER 1970

One thing that I was happily tasked to do on Thanksgiving 1970 was to take Thanksgiving dinner out to every outpost with an American and every American out on a patrol away from a base in the Seven Mountains Area. Not only did the dinner consist of turkey, mashed potatoes, gravy and corn but also shrimp cocktail, cranberry sauce, hot apple pie and coffee.

We began early in the day and delivered the wonderfully smelling meals all day until we served the last morsel. All day every time we opened the containers the smells reminded me of home. We didn't sample anything for fear there wouldn't be enough for those troops away from the main bases. We were correct in our thoughts because they were scraping the bottom of the containers at the last outpost. We couldn't wait to return to B-43 to get our Thanksgiving Dinner.

It was 1900 hours when we landed but there was no food left waiting for those of us who spent the entire day delivering meals to everyone in the area.

We hurriedly flew to Chau Duc to refuel for our trip back to Vinh Long and a Thanksgiving dinner there. Alas, they had expected us to eat with the Green Berets at B-43 and had saved nothing for us.

The cupboard at Vinh Long was also bare. No turkey dinner for us!

Frank Strobel
"Knight Hawk 6"

SHOT DOWN ON PHUC QUOC ISLAND

Phuc Quoc Island was about 65 nautical miles west of Rach Gia. For those who never got out to Phuc Quoc Island, you'll never know what you missed. Phuc Quoc was a beautiful island in the Gulf of Thailand. It was about 30 miles long and shaped like a large turkey drumstick.

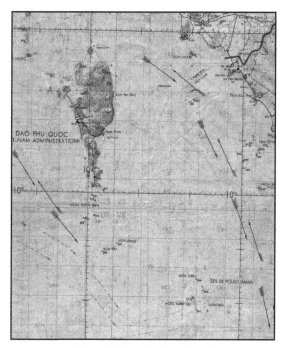

Map Of Phu Quoc Island

The southeast side of the island was one secretive cove after another all along the coast. Everyone was different; some had sandy beaches but most very rocky with large boulders, yet all were the same in their beauty. All of them looked pristine. The southwest side of the island had a long straight white sandy beach with white capped waves rolling up the shoreline. If you flew about 50 feet above the breaking waves the beach looked as if it went on forever. One day we even saw a small pod of whales off the western shoreline.

Occasionally, flying up the west coast you would see a small lonely hut. It was that way until you went one half of the way up the coast to the village of Duong Dong. This fishing village was as beautiful as it was unique. At the village was a small stream with a 150' peninsula jetting westward in a small curl out into the Gulf of Thailand. That small piece of land was large enough to protect the island's small fleet of fishing boats from the weather. Part of the way out the peninsula was a 15' high statue of the Madonna and Christ Child. Towards the end of the peninsula was a small beautiful pagoda. I assume they were there to bless the fishing boats on their way out to the fishing grounds and welcome them back when they came home.

Madonna & Child and Pagoda

I was lucky enough to have had half a dozen missions to the island. They were all a few days and long enough to really get to enjoy the time there. It was a completely different world, although there was still a war wherever I would go. It was a real dichotomy. In fact I did not officially take an R&R (Rest and Recuperation leave) while in Viet Nam but one time I hitched a ride on a C-123 and spent four days there at the Navy base at An Thoi. Yes, I took my bathing suit.

There was one thing that I wasn't too fond of and that is the fact that while on the island, there was only one helicopter. Mine! If something happened to me, there was no help nearby. Help was many hours or days away. The mission while on the island was mainly "ash & trash", moving people and supplies. On several occasions I dropped patrols into different parts of the island. On two occasions, I did medical evacuations.

The only other aircraft stationed on the island was a lone fixed wing Bird Dog (L-19.) That small aircraft would fly a high cover for me in the event I was flying into a known hot area. The only thing he could do for us was to fire the four 2.75" rockets he had mounted under his wing that were normally used for marking targets with smoke. After that, all he could do was contact someone on the mainland to send help. He loved shooting the rockets. When I was there it was the only time he loaded High Explosive rockets instead of Smoke.

The second medical evacuation was the one I remember the most distinctly. A patrol was ambushed in the center of the island, in a valley between the villages of Duong Dong and Ham Ninh. Three RFPF soldiers were injured in the first of several small firefights. An American advisor from Duong Dong called me and asked if we could do an evacuation of the injured soldiers. Tactically, I was told that the Viet Cong were two tree lines north of the patrol and there was a good clearing for me to land right at the friendly position. The winds were not favorable though.

As I approached, the wind was blowing very hard from the south so I didn't feel a downwind landing would be safe. I made a downwind approach and did a steep 180 degree turn at 30' AGL to turn my nose into the wind. I used the southern of the two tree lines for a little cover as I crossed their position with the intent of sitting down immediately. Unfortunately, in the time it took me to get to the area and begin the approach, the enemy soldiers had moved into the tree line I was using as my cover. In effect, I bled my airspeed to zero while completing my 180 degree turn immediately over the trees sheltering the Viet Cong. In effect I was sitting completely stopped immediately above them. They didn't even have to aim I was so close to them!

The results were not good. We got heavily peppered with small arms fire. It was immediately obvious that we were hit many times in just a few seconds. I didn't land. With this surprising change in enemy location, not being able to talk with the soldiers on the ground because of the language barrier and also not knowing where else the enemy might be, I pulled pitch and returned to Duong Dong. I needed to check the damage before I stressed the helicopter too much. On the five minute trip back we did a quick inventory and ascertained that no one on board was hurt and that the Huey was flying okay. I was surprised that we weren't shot down in that clearing! We were very, very lucky.

After setting down and seeing the number of times we were hit, we were very surprised that none of the bullets seemed to have hit anything vital. We stopped counting at 40. That was before we checked the tail boom! Numerous hits were taken in the area where the tail boom attached to the airframe. Of the four bolts that secured the tail boom to the body of the aircraft, one nut was completely blown off and two others were hit; one nut half missing and one cracked severely. The aircraft was definitely a "RED X" for maintenance. It could fly no more!

I climbed into the Bird Dog and we climbed to about 8,000 feet before his FM radio was barely able to reach Knight flight operations at Vinh Long. We actually had to have another aircraft relay parts of our message to Knight operations. They agreed completely that it should not be flown before it was inspected and repaired by maintenance. They told me that Road Service would be sent as soon as they could get the parts organized.

After landing in the Bird Dog, I was immediately approached by the local South Vietnamese Officer in the area and his American Advisor asking if we could try again. I explained the problem with the aircraft and that it wasn't safe. We took too many hits in a vital area. We needed to stay put at least until Road Service replaced the tail boom bolts and evaluated the other damage. The last thing I needed was my tail boom to flex while flying a rescue mission.

They were incessant, however and we went round and round for about 30 minutes. Then they hit me with, "The most seriously wounded soldier was the village chief's son. He was bleeding badly and if he did not get evacuated soon, he would die! He had been wounded so badly they didn't feel that he would last the few hours it would take to make a forced march out of the valley."

I then spoke with the rest of the crew and we discussed going back out again. I was not going to force anyone to go. The basic questions centered on the damage to the Huey's tail boom and the resulting flight worthiness of the Huey. It was never the combat situation. Nothing was mentioned about the enemy! The entire round trip flight would be less than three clicks. I told them that the criteria I had always used to evaluate the situation before making a medical evacuation was a question that I asked myself, which was, "If I was on the ground wounded, would I want me to try?" Funny thing the answer always came up, "yes".

If any one member of the crew refused to fly then no one would fly since we needed a full crew on both sides of the ship. Not surprising to me, everyone volunteered to go. I told the advisor that if they moved the wounded a couple hundred meters to the south where there was a larger field requiring little "peddle work" and therefore less strain on the tail boom, we would go. There we could make a simpler approach and departure. The patrol had already been moving south trying to flee the enemy soldiers and would be ready when we arrived.

We took off, not climbing above 200 feet. Gingerly, we made the approach only receiving some sporadic fire. The only problem with sporadic fire is that any one of those bullets could still be that "Golden Bullet" you don't want to see. The patrol was where we expected them to be and with the exception of that small amount of fire, we made the evacuation without further incident. When we returned to the airstrip we were greeted by many members of the village, the village chief and his wife.

Several hours later that afternoon, Road Service arrived and after their inspection and some quick repair (replacing two of the tail boom bolts), we traded aircraft and they flew mine back home to Vinh Long for repair while we stayed with the Road Service ship to continue our mission on the island for the rest of the week.

There was a great celebration that night in the village. The whole crew was invited to the village chief's house and we were treated like kings. Well, maybe not exactly like kings but we were treated very well. The food was great tasting and much more seafood and pork than we could think of eating. The drinks were freely flowing and the party lasted into the wee hours. As a gift, I was presented with a quart of locally made Nuoc Mam which they claimed was Viet Nam's best.

Village Of Duong Dong Looking South

It would be wonderful to revisit that island someday. My photo skills do not do that wonderful island justice.

Over a year after I returned to civilian life, I surprisingly received a letter saying that I was awarded a Distinguished Flying Cross for the mission. I had no idea that any paperwork had been ever presented for that mission. To me and my crew, it was just one of those days that we had like so many others over there.

Frank Strobel
"Knight Hawk 6"

TROOP MORALE, SON-A-DOC AND CRAWFORD & HULSEY

I left my home in Erie, PA, for Viet Nam at 11:00 AM December 26, 1969. I arrived in Nam at the 4th Replacement Company at Long Binh a couple days later and was assigned to the Knights, January 3rd. I reached the Knights on the 4th of January.

I was trying to get my feet on the ground and found that an orphanage run by Irish nuns was next to the base. I was over there numerous times. I helped them do some repairs in one of the dormitory rooms and took some U. S. Army "goodies" over to them a couple of times. Those goodies were hard to come by but it could be managed. But that was about it. The nuns stayed a bit distant from me though. I assumed it was because of threats from the Viet Cong.

Troop morale was always a concern to me. Personally, I had very little problem with either Officer or enlisted Knights. While there though, we had two Warrant Officers transferred into the Knights that truly had personality disorders. They had been transferred into the Knights from other units that had had problems with them. Both of them had detrimental effects on their assigned platoons (1 Red Knight, 1 White Knight) and both did some damage but luckily neither lasted long in the 114th.

The White Knight Mascot "Son-A-Doc"

The pilot transferred into the White Knights was regularly smoking pot; the one in the Red Knights was just plain anti-social. The Red Knight had been in my flight school class at Fort Wolters, Texas. He was not one of my favorite people then; maybe that was just his regular personality. After arriving in Viet Nam he completely went off the deep end. He killed Son-a-Doc one night, our White Knight mascot after crawling into its cage in a drunken rage. I med-i-vaced it to a veterinarian in Can Tho but he was unable to help and put it to sleep. The pilot was transferred out of the Knights a couple hours later before he was killed by the whole angry White Knight Platoon. Both were instances of problems transferred into the Knights from other units.

In another situation, the night before Crawford and Hulsey were killed, they both were over to my room and spent a couple hours. Crawford, who was black, was a super guy. He really had his head on straight. I was very happy to consider him a friend. We talked about a growing problem with blacks on base having demonstration marches claiming that it was unfair to have more African-Americans facing death on a daily basis than whites. At times I heard their anti-white chants and was very happy to be away at night when they usually got together for their demonstrations. That was scary, knowing that if they somehow got out of control that they had access to weapons. That was a real fear at the time. Imagine feeling safer flying out in enemy territory at night than in your own bunk. I had truly forgotten about this until I started writing this note.

The day after Crawford was killed, there was a mass demonstration of blacks on the base at Vinh Long claiming that he was put at risk and not enough whites were. Three whites died along with Crawford in that crash. The argument was not reasonable but nevertheless professed. I know that he would have rejected their arguments.

I was unaware of any large use of drugs by any of the Knights but have heard some stories only after I left Viet Nam. Of course other than sleeping, I spent little time at Vinh Long. I flew as much as I could. I never had any need to question if anyone with whom I was flying with was using drugs. I was always proud to have been with the guys I served. Had I known about someone doing drugs he never would have been allowed to board my ship.

In slightly more than 11 months of flying, I logged over 1,300 hours. I personally saw no in-flight drug problems; maybe I was too busy to see those things. My missions dominated my time.

Between flying my missions, the briefings and planning and paperwork and the fact that I never had a maintenance problem of any kind that needed my attention, I guess I had no need to look for a drug problem. If there was it didn't affect me. I didn't need to look into the workings of other platoons within the company. I was busy; my needs were continually met; I was happy.

The biggest problem I remember is the politics that permeated everything we did. We were sent over to fight a war and had more and more restrictions as time went on that went beyond fighting a war. It got to the point that at times, if we followed the rules, we could not even defend ourselves. That became my big fear. I knew that, had I done something that the "brass" considered wrong, I would be on my own. That is very sad for any soldier to contemplate. Most of us were not in Viet Nam because we wanted to be, yet we could be sacrificed for somebody else's career. I had no doubt in my mind that a situation would be handled that way. I didn't necessarily want to be fighting a war but the rules we were required to follow were crazy! If our county is going to fight a war, let the military fight it. It was obvious the politicians didn't know how!

We had strict rules to follow and the other side, our enemy, had none. They could do anything they wanted to do. That did not make sense and it did make me angry—angry at our politicians!

Frank Strobel
"Knight Hawk 6"

FLYING THE CHAU DUC SWING SHIP

One beautiful sunny day I was assigned to fly the "swing ship" mission for the Chau Duc area. I spent the morning flying basic resupply sorties going from outpost to outpost dropping off food, ammunition and some mail.

In the early afternoon we were resupplying the outposts further to the south, with the last outpost on the southwest side of Nui Coto. When flying near that mountain in the daytime I always flew low and close to the mountain's base since the Viet Cong had at least one active .51 caliber anti-aircraft gun mounted near the summit at all times. It could not rotate enough to shoot downwards easily, so flying low and close to that mountain was flying safely.

We were empty and heading east to round the mountain and head back to Chau Duc and what we thought was an early release. My crew chief said through the intercom, "Mr. Strobel, I see some Viet Cong with rifles sitting on large boulders at the base of the mountain." I banked hard and immediately saw them as they began to scramble and hide.

This was very unusual. I never saw groups of Viet Cong during the day. We weren't prepared for a large battle. We had been carrying heavy resupply materials not a great deal of ammunition for our machine guns. Each gun had only 1,500 rounds available. That was normally adequate for a swing ship but not for an active firefight.

We began to receive heavy AK-47 fire as I had my crew chief open fire on them. I expected the Viet Cong to quickly disperse but they surprisingly stayed together to fire at us. After a few passes from both sides of the aircraft we were beginning to run low on ammunition and on fuel.

I made a general call for help on my UHF radio. I quickly received a response from another unit's Command and Control helicopter that was nearby and could lend some help. As I was beginning to leave the area I gave him a quick briefing over the radio about the tactical situation and reminded him of the anti-aircraft gun(s) on the top of the mountain. He replied that he would fly the mission the way he wished. I then left the area since I was low on fuel. I left the fight in his hands.

I heard the next day that he was shot down by an anti-aircraft gun on his first pass and had to be rescued by the other aircraft he had been controlling earlier. What a waste.

Frank Strobel
"Knight Hawk 6"

BODIES FROM AN OVERRUN
OUTPOST NEAR TRI TON

One of the most unpleasant tasks that I was required to do several times while in Viet Nam was to transport body bags. One occasion required a couple of flights of ten body bags each from a small outpost that had been over-run.

The outpost was south of Tri Ton, nearer to the hamlet of Dong Hau but still even a little further south. It had been over-run a few days earlier by enemy soldiers who surged off of the mountain, Nui Coto. They over-ran the base and then immediately retreated back onto the mountain. I had heard thirty or so ARVN soldiers were removed from the outpost during the fight and were saved. Those who were left were either dead already or were killed by the Viet Cong in the last minutes of the fight. I was not part of that fight so I don't know the exact details. I was just part of the cleanup.

It was the first day anyone was able to get back into the outpost. It was a grim task. Cleaning up what the Viet Cong had left was not pretty. A company of ARVN troops moved in to secure the area and did the unpleasant work. The bodies had been laying in the hot monsoonal weather for three or four days. I thanked God that I was not part of placing them in body bags.

Later that day, I was called in to fly out the full body bags and take them to Chau Duc to the MACV compound. It was not something I was really excited about doing but it had to be done. Soon, I was sitting on the ground outside the small outpost.

The stench from the bodies before they were even loaded was horrifying. The ARVN soldiers stacked the bodies in my helicopter. Onboard it was all we could do just to breathe. I took off as quickly as quickly as I could just to get some air movement flowing through the ship. As I climbed to altitude for the twenty minute flight to Chau Duc I received a call over the intercom from my crew chief. Although the air movement helped the two of us up front a little, it did nothing for my crew chief and gunner in the back.

The only thing I could do was to push the right pedal and fly sideways and out of trim to have fresh air blow directly on my crew chief until my gunner could take the smell no longer. Then I pushed the other pedal to give him some fresh air. I alternated flying that way the whole flight to Chau Duc. That maneuver places a great deal of pressure on the tail boom. I prayed that it wasn't too much stress.

When I was approaching Chau Duc I called and requested that an ARVN truck and a few soldiers meet us to recover the bodies. When I landed there was only one soldier and no truck. I shut down the engine and climbed out to a very unsettling sight.

The ARVN soldier grasped the top body bag, gave it a pull. It quickly slid it off the pile, out of the helicopter and it slammed onto the hard ground making an ungodly sound. I was again horrified. How could you treat anyone that way? Dead or not, they were not bags of rice. I yelled at the soldier, knowing that he didn't understand a word but he did understand what I was saying. I was so angry; I immediately made a fist with my right hand and began a swing to punch him in the face. I stopped short but just barely.

Although I didn't condone what he had done, his superiors sent out one five foot tall 90 pound private for this job. They were the problem, not this poor private. I did push him away from my helicopter and my crew and I emptied the chopper of the body bags, gently placing them alongside the helicopter in a row. I am sure my crew (my co-pilot, crew chief and gunner) didn't like the job but not a word was spoken while we gingerly completed our task.

After my last trip to the outpost, I flew my helicopter over the short distance to the Mekong River and we washed the blood out of the ship before it dried. It was another part of the war that was very unpleasant but necessary. We then continued our mission just like any other day.

Frank Strobel
"Knight Hawk 6"

Chau Duc—The MACV Compound

MY BURNED OUT STARLIGHT SCOPE

The Viet Nam War was a strange mixture of old and new. A great number of the weapons and other armaments were WWII vintage. The Viet Nam War was a good way for the United States to use up a lot of military "stuff" that was left over from the Korean War. The military was able to clear the inventory of the old equipment and to test the new technological items, many that were in the final stages of development. For those unaware of it, the Soviet Union and the Red Chinese did the same through the North Vietnamese. One of the new items that I was able to use was the Starlight Scope. That was the night vision scope that I used in Viet Nam, though was nothing like the equipment that was available twenty years later.

The Starlight Scope of the Viet Nam Era (first generation night vision scope) was very large, unwieldy and very, very fragile. The Scope itself could be more precisely described as a nighttime spyglass. It was about 30 inches long with a rubber eyepiece on one end; the other end was about 12 inches in diameter. It had a snap-on cover over the large end to protect the insides from too much light. Just a flash of day light would burn out the delicate electronics. It was amazing to us to see just how well we were able to see at night through that equipment. It worked well. I was told that they cost the Army $30,000 each, though I am not sure. That was big bucks in 1970. I have no idea what today's cost would be.

One morning while refueling at the Chau Duc Airfield, the Starlight Scope Cover accidently was bumped and its cover popped off. Its electronics were immediately fried. So instead of flying back to Vinh Long that morning we kept right on flying east to the repair depot at Long Binh, northeast of Saigon. When I carried the scope into the repair facility I met a sergeant who took the scope and gave me a receipt. He told me it would take a week to repair. I told him that I would be back to pick it up. I turned to walk out but he stopped me saying, "Do you want me to lend you another one, while we are repairing yours?" He proceeded to tell me that he had three scopes that were on no one's inventory and I could have one while mine was being repaired. I grabbed it in a flash. What was even better, since it was not on anyone's inventory, I didn't need to sign a receipt.

About ten days later, I flew back to Long Binh to pick up my newly repaired Starlight Scope. I purposely left the borrowed Starlight Scope in my helicopter and went into the repair depot to pick up my old one while holding my receipt in my grubby little hands. When I arrived at the counter the sergeant I met the week before was not there. When I asked for him I was told that he was transferred elsewhere and he would not be returning. I was given my Starlight Scope and I returned to my helicopter. Suddenly I was one extra starlight scope to the good. We now had a starlight scope for each side of the helicopter.

Towards the end of my tour as I was preparing to go home, I now had a starlight scope that didn't have a home. It obviously wouldn't fit up my sleeve during my flight home. So during my last week, on one of my last flights out to the Seven Mountains Area, I dropped in unannounced to Ba Xoai. In my view they were one of the outposts that were attacked by the Viet Cong at night very often but were not authorized such an expensive high tech piece of equipment. When flying the Night Hunter-Killer mission I often gave them air cover. I gave them my extra Starlight Scope, with a few extra batteries and the proviso that they would destroy it immediately if things became dire some night. They felt that it was an easy promise to make and I was on my way.

Frank Strobel
"Knight Hawk 6"

BOM-MI-BAI AT NUI SAM QUARRY

One very hot day while waiting for General XI at the Nui Sam Pier I decided to take a walk. The road there was the narrow two lane Highway 2 that ran to Chau Duc. As I started walking down the road I began to notice the empty barges that were waiting their turn at the pier to load gravel. I passed a couple barges and then saw one of them with about 20 men sitting in a circle on the bow talking. Several began to wave to me inviting me to board.

It was just at the end of the monsoon season and the water was still pretty high. The only access was a long 3"x 6" plank that was reached from the bow to the ground. It was almost to the road. It was at least 25 foot long and at its highest point was about 20 feet above the water. Gingerly, I began to walk up to board the barge, all the while hoping that my balance wouldn't fail me!

When I arrived on deck I was warmly greeted. They made an opening in the circle, large enough for me to join them so I crossed my legs and sat down. Initially, as I sat there looking around, I wondered how many, if any, of those men had seen me flying the Night Hunter-Killer Mission, or had possibly fought against me one of those lonely black nights.

Caption: Nui Sam Quarry

The next thing I knew was that I was given a small clear glass and from the far end of the circle a bottle was being passed around. All

I could think about was that I was not really a drinker. I couldn't handle my liquor. I just hoped that it wasn't too strong.

The bottle reached me and I took a quick look at it. It looked like vodka and I could see a couple of rice husks floating in it. I poured a small drink and passed on the bottle. All eyes were on me. That was my clue! I put the glass to my mouth. My upper lip immediately began to burn like fire, my eyes started to water and my nose began to run. All this and I haven't had a taste of it yet! They all had a good laugh at me. They all started saying at once "Bom-Mi-Bai!" I had heard of it before but had never had any. It was a rice whiskey, sort of like our white lightening here in the States but brewed from rice and maybe some sugar cane, not white sugar, corn or other grains.

A man at the other end of the circle started to motion to me. He obviously was going to show me how to drink the stuff. The bottle reached him and he poured a healthy glass of the stuff. He sat the bottle down and made an exaggerated gesture of drinking. He didn't let the drink touch his lips it just hit the back of his throat and down it went. He then motioned across the circle back to me. It was my turn.

Reluctantly with all eyes on me I did the same. Surprisingly I didn't choke, though it burned like fire all the way down. A quick cheer was made and all went back to the important activity of the day, talking, laughter and the bottle. Before the bottle returned to me, my crew chief called to me from the road saying that General Xi was on his way. It was probably a good thing.

I stood up and said my good-bye's and began making my way back down the plank. No sooner did I reach the helicopter than General XI arrived. I climbed aboard the chopper and started to strap in. All of a sudden I started to feel the effects of that one drink. I started to get that tingly feeling, first on my tongue, then on the tips of my fingers. Next it was my biceps, triceps and the calves of my legsband I started sweating profusely. Damn, I was drunk.

I started the helicopter and with sweat beading on my brow, I told my co-pilot to fly the General home. He picked the helicopter up into a hover and did a pedal turn to face east for takeoff. It was a perfect position for me to wave goodbye to my drinking buddies on the barge. There were waves in both directions as we flew off, **away** from the sunset.

They are probably still laughing at the American who couldn't handle his **"Bom-Mi-Bai!"**

Frank Strobel
"Knight Hawk 6"

HOLDING HANDS ON FINAL

I didn't fly troop insertions regularly because of my Night Hunter-Killer missions but there were times that I was assigned to do just that. Some of the things that the crew always carried were old unusable heat warped M-60 machine gun barrels. Why?

On occasion one of the ARVN soldiers, usually out of fear, wouldn't want to get off the helicopter when we arrived at the landing zone. The crew would use those barrels to hit them on their metal helmet "to ring their bell." This never failed to encourage their departure. I didn't like the process but it did work. I always asked my crew not to hit them too hard, just hard enough!

I often tried to think of different ways to get them out of the helicopter without beating on them. One day I had an idea. I told my co-pilot that on short final, the last 15 seconds or so to "Hold my handand we will gaze longingly into each other's eyes as if we were lovers." He thought I was kidding but I convinced him to try it once.

So, on short final, we held each other's hand and looked longing at each other. When I brought the ship to a three foot hover the ARVN soldiers were instantly out of the ship.

As we were taking off out crew chief came onto the intercom laughing heartilyand told us that we were instantly noticed. Our acting in the front seats of the helicopter was pointed out to all who had not seen it on their own in a matter of a couple seconds.

There was enough concern that they were all happy to get off the chopper as soon as they were able and no one had a headache! We were probably the topic of conversation all day.

Frank Strobel
"Knight Hawk 6"

MARTHA RAE AND ME!

Martha Rae had a wonderful relationship with the Green Berets. She had adopted them and vice versa. Throughout Viet Nam she would often do special shows for them and even performed duties of a nurse when needed. She was a nurse in WWII and I had heard she had done those duties in Viet Nam as well. She was very competent.

One morning after a particularly long and stressful night in the Seven Mountains Area, I helped with the ship clean-up for a short while and then proceeded to walk the quarter mile to operations and complete my after action report. My after action debriefing normally would take an additional 45 minutes to an hour. I was exhausted but that was not unusual. A 16 hour day away from Vinh Long was close to normal.

No sooner had I crawled into my bed than I was asleep. I was sound asleep when the company clerk was knocking on my door. I was told to report to the Commanding Officer as soon as I could get my uniform on. It took me about 10 minutes to report. I couldn't figure out what I had done! I was then told that every ship was away on missions and I was the only ship available for a special mission.

Martha Rae was at the Green Beret compound at Can Tho and needed transportation but to where he didn't know. Happy to be flying a Hollywood star, I quickly went back out to my ship where my crew was already waiting for me. I was to report to Can Tho as soon as possible and take her wherever she wanted to go. I was given a special frequency to use along with an unfamiliar call sign and was to call them enroute to Can Tho to let them know that I was on my way. I did so and was told that the tower would give me instructions when I arrived.

Upon arriving at Can Tho I was instructed to sit down on the VIP pad and remain running at flight idle; she would be right out. It was a bright sunny and hot day; the humidity had to be in the 90's. At least with the rotors turning we had a fan moving the air a little. I pulled pitch very slightly and frictioned down the controls to give us a little more air movement. The sun flickering through the spinning rotor blades was not very comfortable though. That flickering was an easy way to make everyone sick to their stomachs. After half an hour of just sitting there with the chopper running, I called the tower. I was again told, "She's on her way." We again sat there until we were almost out of fuel.

I called the tower again and asked for clearance to move to the POL area for refueling. I asked him to call again to find out what the plans were. We were cleared to hover across the main runway to the POL area. After refueling and while returning to the VIP pad, he told me that all they would say is that she would be out as soon as she could. I asked him for a place that I could sit down and shut down. I did so. At one point a Green Beret sergeant whom I had never met came out and told us she was being entertained by some Green Beret Brass.

We sat there through lunch. The temperature was near 100 degrees and the humidity was almost as high. We asked for some water to be brought out to us in the helicopter; it wasn't. The heat was almost unbearable in the bright pounding sun but we were requested not to go to the mess hall because she would be out shortly. So now tired, hot, dry <u>and</u> hungry, we sat there another two hours. She never showed. At 1500 hours I called the special radio frequency again and told them that I only had a maximum of two hours before I had to prepare for my regular night mission. Five minutes later a jeep came out to the chopper but no Martha Rae. She would not need any transportation that day. I was released to go back to Vinh Long.

Angry was not the word. My whole crew had been up and working now for well over 24 hours. The only rest I had was the short nap I had in my bunk. We left Can Tho for Vinh Long to prepare the ship for that night's mission. There was no time to relax once we landed at Vinh Long. We prepared the ship and left for the night's work and at least another 16-18 hours before we could get some real rest.

Martha Rae did great things for the soldiers in Viet Nam and especially the Green Berets but it didn't extend to us that day.

I never met Martha Rae.

Frank Strobel
"Knight Hawk 6"

ARVN SOLDIERS TAKING ITEMS—A
CAMERA AND AN ENGINE COVER

I always hated hearing others speak badly about any group of people, no matter who or what they were. Yet, in all of my life there is one group of men about whom my mind always does. It is not only from the many stories I had heard but, alas, from personal experience also.

It was the ARVN & RFPF soldiers. They were always very nice and polite when meeting them face to face but when you were not watching them, especially when we were transporting them in our helicopters, anything could come up missing. I could understand if they stole a can of C-rations that they would find sitting around but they would steal items that they could have no use for at all.

One day towards the end of the monsoon season I was flying trail while doing troop insertions with the Knights. We had just picked up a group of ARVN troops and were returning them to their base. When we arrived we made a normal formation approach to the base but as we touched down one of the helicopters stayed at a 25 foot high hover. Being in the trail position I made a radio call to him asking him, "What's the problem?" His answer, "My new $400, 35mm SLR Camera is missing. It was on my radio console. If I touch down I will never see it again. I am not coming down until I get it back!"

He said that his crew chief was going through the cargo compartment looking through everything. Three or four minutes later he came down to a 15 foot hover and I saw a body come sprawling out the cargo compartment door. This body with its arms and legs flailing came to a splashing halt in the deep water and mud of the flooded rice paddy below. The soldier slowly stood up and walked over to his buddies. He did seem unhurt and he now had no camera. It had been recovered from his back pack.

I did get angry with an ARVN one day. Three Knights had already reported items missing from their ships. On each of the first two sorties that day we were missing items needed for the helicopter, including the rotor blade tie down strap. On the third sortie I told my crew to be extra diligent watching the ARVN's while we were giving them a ride.

A few minutes after we took off my crew chief told me that the soldier immediately behind me had taken our engine exhaust cover and put it into his bag. All I said was, "What the hell could he use that for?"

Once we leveled off at our flight altitude I gave control to my co-pilot and unbuckled my seat belt. I turned around and climbed up kneeling on my seat facing the cargo compartment. I tapped the soldier on his shoulder and when he looked at me I motioned that he give me what he took. He shook his head like he didn't know what I was talking about. I then most sternly motioned that he give me what he took. He again motioned that he didn't know what I wanted.

Over the intercom my crew chief then said, "Mr. Strobel, I watched him put that engine cover in that bag on his lap." What I did next may sound drastic but you must remember I had ten ARVN soldiers onboard with loaded semi-automatic guns. I pulled my .38 caliber pistol out of its holster and placed the barrel against his right temple. In English I yelled at the top of my lungs and over the rotor noise, "NOW!"

With a shocked look on his face he reached into his bag and gave me the engine exhaust cover. I told my crew chief and gunner to hold their machine guns in the direction of that soldier and make it obvious just to discourage any surprise retaliation from <u>anyone</u>. I didn't want an errant bullet accidently brushing my helmet.

We were all very happy when we dropped them all off in a rice paddy. I didn't tell anyone that I kept one barrel of my .38 empty, just like Barney Fife, so I wouldn't accidentally shoot myself in the foot!

Frank Strobel
"Knight Hawk 6"

ANGELS POINT ZERO ZERO TWO FIVE

For anyone reading this story who is not a pilot, let me explain one term. U. S. Air Force pilots, because of the heights at which that they fly, have added a word of jargon to their vocabulary. It is the term "Angel." An Angel is Air Force speak for 1,000 feet. When reporting an altitude over the radio they can simply say, "I'm at Angels 29" instead of the much longer, "I'm at twenty-nine thousand feet". It's simpler to say and easier to understand if radio contact is not clear. Or, maybe those Air Force pilots don't like using all "'dem big words." I really am not sure but anyway the following is a brief radio encounter of mine.

As always at night, I used Border Control Radar located in Chau Duc for flight following. We were always looking for ways to relieve some of the stress that always had its head lurking about. We were even known to break strict radio protocol from time to time in an effort to relieve that built up tension.

At one point, in the middle of the night, I heard an Air Force jet jockey contact Border Control to let him know he would be in the area for a short while at "Angels 10," just in case anyone needed him. As he ended his transmission, I started mine.

"Border Control this is Knight Hawk 6. If he needs me, I'll be here at Angels Point Zero Zero Two Five!" (25 feet above the ground).

All I heard, (I assumed from up above) was, "Now, that's a new one!"

Frank Strobel
"Knight Hawk 6"

SOLO NIGHT FLIGHTS INTO CAMBODIA FROM PHU QUOC ISLAND

There were a couple missions I flew into Cambodia that were against what my normal orders were. Both missions were flown in the middle of the night in situations that were very strange to our basic operating rules which required a full flight crew. Both missions were flown from Phuc Quoc Island (An Thoi Airfield) and without the crew that flew with me to the island. They were the only times that I flew a Huey solo while in a combat area.

They were somewhat strange and different missions that were never fully explained to me other than I was "picking somebody up." I was told at the time that the flights were to be kept secret from my crew and I was not to log the flight time in the aircraft's log book. I assumed that they were flights similar to those flown by "Air America" but why me? That has always been a question in the back of my mind. The only thing I was ever able to guess was that I had flown and navigated many night hours (over 300 hours) as commander of a Night Hunter-Killer Team and was I very comfortable doing so at night. I assume someone must have known that fact.

An Toi Airfield: Approaching from the East

The first time I flew the mission, I was approached by a young dark haired man in his late 20's or early 30's, dressed in civilian clothes. He asked me to take a walk with him out the runway to the west end at An Thoi while my crew refueled helicopter. That refueling was a long project because there were no electric or gasoline powered pumps and only a hand pump was used in a fifty-five gallon barrel of JP4. If I was empty it took four full barrels. It was a long process.

As we walked out the runway he introduced himself and told me just to call him John. I have no idea if that was his real name but probably not. He wanted me to fly him west of Phnom Penh, Cambodia to pick up something and bring it back to An Thoi. The unsettling thing was that I was to tell no one about the flight nor log any of the flight time and most of all I could ask no questions unless it pertained to my operation of the helicopter.

I was then asked, "Would I do it?" I had many questions but didn't ask any, probably because I realized they wouldn't have been answered anyway. I didn't expect that someone would be there on the island base without authorization and being in civilian clothes he was probably with the CIA or NSA or one of the other alphabet soup organizations. We all heard of "different" things happening in Laos, Cambodia and Thailand, especially the exploits of the Air America organization. I often saw Air America aircraft at the air field at An Thoi. So figuring that I might be getting myself into something interesting, I said, "Okay!" Who, knows, maybe I'd even receive a job offer after my 12 month tour was over.

It was interesting. A few cold cases of beer (a French beer called, Export 45) were made available to my crew after the ship was prepared for the next day's flight. The beer was well away from the flight line in a small building in which we were to sleep. A few Navy guards were near the helicopter for security, so all was comfortable and relaxed. At 2300 hours I told everyone that I was going to take a walk on the beach. I had managed not to drink any beer and they laughingly told me that they weren't going to save me any of the beer if I left. They would drink it all while it was cold since it wouldn't be any good warm.

I walked down to the runway and got my first surprise. My helicopter was missing! Almost immediately, a guy I had never seen stopped in a jeep and picked me up. He took me to the far eastern end of the runway where my helicopter was sitting. They had just finished moving it so that my crew would not hear me start it or take off. Then I had my second surprise. They had changed the radio/battery (nose) door and had replaced it with a plain one without the Knight Logo. They obviously had done this before.

The five inch "United States Army" printed in a bold Arial font letters on the tail boom had been painted over earlier by the 114th so there was nothing on the outside of the helicopter identifying it as from the United States. Although, who else would it belong to?

Then my third surprise. "John" handed me a set of civilian clothes including sneakers (that were a couple sizes too big) and asked me to change. The bluish plaid shirt was pretty ugly and too large but then again, who was going to see it? The clothes were comfortable. After I changed my clothes, I thought that I was ready and then John asked for my dog tags. He wanted my dog tags? What had I gotten myself into? I guess I shouldn't have been surprised. If we went down there would be no identification on the bodies, that is if they would even find the wreckage . . . if they even looked! I briefly thought of that John Wayne movie title "They Were Expendable!" They even took the logbook out of the aircraft.

John then spread his map over the cargo compartment and with an olive drab right angled flashlight with a red filter showed me exactly where he wanted to go. It was southwest of Phnom Penh, Cambodia. We were to land to a hand held battery powered strobe light, the kind that was used to signal rescue aircraft in an emergency. It was definitely a clear night with a bright moon. He said he had been there several times so he would ride in the left seat to assist me in navigating. I asked him what we were going to pick up and he told me I only needed to know that it was one person that weighed less than 150 pounds.

John told me that my flight plan was to be this. Lift off and depart to the north as low as possible so that the noise would be minimized by the hills on the east side of the island and not be heard at the base. Stay below 200 feet AGL unless necessary to miss any obstruction but preferably go around it. He said that he could get me close to the landing zone but then we would have to look for a strobe light. I had the same kind of feeling I did when I first had a mission with the Navy Seals but at least that was in the daylight. I would be refueled at the time of the pickup.

It was a fairly simple plan except for a couple things. I actually had some questions. What if we got shot down somewhere or couldn't find the strobe? The simple answer was that we would walk out. As I started the engine, I was thinking, "Is this smart, or am I just plain stupid?" I wasn't trained for anything like this . . . but was anybody? The only way I could justify the danger was that I was prepared for it, probably better than anyone else in my unit because of the Night Hunter-Killer missions that I had flown for so long.

As I flew I quickly saw the lights of Phnom Penh. Luckily for me the mission was fairly simple and straight forward. I remember being surprised at how much moonlight there was. The moon lit the ground up pretty well and the number of small hamlets and hooches with lights made it very easy to differentiate up from down and reduce the opportunity for my biggest fear, night vertigo. I was astounded at the light that emanated from the City of Phnom Penh. I was not used to that. I was too far away from the city to see anything specific but the light did dominate the horizon.

I was pleasantly surprised to see the strobe light less than 2 minutes after John told me to start looking for it. I sat the helicopter down at the strobe light and right beside four 55 gallon drums of JP4. We were already being refueled as I rolled the engine down to flight idle. Our reluctant passenger was hooded and placed onboard in less than a minute. The two gunners who accompanied us on our flight moved from their seats in the well to the ends of the passenger bench seats to protect our passenger. Interestingly it was the only time that I saw a POW (I assumed) with a chain around his waist that was locked to one of the cargo rings ensuring that he could not jump out!

The flight back to An Thoi was relatively uninteresting, at least as far as I was concerned. The navigation was simple and the flight was what I considered quiet. I landed at the east end of the runway and quickly shut down. I changed back into my flight suit and quickly got into the jeep waiting for us. John and I rode in the jeep back to the base on the west end of the runway.

The next morning my helicopter was back at the east end of the runway with the correct nose cover on it. It was fueled and ready to go. I usually did a good preflight inspection but that day it was a super thorough preflight. My crew probably thought that something was wrong with me that I didn't trust them about anything. Little did they know that the machine had a few extra flight hours on it and other people had worked on it. I never did find out to whom we gave a ride. Since there was a POW camp located on the island, I can only assume that he (?) was a "special case"!

DINNER IN A TENT—A VIETNAMESE CROSS OF GALLANTRY

Shortly before going back home to Erie, I was invited to a dinner General Xi was giving near Chau Duc. It seemed strange that I was given map coordinates and not the name of a building in Chau Duc, or someone to pick me up to take me to a building. But, who was I? When given map coordinates, I go to the map coordinates.

As I approached the destination in my helicopter, I saw two small tents and one large tent, set up in the middle of nowhere. Actually it was in the middle of a dry rice paddy. It was at least a mile in any direction to the nearest bush or shrub. It was a strange place but again, who am I to question? I landed about 100 yards away from the tents so that I would not blow them over. I left my crew to secure the ship and began walking to the tents. I was with Wendell Jarrett of the White Knights who often flew with me. He was also invited to the dinner.

About halfway to the tents we were warmly greeted by a South Vietnamese Colonel and were assured our crew would be taken care of at dinner time. He briefly apologized about the tents. He said that they didn't often do this but with the large number of officers who were invited, security was much easier out in the open. It made sense to me.

After having a glass of wine, I was seated next to the South Vietnamese Colonel on one side and on the other side a South Vietnamese Major whom I had supported many times while flying the Night Hunter-Killer missions. Both spoke fluent English and I had a lively conversation in both directions. Soon, some South Vietnamese soldiers dressed in khaki uniforms started filing in carrying trays of chilled shrimp cocktail followed by a nice but simple salad. Then came the main course. Trays were being carried in with dishes of steak (about eight ounces) and lobster. I couldn't believe it. For most of the year, my main nutrition came from an Army green tin can of C-rations and now this! I leaned over to the Major and said, "Surf and Turf. I haven't had steak and lobster since I have been in Viet Nam!"

He smiled and said, "Surf and Turf, yes. Steak and Lobster, no." As the plate was lowered to eye level, I took another look at the plates being served to us. Yes, there was steak but it was not lobster alongside. It was one very large shrimp. It was larger than the piece of steak. The major told me that it was brought up from Rach Gia. Rach Gia was a nice sized fishing village on Viet Nam's coast along the Gulf Of Thailand. Dinner was excellent. I had been told that the Gulf Of Thailand was a very rich fishery that was not commercially fished. That shrimp was amazing.

When dinner was over, General Xi stood up and spoke briefly of what had been accomplished in the 9th ARVN Division Area in the last year. He listed a number of accomplishments and said that Wendell and I were a very large part of the successes. The major ones were the removing of the enemy from the mountains of Nui Cam, Nui Dai and Nui Coto. They were the three largest mountains in the Seven Mountains Area.

He then called Wendell and me up to the main table and presented each of us with a medal. It was the "Vietnamese Cross of Gallantry with the Bronze Star." I was stunned. I was honored that I was invited to a dinner by the General that included most of the people he had worked closely with the past year. The people he had depended on. I had not expected to receive a medal.

As I look back on my military service, that moment has become one of my proudest. Why? Certainly I had earned a number of awards for my combat service, most of which the US Army awarded to me after I was a civilian again.

It was specifically because that medal was awarded individually to me by a foreign government, a foreign culture. People whom I had never met before and would never see again. They were people from halfway around the world.

They appreciated what I had done for them and thanked me for just that. For that reason, that award will always be very special to me.

Frank Strobel
"Knight Hawk 6"

Turning Final - Vinh Long AAF 1970

Flying Back "Home" To Vinh Long Army Airfield

FLASHBACKS? YOU BET I HAVE!

I had heard of many veterans having flashbacks to memories of the war and what happened to them while in highly stressful situations. I had a tough time believing that they would be real enough to actually affect a person's normal daily life years later. If it did then there was a problem with the person and how they handle stress, not with the actual memory. I just felt it was an excuse for some kind of personal weakness, that is, until it affected me.

One morning after being home from Viet Nam more than 10 years, I was driving by myself across town to my office. I was a branch manager at a local bank. As I sat at a red light, the song Bad Moon Rising by Creedence Clearwater Revival began to play. I had often listened to it while in Viet Nam. The next thing I was aware of is that I was about three miles closer to my office but there was more.

I was reliving a firefight I had fought in Viet Nam while flying my helicopter, yet I was in Erie stopped at a red light. I was in a full sweat (in January) in the middle of a radio call that I had actually made 10+ years earlier! I "woke myself up" when I heard myself say out loud, right in the middle of that radio call I had actually made, "What the hell are these red lights doing up here?"

I was stopped at a red light with my turn signals on. I couldn't remember how I got there. I was confused to say the least. As I sat there a sense of fear flushed over me. The light turned green and I stepped on the gas and I gingerly made a left turn just as my turn signal was already indicating. I immediately pulled off the road and onto the grass of the Erie General Electric Company factory. I hoped no one would report me for parking on their lawn. I didn't feel I should be driving. I sat there for awhile trying to figure out what had just happened to me.

All I could ascertain was that the music on the radio triggered a memory flashback. It was something I didn't believe could or would ever happen to me. In my mind, I was back in Viet Nam reliving a long forgotten memory. I traveled across downtown Erie, during morning rush hour, totally oblivious to the fact that I was driving a car. It was very unsettling for me.

I had obviously driven through town but did I follow the traffic regulations? Had I caused any accidents? Did I do any damage? But most importantly, did I hurt anybody? There were so many questions flashing through my head. I then realized that I had been sitting on the grass for almost ½ hour and I had better get to work.

I arrived at my office and checked my car for any damage and after opening the office, I turned on the radio in my office to listen if there was any report of a "crazy man" driving through Erie and causing a great deal of damage. Thankfully, nothing was reported on the news and no police stopped in my office that day. I was happily surprised.

To this day, I do not remember driving those three miles. I do believe in the power of a memory. Now, I also believe in flashbacks. I have had numerous once since.

I Do, I Do, I Do, I Do, I Do, I Do, I Do!

Frank Strobel
"Knight Hawk 6"

3053 BACK HOME IN ERIE, PA AKA . . . THE POPCORN INCIDENT

Thanks to President Nixon's "Early Out" Program, I only spent 50 weeks in Viet Nam instead of 52. Anyone who had an expected date to return to the States between December 20 and December 31, 1970 could depart between the 10th and 20th if orders for a permanent change of station were in hand. This way those individuals could be home for Christmas! It cost me two cases of beer to bring in a clerk from battalion to prepare my orders on a Sunday afternoon. My family was expecting me home the week after New Years (1971) and I didn't want to get their hopes up, just in case of a SNAFU with all of this "fast paperwork", so I didn't mention the possibility. They needed no disappointments during the holidays. Things began to move quickly though.

Soon I flew my last mission. It was just a simple troop insertion mission but for the first time since I was new "in country," I flew very cautiously. It was the first time I flew so carefully that I was almost dangerous; maybe I **was** dangerous. Now I was the short timer I spoke of early in this book. I was too close to be going home to have a problem; I was going to be careful. I was not going to take any chances. It was probably my longest preflight of the year. Everything was going to be exactly right before I flew. Soon the mission was completed, although it seemed to last an extraordinarily long time in my mind. My crew had a beautiful wall plaque made and presented it to me that evening. It immediately became one of my most precious possessions. It proudly hangs in my office.

Early on the morning I left, after packing my last bag, I carried it out of my hooch and paused for a moment. I looked around for the last time at the area that had been my home for the last 12 months. The area was deserted. Everyone was away doing their job, flying. Even the mama sans, for some reason, were not there.

It felt very strange. In a funny way I felt a little sad. I felt a little lonely too. Everybody was out flying but me.

This was the place that took a 22 year old who had lived on his own for a couple years and thought that he was pretty callous to the ways of the world but Viet Nam showed him differently. I had considered myself a full grown and mature man when I arrived in Viet Nam. Only a few days later I realized that I had some thinking and more growing to do. Growing that I was not expecting needed to be done. My first two weeks in Viet Nam were a real wake up call. It was almost as if God grabbed me and slapped me a few times across my face and said, "Do you understand what this is all about now?" I couldn't then and can't now imagine being 17 or 18 when I arrived, as so many others in my unit had been. Twenty-two was young enough.

It's funny! At the Columbia, Missouri, reunion Bill Mattler (a former gunner of mine) told me that they called me "Pops" behind my back all year in Viet Nam. He said that the guys felt that I had my head screwed on straight and when someone had a problem they felt I could help with, I did. How satisfied those words made me feel.

Had they only known how frightened I had been, oh so many times that year, worrying that I had made the right decision for those onboard as well as those depending on me on the ground. Had they seen the beads of sweat under by my visor? If they had actually seen me sweat, they may have felt otherwise. If they did see the moisture on my brow they must have thought it was the heat. Had they asked, I'm sure I would have told them that's what it was.

How different I was from the first day I arrived in the Knight compound. As I picked up my bags to head to the operations building, I had a strange feeling come over me that I no longer belonged at the 114th. I wasn't part of the "club" anymore. I remember thinking that it was a very strange feeling. How could I not belong?!! This part of my life, for whatever reason, was over.

I felt sad but somehow comfortable with that idea on my short walk to operations. I knew I had done the best I could. There were so many ambivalent feelings for one guy to have. On that short walk, my head was constantly moving, looking at things I would never see again.

Nothing I saw was really important, probably the same things that I had looked at the first day while I was there trying to get my bearings. I guess I was just solidifying memories as much as anything else. I really couldn't imagine not seeing that place again. I had only been here a short year, less than 5% of my life but I knew that it would remain a major hallmark of my life. I was not wrong in that thinking. A few more minutes and I would be climbing into the back of a Huey leaving the Knights just as I had arrived a year earlier. I was now just part of the baggage again.

I had seen so much hurt and so much death in the past year. Among those who suffered were not only the enemy but also my friends. They were people whom I knew, people that I was close to, people with whom I ate and laughed and cried. Cried with?! What a strange thing to say. At that time in my life, I would never have admitted that. There were so many conversations about who was hurt and who was dead. We never would have admitted to crying. I guess those sad conversations were crying on one level even if no tears were showing.

How lucky I felt Bert Lorentz and Jeff Carr were after they were shot in the leg and sent home to recover. Lucky? What terrible pain that had to be but they were truly lucky they were alive. I wonder if they ever thought they were "lucky." Butcher, Crawford, Hulsey and Akana, they weren't lucky. Their lives were, well their lives were quickly whisked away. Was it an accident or luck or fate or the odds or God? That they went through what they did and yet I'm walking down the walk to begin my flight home. How can you explain it? What was wrong with me that I would even think in those terms? I felt a little guilty 'cause I didn't know the answer to "why me?" Why was I permitted to go home?

I signed out of the company and was told my Huey was waiting for me. I had to file my last flight plan and fly myself to Long Binh. I wasn't baggage after all, I was flying front seat. It was hard to believe it but it all worked. Everything fell into place and my last flight in Viet Nam was flying myself to the pad at the 93rd Replacement Company in Long Binh early that day. When I arrived in Viet Nam I spent a couple days at the 93rd and saw several Hueys landing at that pad and thought, "Now that's the way to head home!" Now it was my turn on that pad.

Most guys arrived at the replacement company to go home in a Jeep, a bus or a truck but here I was flying myself to that same VIP landing pad I had seen when I first arrived. It was so nice of the 114th to allow me to fly myself to Long Binh. Damn, that felt good. I flew left seat flying myself all the way and sadly thinking that this would be the last time I would touch the controls of a Huey. Thank goodness I was wrong in that thought.

At Long Binh I cleared my paperwork in an extremely short time and within a couple hours I was on a bus headed to Tan San Nhut Airport. The brass must have been in a great hurry to get rid of me because soon I was walking out to a Flying Tigers chartered DC-8 passenger jet and on my way home. I couldn't believe how lucky I was. Richard Nixon must have put a great deal of grease on the gears of the U. S. Army. I was shocked for two reasons: first, I was actually boarding the plane that afternoon and second, as I boarded many of the guys from my flight class with whom I flew over were boarding along with me. It seemed too good to be true. We knew that we would party and exchange war stories all the way back.

You'll never guess what happened but then again maybe you will. Shortly after the pilot said that we had cleared South Vietnamese airspace a huge cheer went up and we all went to sleep. I think it was the first time in a long while that we let ourselves really relax. We had done our jobs, now we could sleep. After I awoke it started to sink in that I had actually finished my year in Nam. It had been a very long time since I ever thought that would really happen. What I thought mostly was, "I'm on my way home!" I wasn't sure I deserved it. Too many guys were not coming home.

After a few hours everyone began to wake up and the party began, although it was less enthusiastic than I thought it would be. We exchanged experiences. We spoke and learned of those who were injured during their tour and those who didn't make it. When I told everyone Gale Butcher's story, all went silent for a moment in disbelief. All that work getting through flight school and he died on his first mission. He had only been exposed to the bad (hard) side of flying. He never had the opportunity to kick back, enjoy and reap some of the benefits of all that sweat. He never got the chance to take a few moments off, relax a little and feel "fat, dumb and happy" for just a few moments up in the sky somewhere. We were much more reserved in our partying than I had expected. We were different people than we were a year earlier.

We landed in California and were advised to quickly change out of our uniforms and into civilian clothing. It seemed that many servicemen were attacked and some were beaten by members of the anti-war (peace) movement. I refused to change, as did many others. I respected my uniform too much to hide it. We said good-bye to each other and we all went off in our own earnest efforts to get home. The good-byes may have been different if we realized that most of us would never see each other again.

My flight connections worked and I landed in Erie on Christmas morning around 9:30 AM. I made it, I really did. I still hadn't told anyone that I was out of harm's way. I decided I just may as well make it a complete surprise. After picking up my bags, I went to the Yellow Cab taxi stand. I threw my bags into the back and sat down in the front seat. Boy did that torn beat up leather seat feel good. I spoke with the driver and he asked me where I was stationed. When he found out I had just left Nam he questioned me all the way home. Once home he said, "Merry Christmas" and that the trip was on him. Home looked pretty good. Seeing home just reaffirmed to me that I really had made it.

Man, was I shocked though when I looked at my parents' home. There was a 10+ foot in diameter lighted Christmas wreath hanging on the front of the house. It was in the form of the anti-war protest movement's peace symbol with multi-colored Christmas lights woven in and out. My mouth almost dropped into the snow.

Later that day, I explained to my father my feelings that it was the symbol of the protest movement and I felt that it was the ultimate reason why the war was extended and the reason many of my friends were killed and injured in Viet Nam. They had put it up thinking that the sooner the peace, the sooner I would be home. Although I didn't see it being done, it was down the following morning. It's funny how I still feel that way about that symbol. I see it as a symbol of death.

I walked in the back door carrying my bags and directly into the kitchen. It was about 10:00 AM and everyone was running around getting ready for church. My mother was combing my youngest sister's hair as she looked up and saw me. She dropped the hair brush and almost passed out! I guess it wasn't a good idea to make my homecoming that much of a surprise. All activity stopped as "Welcome Homes" were given to me by my parents and my seven siblings still living at home.

My Dad then said, "Let's get moving or we'll be late for church." I hadn't heard that one in a long time. I was still in my TW's

(Tropical Weight uniform) that I put on in Viet Nam two days before. They were not very crisp or clean. They looked as if I had slept in them, which I had actually done several times over the last two days. At church my dad led me into the sacristy to say hello to Father Gallagher, our Pastor. As we returned to our pew Mass was about to start but Father didn't start Mass, he walked to the pulpit.

He told the packed church that I just came home an hour ago. The church erupted in applause and when it began to die down we all joined in prayers of thanksgiving. I quickly forgot that my TW's were a mess. He then announced that the Mass was said in thanksgiving for my safe return home. When Mass was over it took us almost an hour to leave the church. I had more hugs and handshakes than I had ever had in my life.

Part 2, . . . Yes, again there's a part 2!

On returning home my youngest brother, who was about seven years old, along with my other brothers and sisters quickly accepted my homecoming, changed out of their church clothes and were gone to enjoy the day. This left my parents and me to catch up on what had transpired the past year. Many, many questions were posed.

I heard stories of men who returned home from Europe after World War II. It took many of them six to eight weeks or more to get home on a crowded Liberty ship. I now realize what a great name that was for those ships. It took many other men from WWII, six to nine months or more before they returned. A long trip back would be a great way to decompress at least somewhat from the immediacy of the profound experiences they had been through. It probably drove them crazy that it took so long to get back home. As I look at it now, I think it was a very good tonic for them.

We didn't have that luxury but we didn't know it. I assumed that I would get back home and **SNAP** everything would go back to normal. Little did I know!

The moment of truth, well at least one of them, was here.

While in Viet Nam, not wishing to scare any of my family, I only wrote home detailed stories about USO flights I made with Norm Snead and other members of the Philadelphia Eagles, a Country Western Singer, a couple of singing troupes and then my personal problem with Martha Rae. My mom didn't know I flew real combat. She had told everyone I was lucky enough to get a job flying for the USO. As the day went on she had a little better idea. I told her that I flew nights because it made me feel more at home since I was up the same times everyone was up back in Erie, Pennsylvania.

After dinner, we all gathered in our large living room. It had to be large with that many kids in the family. There were two large couches and several overstuffed chairs in the room and, of course my dad's recliner. A couple neighbors joined in and soon we had a house full. Our next door neighbor, who was a retired Marine Colonel, was there. My mother sat beside me on one of the couches rubbing my left hand between both of hers all evening, just happy that I was home and maybe reassuring herself that I was actually there. After a couple hours of lively discussions, my brother Tom, who was about ten, decided to make me a treat for my first night home: my favorite, popcorn. Unfortunately he didn't tell anyone.

To me, popping corn on the stove in a light aluminum pot and lid, sounds the same as small arms fire piercing the thin metal skin of a Huey. When the popping started, I did not respond as a civilian back at USA would respond. As the first couple of kernels erupted, flinging themselves across the covered pot and banging into the lid, I instantly flung myself on the floor looking for cover but it was worse than that.

In a war mind set, when you hear rifle or mortar rounds impacting nearby you react instantly and just in case your buddy next to you didn't react, you "assisted" him to cover. Well my buddy sitting beside me in my living room was my mother. I instantly flung myself off the couch heading for the safety of a nearby coffee table and I pulled my mother with me. Before she was completely on the floor I realized what I was doing and stopped. In half of a second, things had changed. She started to cry quietly, realizing in some small way what had happened. She knew her baby boy would never be the same. Sheepishly I apologized to all the room and re-seating myself we went on with no further explanation. Soon my brother Tom proudly came into the room with a large bowl of my favorite, hot buttered popcorn.

About a year later, I received a letter from the Department of the Army. Since I was off active duty my mother was sure they were calling me back up to head back to Viet Nam, so she opened my mail. I was married by that time and lived near the campus of the college I was attending. She called me all excited and all the while apologizing that she had opened my mail. I was awarded my 4th through 37th Air Medal and a Distinguished Flying Cross.

Later that year in the ceremony awarding me the medals, the citation was read. While standing there in my uniform, I could see my mother out of the corner of my eye. As the reading went on she got more and more upset. When the ceremony was over, she grabbed me by my uniform lapels and pulling me close to her, said to me, "You never told me you were involved with any of that s—t!!!!"

Now, that shocked me more than many things I witnessed in Nam. My mother never used any kind of foul language. Up to that moment, I didn't know she had ever heard the word let alone used it!

Over the following months, I slowly and carefully filled her in with a little more detail than I previously had, though still leaving out most "unnecessarily messy" details. Soon my mother and my wife started urging me to write my stories down, to write a book. I always insisted that I was just one guy that had been to Viet Nam and there were hundreds of thousands of guys that are Nam Vets and they all had their own stories. No one would be interested, especially with the anti-war/peace movement that was so active. Peace movement? Huh! It was not very peaceful from what I could see. It was not until November 2000 when I learned of the Knight forum where I would begin to relate my stories.

I think I have written down most of my "interesting" war experiences, although I admit I still have a many more I could write! As we all do, I have some memories that will never leave my own mind and heart. They are things that I am unable to share and unwilling to put in words.

Thanks, guys and gals of the 114th forum, for your encouragement. It's been a cathartic (ad)venture. There is one last thing. I have had a question asked of me several times this year. Would I ever want to go back to Viet Nam for a visit? That is a really hard question. Part of me immediately and emphatically says, "No," yet there is a little part of me that feels it would be a really interesting trip! Where would I start? It would probably be Vinh Long, I guess but then there is the Seven Mountains Area, Moc Hoa, Chau Duc, Phuc Quoc Island, the U Minh Forest . . .

Frank Strobel
"Knight Hawk 6"

MY TIME IN THE PENNSYLVANIA ARMY NATIONAL GUARD

PAANG—MY ENGINE FAILURE AKA . . . IT'S JUST A MATTER OF PERSPECTIVE

I joined the Pennsylvania Army National Guard for awhile but the closest flying assignment available was 150 miles from home. They had no quarters or mess hall so it was too far and too expensive for me to serve long term. I did have some good times for a couple years though. I was transitioned into the OH-6A. It was a fun machine to fly. I was assigned to a flight detachment that was attached to an Infantry unit.

We had a couple of UH-1H's and a few OH-6A's and basically did only VIP flights. The VIP's didn't like squeezing into the smaller OH-6A, so 99% of their flights were in Hueys. That being the case I usually had no assignment, so I just took my little helicopter and did my own private training missions. For the most part if there were no missions and as long as I kept off the base and completed all of my required training, I was left alone. If I kept out of sight and out of trouble, my helicopter was mine to do with as I wanted. I did static displays at air shows and safety training at non-aviation National Guard units around Western Pennsylvania. That was about it. It was almost like having my own private helicopter with someone else paying for fuel and maintenance. What a job!

Then some disgruntled Air Force crew chief flew a Huey from Andrews Air Force Base and landed it on the White House lawn. New rules and new regulations were implemented. All helicopters were retrofitted with an ignition key. The next step was placing heavy padlocks on all aircraft. Things changed; there would be no flying without a specific mission. Then there were fuel shortages and even more restrictions. There was just enough flying to keep up the basic required flight minimums. There were many days I would drive from Erie, PA, to Washington, PA, 150 miles and just sit in operations. It was a major waste of my personal time and money. My monthly pay would barely cover the cost of the travel, lodging and food expenses. I could be home with my family. It would have been much different if I had lived near the base.

One summer camp in the early 1980's at Fort Picket, VA, I had an engine failure on a training flight when flying at about 200 feet AGL over a pine forest. My crew chief Sgt. Garofalo was a school teacher from Brownsville, PA, who had flown with the National Guard for about 14 years with nary a warning light flash the whole time. I did a side slip autorotation onto an old tank trail with my skids just clipping the tops of the trees as we slid over them. We rapidly approached the ground.

We touched down and he quickly got out, ran around the front of the chopper and tried yanking me out as I was turning off the last of the switches. I told him to relax; I would climb out on my own. Moments later as we walked around inspecting the helicopter for any damage he asked me how I could be so cool in an emergency situation. I told him it was easy. "I didn't have to worry about anyone shooting at me once we got down on the ground." It's funny how life is all just a matter of perspective.

CW2 Frank Strobel and Sgt. Carl Garofalo

By the way the engine failure was caused by fuel contamination. They found an old hose being used by the refueling truck that was shedding pieces of rubber off the inside of that hose. All helicopters were grounded for a couple of days until everything was inspected and cleaned and a new hose was attached to the truck.

Frank Strobel
CW2, PAANG

PAANG—THREE MILE ISLAND

I was only activated on one occasion while a member of the National Guard. It was on March 28, 1979. At the time I was a manager at a local bank in Erie, PA, about 150 Miles away from the National Guard Base that I was stationed. Shortly after I arrived at work I received a phone call, telling me that I was activated and they expected me at the base shortly after noon. After receiving the phone call, I made the necessary arrangements at the bank, called my wife and packed my bag. I changed into my flight suit, grabbed my flight gear and I was on my way.

As I drove, I heard on the radio in the car about the accident at Three Mile Island but was unaware of its severity. I had been told to get there as soon as possible so I did break the speed limit on Interstate 79 a little during my drive to "Little" Washington, PA, the location of my unit. I arrived at the airfield about 1230 hrs. still not exactly sure why I was activated.

I was given a quick briefing in operations. I was told that the accident at Three Mile Island was far worse than I had heard on the radio. There was a possibility of mass evacuations of people in the immediate area of the accident. How large was the area? They had no idea.

My mission was to fly to the Harrisburg area and contact the National Guard unit located at Ft. Indiantown Gap on my way. I was to make myself available for anything they needed but it probably would be the evacuation of people in the immediate area of the accident.

I collected my gear, the radio frequencies I needed, filed my flight plan and then left operations for the flight line. Two maintenance men that I knew well were at my helicopter. They had gone over it for me and made sure it was fully fueled. I still did my preflight inspection but it was a great deal faster than I normally took. I cranked up and took off heading east by myself towards Harrisburg.

Now, for the first time as I flew, I had time to do some thinking. Here I was heading towards Three Mile Island to what they were now calling a nuclear disaster. They were expecting to call for an evacuation and I was flying towards it. It didn't sound too healthy as I mulled it over in my mind but this kind of "stuff" is why I volunteered.

Just as I approached the Appalachian Mountains I received a call from my unit back in Little Washington. They had just received a phone call from Ft. Indiantown Gap. My mission was cancelled and I was to return to Washington immediately. No evacuation would be called. I turned the helicopter around and headed back, though with some mixed feelings. I had myself really pumped up for doing some exciting flying over the next week or two even though there would be danger involved.

As soon as I landed my helicopter I went to operations and was immediately released to go back home. I was told that the flying I did would just be counted as one of my regular monthly training periods.

So goes my only activation while in the Pennsylvania Army National Guard.

Frank Strobel
CW2, PAANG

PAANG—RICK FONNER'S FIRST HIGH OVERHEAD APPROACH

Back in the early 1980's, I was flying OH-6's (Hughes 500) out of "Little" Washington, PA. My crew chief this day was Sgt. Rick Fonner. Rick had served with the Marines in Viet Nam, in I Corps in 1969. One weekend we were flying near the Wheeling, West Virginia Airportand I said to Rick, "I haven't done a high overhead approach in a long time; I think I'll try one."

He asked, "What was a high overhead approach?" I explained that this type of approach was used in Viet Nam for landing at a base where a normal approach would be too dangerous because of nearby enemy activity. It was setup by heading the helicopter into the wind directly above the compound at 1000 feet above the ground. After reducing power to a minimum we begin a tight 360 degree turn, touching the ground or coming to a hover at the completion of the turn. Obviously that reduction in power resulted in falling out of the sky very quickly. It is slightly dangerous but very expedient.

If the ship was shot down during this type of an approach, it would be near the immediate protection of the base, not a long distance away and in jeopardy.

I told him to hang on. I asked him to help by watching my engine and rotor RPM needles and let me know if they begin to split. We didn't need a rotor blade over speed.

CW2 Frank Strobel and Sgt. Rick Fonner

After receiving tower clearance over an inactive runway at the Wheeling, West Virginia Airport, I proceeded to talk him through the procedure, as the bottom dropped out of his seat. He started crowing like a cowboy on a bucking bronco. I could hear through the helmet yelling, "Yeeeeee Ha!" all of the way down. After that day, it was his favorite type of an approach.

Frank Strobel
CW2, PAANG

PAANG—MY FAMILY HAD
NEVER SEEN ME FLY

No one in my family had ever seen me in a helicopter. In 1979 my mother was dying from cancer and had pointedly mentioned several times the fact that she had never seen me fly. She was still able to get around with a great deal of pain and assistance, so I decided that I would see what I could do to fly up to North East, PA, (near Erie, PA) during one of my weekend flight training periods. I would just have to make sure it was a day that there were no missions that needed to be completed and that the weather would be decent. I could use the flight then as a navigation training mission. For several months schedules didn't mesh.

The Pennsylvania Army National Guard didn't make it easy though. I could fly anywhere I wanted when I was on a training mission but I did have to be refueled at airfields with government contract fuel. That normally wouldn't be a problem but the closest airports to Erie that had contract fuel was either "Little" Washington, PA, (south of Pittsburgh) or DuBois, PA, closer to the center of the state. I wasn't able to fly round trip from Washington to North East without refueling but I could fly, just barely, from Dubois. It was quite a bit out of my way but it could be done. One Saturday in July 1979, when there was nothing scheduled, I filed a flight plan to practice my cross country skills.

With my planning I figured I had a maximum of 15 minutes of extra flight time over North East before my 20 minute low fuel low warning light would be illuminated on my return to DuBois. I called my wife before I took off to tell her of my plans and when I expected to arrive in North East. She called my father and plans on the home front were made.

I began my flight and refueled as planned at DuBois. I flew to North East and landed on my parents' 40 acre spread off Route 89. My Crew Chief, Sgt. Carl Garofaolo and I had a nice lunch and posed for a few photos. We took off for a 10 minute airshow over the property and then flew back to Dubois for some badly needed fuel.

Frank and Family

My mother died six months later, January 8, 1980.

I heard once . . .
"What doesn't kill you makes you stronger!
All the crewmembers of the 114th Assault Helicopter
Company" Must be Gorillas!

Frank's Portrait

At the End of this book, I present the Epitaph
I wish to have on my tombstone:

**I Have Lived My Dream,
I Had My Moment In The Sky . . .**

APPENDIX 1

Communication I Have Received About Individual Stories

3324 HOW'S YOUR MATH? . . . SISTER ANN STEPHANIE, MY FRIEND

3325
From: John Laughinghouse
Subject: Not quite a "War" story

"Francis"- Thanks for another very interesting story. You know it is amazing that when someone said that truth is stranger than fiction, they were right. Did you really go to an all girl Catholic School?

John

305

3326
From: Frank Strobel
Subject: Not quite a "War" story

John,

If only I could have!!!! I went to a parochial school through 8th Grade. I went to public High School, my sister went to the all girl's Catholic high school where Sister Ann Stephanie had been transferred.

Besides, I couldn't pass the physical!

Frank

1094 MY FIRST WAR STORY AKA . . . MY FIRST TWO WEEKS IN VIET NAM

1103
From: Charlie Brown
Subject: My First War Story

Great job Frank. Keep at it and help Steve Stibbens (Editor of the 114th History Book) when he calls. I know he will.

Charlie

1105
From: Miles Hedrick
Subject: My First War Story

Way to go Knight Hawk Six. Now do some more and let's get the rest of that 1970-71 bunch writing. They sure can talk at reunions. Surely they can write too.

Miles Hedrick

1109
From: Ginger Shannon
Subject: My First War Story

Frank, I sure would like to see that photo of the "Flying Coffin" and I didn't get the attachment! Can you please, huh??? Thank you kindly Sir. I need that little icing to add with your story going into the newsletter! Thanks,

Ginger

1114
From: Gary Jones
Subject: My First War Story

Frank,

Great story and we all can relate to your loss of a friend. The days of Knighthood, regardless of when, is something we are all proud of. I have never served in a unit that could compare with the 114th.

Gary Jones WK 2 1965

1259 MY SECOND WAR STORY AKA . . . NIGHT VERTIGO

1260
From: John E Laughinghouse
Subject: My second war story!

Great story. Were you instrument rated when this happened? Also, were you a Red Knight? From 1964 to 65 Red Knights had the flare ship mission assignment, when did this happen? Thanks for sharing this with us, I know there are more stories out there. This is a good time to tell a war story, there is plenty of space and time on this net.

John

1261
From: Charlie Brown
Subject: My second war story!

Good job Frank! Charlie

1262
From: Miles Hedrick
Subject: My second war story!

Great story Frank. I suspect we all had that problem at some time or another. I would have sworn I was falling out of the sky over Nevada one day and kept pulling back on the yoke. Just before stalling that old U-6 out, my kindly old Major boss and Aircraft Commander took the ship and it took a while to convince me. We have all come close and are lucky to be able to tell it.

Miles

1274
From: Gary Jones
Subject: Reply & More to John L.

Frank, Great story and we are glad the it had a happy ending. Back in those days we are all lucky to have survived some of the situations we found ourselves in. This may get some more good stories going, I know they are out there.

Gary Jones

2661 MY TOO CLOSE OF AN ENCOUNTER . . . WITH A RAT!

2662
From: Parker Evans
Subject: The Rat Story

You know Frank, we just can't say how many times we all ate the "rat". Of course, I'd prefer not knowingand I know you didn't like the mess hall but at least they didn't serve rat. Did they??

cobra599

2663
From: Charlie Brown
Subject: Food!

Frank, I assure you the mess hall wasn't always that way! We were not exaggerating at all when we said that the mess hall was top notch. I'd skip a good restaurant today to go into that chow hall again.

Charlie

2664
From: Frank Strobel
Subject: Food!

Parker,

You are absolutely right! After something is "prepared" it is hard to know what you are eating. To be quite honest, it really didn't taste bad, it was just the "idea"! I know that I had dog while in Nam and it really wasn't bad either! It was quite good. Our culture just isn't in tune with subsistence living! We are just a bit removed. We're not really all that far away from it though; talk to people that had a hard time during the depression or those coming here from eastern Europe. To many it is one generation, or maybe less, removed!

If Nam taught me anything, it is that we really do have it good here in the States! It would be an excellent learning experience if everyone in this country would be "required" to spend some time living in the environment and on the economy of a third world country. Many eyes would be openedand this country would become even better off than we are because some people who just spend their life "coasting" over here would suddenly become productive! People would call it a miracle. I would call it motivation!

I read somewhere 80% of the homes in the world don't have running water and most of those that have it, only have cold! Just kinda makes you think! Dosen't it!

Frank

2666
From: Parker Evans
Subject: Food!

Frank,

Prepared, required and motivated. You are exactly right. But what it comes down to is "taking everything for granted". It's easy when you don't know any better. I know times are tough for all of us but thank God we live where we do.

I once toured the Civil War Memorial at Vicksburg, Mississippi. History has it that those poor folks resorted to eating rats during the siege, IF THEY WERE LUCKY. True, we are not so far removed from the way things are today in a lot of third world countries. Life always finds a way.

cobra599

1276 NIGHT FLARE MISSIONS VS THE NIGHT HUNTER-KILLER MISSION

1277
From: John E Laughinghouse
Subject: Night Flare Missions/Night Hunter-Killer Missions

Frank,

Your mission sounds more than interesting, it sounds exciting. Just a few questions. How many hours did you get during your tour of duty? Was the 140 hours in 30 days a unit limitation and did it apply to all aviators in the unit? If this was your mission, Knight Hawk 6, what kind of rotation did you have for a night

FRANK J. STROBEL

off? What was it like trying to sleep during the day, did it come easy for you after being out all night? When you rotated did you enjoy breaking in your replacement? Did this become a mission that others were envious of or did it stay one that they were glad to let others have? Were you doing this in a D or H model? All of my time in Nam was in a "good ole B model".

John

1278 THE MISSION WAS MORE THAN EXCITING TO ME! . . . AND A LITTLE MORE

1282
From: John E Laughinghouse
Subject: Mission was more than exciting!

Frank-The reasons for my questions were two-fold. 1. I really wanted to know. 2. Our historian is "lurking" out there and getting every word of this for our unit history. We had no flight hour limit that I am aware of. We did not keep a personal record of our flight time, at least I did not, there was no requirement for us to. We also did not have "rooms". Our living areas were separated by a wardrobe (wooden wall locker) and our mosquito net covered bed. We got to know each other pretty good. Our showers were in another building in the area. Love to see the pictures of your room. Sounds like the bunker would have been nice living (scotch and a good book).

I would bet Frank that you probably have more NIGHT TIME than anyone else in one tour. Just think what you would have had if you had not left early. How much of your flight time would you say was night time? 90 %? I bet you hold the record for night time. Does anyone know of anyone close to this? We may have a CHAMPION NIGHT TIMER, Knight Hawk 6. What did you do Frank when you returned to the real world and what do you do now? I look forward to meeting you at the next reunion. John

1284
From: Miles Hedrick
Subject: Mission was more than exciting!

Frank, you got the info right. That 120 and 140 hour rule was from USARV and was effective at least in 66-67 when I was with the 1st Cav Div. (It was regularly violated there). Think the Night Hawk mission was transferred just prior to my taking the company because I remember someone thought it would be a good idea if I flew as an observer with that other nameless company.

You just reminded me of one of my more frightening moments. The two young warrants got vertigo and I still don't know how I convinced them to level everything before we spun it but having just come from teach helicopter instruments at Hunter must have had something to do with.

Keep those stories going!

Miles

1286
From: Gary Jones
Subject: Night Flare Missions/Night Hunter-Killer Missions

Hi Frank,

You have to remember in 1965 the war was completely different, the reason I know is I was back in 1968 and everything had changed. After 1 AM we only stood by on the ground and waited to see if something happened. The only place that got hit was Soc Trang. Vinh Long had not seen A hostile round. I think the VC went to bed about midnight.

Gary

1287
From: Gary Jones
Subject: Night Flare Missions/Night Hunter-Killer Missions

Frank:

Again I am like John, I read what you wrote and it was great. Also like John, after he left in 1965 and I left at the end of 1965 we still had B-Model Hueys. We never had a mission like you guys did at night with the flare ship.

Gary

1288
From: Gary Jones
Subject: Mission was more than exciting!

Frank, again I read about the flying, hours and missions and how life had changed at Vinh Long since 1965. I thoroughly enjoyed the story and hope you will write more. I was also a Warrant Officer in 1965.

Gary Jones WK-2 1965

1289
From: Ginger Shannon
Subject: Mission was more than exciting!

Hi Frank, you can share that photo of your "mahagony paneled room" with us? I just bet the members would enjoy seeing it in Knight Letter! Thanks for sharing so much with all of us. Ginger

1264 MORE ON THE KNIGHT NIGHT-HUNTER-KILLER MISSION

1265
From: John E Laughinghouse
Subject: Reply & More to John L.

Frank, Wow!!!! What a mission. That is an outstanding description of it and your thoughts. This is the kind of thing we really need for our unit history and our history book. I would never have dreamed of a mission of this type without your telling us. I think your ideas and thoughts about it were right on from what you have described. I would not have wanted to fly that type of mission. The "Old" eagle flights we flew in the daytime were spooky enough if you were the low bird. Good ole Charlie taught me to do that. We did have a flight of 10 or more aircraft airborne and loaded with troops, just waiting for us to find a target. In our mission the lone aircraft flew low "hoping" to get shot at enough to declare a target and then mark it with smoke for the slicks to come into.

The flare ship mission we had in 64-65 was to scramble with a full load of flares anytime the Cobra gunships scrambled at night. We were to be airborne at the same time they were and boy that meant highballing it to your aircraft. Of course it had been preflighted by the crew before dark. I liked these missions and got very good at putting the flares where they wanted them. The old standard rate turn was the basic thing for us and then we adjusted the airspeed to make sure the area remained lit while the gunships were working it.

The reception you received the first time you called in as Knight Hawk 6 was very similar to what I received when I called for landing at a Navy base. They asked me the highest rank on board and I replied Captain. They asked would we require transportation and I said yes. Boy did we get a reception, they thought they had a Navy Captain coming in and that would have been the same as a Colonel. I was in an Army aircraft with a call sign of Army 1234 so why did they assume the passengers would be anything but Army? They did let us use the waiting transportation after a little discussion. We were the only ones there that thought it was humorous.

Thanks so much for telling us your story/experience. John

1266
From: Frank Strobel
Subject: Reply & More to John L.

John,

Your mission sounded more like the difference between a fly swatter and a hammer. Having a flight full of troops at your disposal after stirring up some action, could be a real "experience" to those you stirred up. I hadn't realized that my mission was any different than what had gone on before I got there. Now you have my interest. I would like some war stories and details on "how your missions were set up"!

In the meantime, I'll write down some more storiesand post them so long as you don't think I'm talking too much!

Frank

1272
From: Gary Jones
Subject: My second war story!

As a White Knight in 1965 we had some flare mission flights and they were boring. Not much happened and all of ours was single ship. I do remember we would drop flares on the island north of Vinh Long just to wake us up. If my memory serves me correctly we had to fly until 1 am after that we were on standby.

Gary WK-2, 65

1271 NIGHT AIR TO AIR COMBAT . . . A UFO . . . OR WHAT?

From: Bill Glasgow
Subject: Training
Pilots,

One of my friends asked me if we had ever had any air to air combat with our helicopters. Verbal combat was all I could remember. Was that subject ever taught or addressed?

Bill

THE NIGHT I THOUGHT I LOST PAS

This note was written in response to comments about the minigun setup on "C" Model Huey Gunships.

Damn, You guys always find a way to amaze and humble me. If I don't keep up reading these messages and I miss a great discussion or two, or three. How I do enjoy each of these experiences! Back then while flying Night Hunter-Killer missions I often thought, "How clever we were!" Now 30 years later, I find that we were just "Doin' what was dun' before! How "educatun" you guys are!

Frank Strobel

1358 THE NAVY SEALS AKA . . . KIDNAPPING THE VILLAGE CHIEF

1359
From: John E Laughinghouse
Subject: War Story—Navy Seals

Frank- It sounds like you "later" guys got all the interesting missions. One thing I can tell you, this would never have been a one ship mission under Daddy George (Young). We had a radius and anything outside of that was a 2 ship mission no matter what the task. We were never sent on a mission that our operations was not completely briefed on. Sometimes the mission changed during the day due to unforeseen circumstances but at least it started like it should and like we (and operations) had been briefed. Did you complete this complete mission without refueling? Sounds like a long mission from start to back home again.

I don't think I am sorry that I missed that one. Thanks for sharing it with us, it definitely held my attention. John

1360
From: Parker Evans
Subject: War Story—Navy Seals

What a great story, Frank. Sounds like you made the right call all the way on that mission. The Uh Minh was no place to go messing around by yourself. I know the Cobras gave support to the SEALS a few times and once they got on the ground, you really didn't know what they were up to. A bunch of really brave men. Thank goodness for their training.

cobra599 '67-'68

1367
From: Frank Strobel
Subject: Navy Seal Story

John and Parker,

Thanks for your comments. These are stories that I have told family and friends but I have never written them down. With that February (History Book) deadline, I figure it's now or never. I spent the holiday weekend writing more stories down, hope you guys don't think I'm trying to take over this forum. I'll send a couple in every week so they get recorded for the future.

John, most of my missions while in the Knights were 1 or 2 ship. I probably only flew a few dozen troop insertions the whole year I was there. That is probably why I have a hard time remembering who I flew with in many of these stories. Sometimes, five or six nights in a row I would have a different left seat. It makes it hard to remember who was with me on a specific night. I guess whoever lost the coin toss flew with me! Maybe I'm an independant cus or maybe the guys didn't like me flying too close to them! Guess I'll never know!

I do hope more Knights of the "later" years will start sending their stories! I just received a message forwarded to me from Ginger. It was from John Fitzpatrick, who I flew with me on a great number of missions, maybe he can open up and send a few in.

John, if you are listening, let's go! Time is short.

Frank Strobel
"Knight Hawk 6"

1372
From: "Charlie Brown
Subject: Navy Seal Story

Keep writing Frank. Your stories are great. Charlie

1393 THE OLD MAN FROM HONG NGU

1395
From: Ginger Shannon
Subject: Things are pretty quiet so here I go again

Frank, I for one, am so glad you shared this compassionate story with us. War is not all hate and ugliness. You showed your warm and understanding side to these people, something they probably saw little of, even among their own. I respect you highly for this deed, even tho it was against all military regulations. Ginger

1403
From: Charlie Brown
Subject: Things are pretty quiet so here I go again

I concur with you Frank. We all had little regulation glitches but yours is better than most.

Charlie

1407 WENDELL JARRETT & HIS DAD AKA VIEWING THE WAR FROM ABOVE

1414
From: Charlie Brown
Subject: One more short story

Another great story Frank. Keep it up!

Charlie

1453 MOC HOA . . . IT'S A SMALL WORLD—DEE THOMAS & DENNIS FENNESSY

1454
From: Tim Meitin
Subject: Here's another one . . . Moc Hoa Airfield

Re: Franks story about MocHoa, I can confirm every last bit. I was the platoon leader at the time and had to have a little discussion with Sgt. Thomas, concerning that incident. Frank was not the only pilot that became a victim of Sgt. Thomas. Sgt. Thomas was a top notch CC. And he knew how to lighten up the pilots.

Tim Meitin
White Knight 6

1455
From: Ginger Shannon
Subject: Here's another one . . . Moc Hoa Airfield

Frank, these two stories are just too too great for you to have kept from us! I laughed loudly at your first one and shake my head in wonder at your second, what are the chances!

Thanks again for sharing so much with us,

Ginger

1456
From: John E Laughinghouse
Subject: Here's another one . . . Moc Hoa Airfield

I don't understand how a guy that was enjoying life so, could even think about going back to being a civilian. Frank, did you find civilian life boring or just restful? John

1457
From: Frank Strobel
Subject: Here's another one . . . Moc Hoa Airfield

John,

To tell you the truth, I always missed my (lack of a) career in the military. I got out of the Service in 1971 in order to get my College Degree. Hate to say it this way but after Viet Nam back in Savannah, Georgia, I was fat, dumb and happy. It would have been very easy to make a career out of being a pilot. I was afraid of 2 things, first, That I would get too comfortable and not finish my college degree and second, There wasn't an aviation branch! If I was going to make the Army a career, I would have gotten a comission. Had there been an aviation branch there is no doubt in my mind that I would have happily stayed. I just couldn't see myself as an Infantry or Armor Officer. Nothing against those branches but I couldn't see myself "doing my time" in those branches to get my "ticket" punched. I was afraid that I would do my training and then get placed permanently in one of those structures.

I have a younger brother who has retired already with 24 years service as an O-5, my "baby" brother is currently in Germany as an O-5 Battalion Commanderand another brother who recently retired from the Navy. But they all landed in areas that they enjoyed, I had no hope at the time that that would happen to me! I tried to join the Air Force after college graduation, hoping to become a fighter pilot but was TOO old! I was 26 ½ tears old. So I spent a number of years (not enough for a retirement) in the PA Army National Guard and was transitioned into OH-6A, damn that was fun airplane and another story.

At one point, the guys in my National Guard unit were offered transitions into the new AH-64 Apache. They were setting up the first AH-64 units. All we had to do was go on active duty but too many things we going on with my young family for such a drastic change in lifestyle at that time. Two of the guys I flew with, did take the offer but they were single. My wife was ill for a couple of years and I had to leave the Guard to spend time watching my young family. When things changed, I tried to get back into the Guard, but they had new civilian secretarial staff and ALL of my records had been lost. I did send them copies of a great deal of my records but nothing ever came of it

In my attempt to get back in, I had to "re-swear" my allegiance to the United States because they had no records! A Distinguished Flying Cross, 37 Air medals (2 "V" Devices), a Bronze Starand an individual award from General Xi and the Government of South Viet Nam of the Vietnamese Cross of Gallantry w/Bronze Star amongst other awardsand I had to re-swear my allegiance to the USA, god, was I angry! After giving them a copy of most of my records, two years later, I gave up fighting!

My Guard unit was 150 Miles from my home, with no overnight facilities. I needed to get a motel room several nights a month plus buy all my meals at a restaurant and of course pay for general travel expenses too! It was just a bit much with that young family. On Several occasions they offered to let me back in o the 'Guard' with no pay until my paperwork was straightened out but they had no idea how long that would take! I told them to call me when it was straightened out. Obviously, they never did!

I received a call annually for about 5 years to "re-up" from several different battalion commanders. I told them, get my paperwork straightened out and I be down the following drill but it never happened. I became sad (there's no other way to put it!) every time I thought of it, so eventually I just forgot the whole thing. I will always miss the flying.

In my civilian career, I have been "right-sized" three times after successive banks I was working for were merged, all three times I had 8+ years service, over 24 years and no pension rights in any of the organizations. I was high enough in each of the organizations to make it worthwhile financially for them to let me go but not high enough to get a golden parachute. We all have our stories. I guess that's life! I had always hoped for a phone call saying that my military paperwork was resolved but I never heard the words, "Come On Down!"

The important thing is I have a great wife that loves meand 3 super kids! That is all I need. I will admit that there has always been a longing to return.

Frank Strobel
"Knight Hawk 6"

1458
From: John E Laughinghouse
Subject: Here's another one . . . Moc Hoa Airfield

Frank-Thanks so much for such an informative reply. We are really getting to know you now. The last sentence in your reply stated: "You have a loving wife and 3 wonderful children and that is all you need". That may be all you need but you sure do have a lot more than that, you may not know how much you have with the members of this net and I am sure that has multiplied many times from your sharing your stories with us. I am sure all of us are looking forward to meeting you at the reunion.

I went the Armor route right out of college ROTC and will tell you some of my Armor stories when I meet you. I also retired as an 0-5 in Dec 75, had my real estate license and sold a house 1 month before I retired. I just finished 25 years in real estate and still going strong with it. Need to go to work now. John

1461
From: David J. Weiner
Subject: Here's another one . . . Moc Hoa Airfield

Frank, You sure add a lot to this Association and I think your stories are fantastic.

1472 THE NAVY SEALS AKA . . . A MESS AT THE NAVY "MESS"

1473
From: Gary Jones
Subject: Here's another one . . . Moc Hoa Airfield

Frank: Great stories, as I think about it, our crew chiefs and gunners, had a tough Assignment. They set back there day after day depending on us to get them back at the end of each day. Then there work began and the aircraft was prepared for another day. I would like to say to all you guys that kept the aircraft flying you are the heroes and us pilots owe our lives and heart felt thanks to each of you.

If I ever locate my crew chief I will travel to where he is and thank him in person.

Gary Jones WK- 2 1965

1475
From: George Young
Subject: Here's another one . . . Moc Hoa Airfield

Amen Gary. Thoughts like that cannot be expressed too many times.

George

1476
From: Carl Hess
Subject: Here's another one . . . Moc Hoa Airfield

I remember hearing of a little "conspiracy" between a crew chief, gunner and the two piliots. The crew chief and gunner exchanged shirts (with insignia) with the two pilots. Then as their passengers approached the aircraft, they (the crew) were arguing loudly among themselves. The enlisted crew (wearing the pilots shirts) said to the pilots (wearing enlisted) shirts: "If you think you are so good, why don't you jump up front and fly this machine home?" You can imagine the reaction of the high-priced brass when the two "enlisted" dudes got in the front seats and flew them home!

1487 CAMBODIA DAY 2 AKA . . . A 155 MM HOWITZER FLIES

1488
From: George Young
Subject: Cambodia 1970, Day 1

You know how it is Frank. Hours and hours of boredom

interspersed with moments of stark terror.

George

1496
From: Frank Strobel
Subject: Hours and hours of boredom interspersed . . .

George, Hours and hours of boredom, interspersed with moments of stark terror.

You don't understand how true that can be until you've been there . . . and I know you have! I did love those "boring" times too though! If you could forget what was going on over there, It was a beautiful country to fly over.

Frank
"Knight Hawk 6"

1486 EXPENSIVE SPAGHETTI

1487
From: Ginger Shannon
Subject: Expensive Spaghetti!

Thanks for the best laugh I've had in a long while Frank! Ginger

1489

From: Charlie Brown
Subject: Expensive Spaghetti!
Same thing happened to me in '64 but I was unaware of the trick. When it exploded, I heard it and put her on the ground via autorotation being sure I was shot down. Crew Chief and Gunner died laughing and I learned how to make a hot lunch.

Charlie

1490
From: Parker Evans
Subject: Expensive Spaghetti!

Jeez, guys. The only way to heat cold "C's" is to use that white bread stuff that no one would eat. You just drained off a little JP4 from the pump into a can of chopped up white bread. It made perfect sterno and you just held your open can of spaghetti, beans and franks, or what ever (I personally preferred the ham and limas, mainly because no one else wanted them) by the lid and stirred it once in a while. I know, cooking is a fine art. Just like flying.

cobra599

1491
From: Charlie Brown
Subject: Expensive Spaghetti!

Anyone remember the cold rice wrapped in a banana leaf the ARVN's used to give us when we got stuck away from home without chow?

Charlie

1492
From: David J. Weiner
Subject: Expensive Spaghetti!

Well since all you pilots have a story about things going bang, here is one for you. I was pulling guard duty at my favorite place in front of Mess Hall Near Main Gate when a can of insecticide {spray type, was place in a container that the individual (Me) had no idea was a smoldering fire, well guess you know what happened next, pasta all over the bunker. well for this 17 year old soldier it was quite a fright as you can imagine, not to say a loud loud bang.

1494
From: Bill Glasgow
Subject: C's

I remember throwing c-rations out to the little kids that would always gather when we landed. Some times they would trade for bananas or mangos. It wouldn't be long before you heard something bounce off the side of the ship. The kid that got the white bread would throw it back at you. Bill

1495
From: Parker Evans
Subject: C rations

Remember that Korean dredge ship out on the river?

When I first arrived at Vinh Long, I had to pull a guard duty shift on that boat with several other guys (back then it was an all nighter).

The Koreans were friendly enough but spoke little or no English. They were very willing to share their chow with us. I opted not to because there was a lot of stuff I didn't recognize in it. And it was so spicy it made my eyes water just catching a whiff of it in the night air on deck. After awhile, even that canned white bread sounded good to me. I didn't eat any of it, though.

cobra599 '67-'68

1497
From: Dick Duerr
Subject: Expensive Spaghetti!

Parker, We Red Knights had a new improved version of the C ration bread can stove. We made 2, 90 degree cuts in the top of the can, peeled the 2 resulting V shaped pieces back to form the stove top. Then perforated the side of the can near the top with a beer opener. With the bread then soaked with JP-4 we had a great stove with air fed through the perforations on the side of the bread can and just sat whatever we wanted to heat on top of our bread can stove. However, there can be a hazard associated with JP-4 and UH-1s and burning JP-4.

One day at Ben Tre I was a long way away from my flight parked on the side of the runway checking on the mission and going over the maps with the company commander, Col Bob Stoverink, the operations folks and the liaison Officer with the 7th division.

There was a lot of fairly tall, dense and dry vegetation and a lot of 55 gallon JP-4 fuel drums scattered around the aircraft My crews were preparing C rations to eat and a fire had started and was leaping up around the aircraft and all those fuel drums. They were trying to put out the fire and I was trying to yell at them to crank up the aircraft and move them away from the fires they had managed to start with their bread stoves. Fortunately they finally got my message, cranked up the aircraft and hurriedly flew them at a very low level to the other end of the field. The move necessitated a couple 180's and one of the guys,.

Jerry Dolin, had a hard over and stuck his main rotor in the pond next to the strip. He got the machine back on the ground safely but it was damaged quite a bit. I don't think Col Bob ever bought the hard over explanation but Jerry did execute a precautionary over at the My Tho strip just prior to the incident because of hard over type problems with his aircraft. Such a long epistle resulting from a jogging of one's memory with C ration bread.

Dick RK Lead '66 & '67

1498
From: Frank Strobel
Subject: Expensive Food

Good Story! With all the damage to Hueys just to get a simple meal, it's a wonder that the government could afford to feed us!

That's 2 stories with aircraft damage just in the hunt for a good hot meal!

Frank Strobel
Knight Hawk 6

1499
From: John E Laughinghouse
Subject: Expensive Food

Maybe I had the safest method. I kept a very skinny bottle of Louisiana Hot Sauce in my ship and with that I could eat "almost" anything and did. My wife hates it when I reach for the hot sauce before I even taste of my food. There are a lot of foods that I know that I want hot sauce on no matter what. Glad I did not go the JP-4 route. Interesting stories.

What is this hard over problem you were talking about? I don't think I have heard of that one. John

1500
From: Parker Evans
Subject: Young and Dumb

Momma says, "Stupid is as stupid does", It could have been boredom, though. Sometimes, during prolonged periods on the ground at staging areas, (some) of us would make little mini-mortars.

Instructions for mini-mortars:

    1 tracer round
    1 sheet, C-ration T-paper
    1 C-ration match (2 or more if windy)
    2 or more bored flight crew

Remove tracer projectile from brass. Pour out about a third of the powder onto the sheet of paper. Take survival knife and cut an X in the bottom of the projectile, exposing the phosphorus. Jam the projectile back into the brass until only the tip sticks out. Fill in the blank area with the powder off the paper. Light with the match and hope the damn thing doesn't fall over and point itself toward something costly. Makes a neat little firework. Like momma always says, "Stupid is as stupid does."

Cobra599 '67-'68

1501
From: Charlie Brown
Subject: Expensive Spaghetti!

Great recall!

Charlie

1502
From: Charlie Brown
Subject: Young and Dumb

Parker, I know you just heard the story but never did the deed, right?

Charlie

1503
From: Parker Evans
Subject: Young and Dumb

Unfortunately Charlie, I'm guilty. It's like my momma had an insight that I was prone to do stupid things on occasion. Also, unfortunately, I still do stupid things on occasion. But thinking back, age has slowed me to some extent.

When I get the nerve, I'll tell all of the guys how I personally knocked my own aircraft out the air and started one hell of a air to ground attack that involved 5 C-model gunships.

cobra599 '67-'68

1505
From: Allen Jensen
Subject: Young and Dumb

Parker

Its nice to see that things were passed on from year to year. Or was this something gunners just needed to do to use up ammo on slow days?

Allen Jensen
Cobra II 66/67

1508 CHAU DUC AKA . . . THE "BORDER CONTROL" RADAR OPERATOR FLIES

1567
From: Parker Evans
Subject: Hunter-Killer missions,

Frank,

Too bad you weren't around in the earlier days. You'd have fit right in with the Cobras flying "C" models. Your exploits flying as Knight Hawk 6 can't be out done but certainly compare well with the old 2 ship fire teams we used along with the Bug.

Your missions sound essentially the same as ours but with a little twist. I'd have been proud to fly with you on my aircraft but alas, I was fazed out. Hell, I'd have stayed longer than I did had it not been for that. Couldn't see going back to slicks or staying on the ground.

cobra599 Mar '67- Nov '68

1583 MY FIRST NIGHT MEDICAL EVACUATION

1584
From: Parker Evans
Subject: Scotch

Frank,

An experience like that would turn even a devoted bourbon drinker (like myself) to scotch, especially if that was all there was. Always listen to the "Doc". Might be he knew the medicinal use of scotch was just the ticket for you.

Since John mentioned the ban on Happy Hour and you mentioned the scotch. Then might I mention that some "numbskull" passed down the order that enlisted men below the rank of E-6 could no longer purchase hard liqueur. This took place sometime during '68. Mind you, I knew lots of E-3's, E-4's and E-5's that were years older than most of the Warrant Officer pilots. For some reason, these fellows took it personally. Can't say that I blame them. Quite frankly, no one thought that order was fair so there were plenty of platoon sergeants and pilots around willing to make a purchase for us. The whole thing was nonsense, I thought.

cobra599 '67-'68

1585
From: David J. Weiner
Subject: My first Night Med-i-vac

Fantastic! I Really enjoyed reading that story. Man you are and were a very brave individual. Thanks for sharing that part of your life with your fellow friends . . .

1586
From: Frank Strobel
Subject: Brave!?

Thanks Dave, But no braver than the men I/We flew with! It always takes more than 1 guy. Not only the men that fly with you but again we come back to those unsung heros that kept our ships in a condition that that allowed you to trust in that machine! I heard a lot of stories about the hanher crew but I don't ever recall having a question or complaint about them.

Whether they flew with us or not they were always with us in their work. I have no doubt that if there was ever any kind if "incident" because of a maintenance error they would take it very personally.

Our crew chiefs have to be included in the "kudos" but they had some incentive, they were up there flying with us! The hanger crew just worked on pride and professionalism. Thank God that it was enough!

Frank Strobel
Knight Hawk 6

1697
From: Charlie Brown
Subject: Brave!?

Frank, I agree with you but we had a lot of truly brave men. We had a few who where really afraid to fly. Some still went flying though; some you couldn't jam in a seat. (We rather they not be there anyway,) The key to me is that when the requirement or opportunity presented itself to put yourself in harms way for others, Knights, grunts, ARVNs or civilians, I never saw a Knight take a step backward.

In other words, I served with 99.2 % HEROES, no matter where they sat in the aircraft or if they were forced to wait on the ramp. (And most of them didn't. They all learned to handle an M-60 and filled in on their days off. Some called it silly, I called it heroic.)

Charlie

1755
From: Frank Strobel
Subject: Brave!?

Charlie,

Just read your note. I have to admit I never saw a "Knight" shrink away from any situation while I was over there. I have always been proud of the men I served with. I guess I have always tried to stay away from the words brave or hero. To me it was always a situation that "you" did what had to be done at the moment.

In particular, I felt that way about medical evacuations. I always felt it was an obligation, a responsibility, because of the position I was in as a pilot.

The Army gave me the training and the tools to help, I feel I have a certain amount of intelligence; it would have been irresponsible not to use them all. I don't look at that as brave, it's just doing your job. I guess there were many situations that I was afraid to die but that was just the times that you had to focus. If you had everything clear in your mind your task at hand, your training/ ability and your logic/intelligence to focus on, things became a great deal easier.

Frank

1614 NUI BA DEN AKA . . . MY FIRST "ARKLIGHT" SIGHTING

1615
From: Parker Evans
Subject: Arklight,

Frank, I can imagine how impressed you might have been seeing your first "Arklight". I was always amazed too. Kinda looks surreal, doesn't it? Day time B-52 missions were impressive too. I've seen a few while flying some distance away. Probably some of the most exciting events I witnessed were air strikes by those old A-1E's that the ARVNS used. They'd dive nearly straight down, like a dive bomber, to make their strikes. I can't say for sure if they hit much but it was sure cool to watch. They reminded me of those old WWII movies.

A US Air Force jet fighter-bomber pilot had to make an emergency landing at Vinh Long just before dark one evening. His choices were Vinh Long with it's short runway, or the river. I remember seeing him jettison his wing tanks before landing. He used up every foot of the runway. Even he said he'd like to have a go with one of those old prop jobs.

Cobra599 '67-'68

1861 MY BASIC TRAINING DRILL SERGEANT AKA . . . WOULD YA LIKE A LIFT?

1866
From: Carl Hess

Subject: Just another "War" story

Frank just to show you what a young dude you are, I left Ft Polk in November of 1962. At the time, I was an instructor with the weapons committee. If you thought Ft Polk was "interesting" when you were there you should have seen it when it was opened for the last time (Oct 1961) I was called to active duty with the 49th Armored Div (Texas National Guard) and Polk was our new home!

Carl Hess

2204 CHAU DUC—THE SINKING SAMPAN

2205
From: Ginger Shannon
Subject: My sampan story

Frank, I usually stay quiet on all that comes thru these pages but I just have to let you know, your memories usually have me holding my breath to the finish. You have a captivated reader here! Thanks! Ginger

2206
From: Frank Strobel
Subject: My Sampan Story

Thank You Ginger.

My Mom always felt I should have written a book, I just always felt that everyone over there had their own stories and mine were significant to only meand my familyand only because I was a part of them. Although many in my family have been in the service, at this point I am the only one in our family to see a great deal of combat. I have felt it to be a responsibility of mine to let them know what it was all about and that includes the good memories and some but not all of the bad.

The good men that I got to know, both American and Vietnamese are often the focus of my memories. There are several stories and incidents that I have never told anyone and I don't intend to do so. We all know war is very graphic and there are things people don't need to see or even hear about. They will stay deep inside me.

I do believe people who were not there should learn from those that were. War is not fun but that doesn't mean that there were not fun or funny (or good) things that happened there. Some of my most vivid memories are of medical evacuations I was involved with, the good done there often was able to out weigh the bad around the same situation.

Thank You again, It's nice to know people enjoy reading them! It's a little cathartic at times too!

Frank

2208 RULES OF ENGAGEMENT

2209 Rules of Engagement
From: Steve Stibbens
Subject: Rules of Engagement

Frank Strobel has posted a pretty good picture of ROE in the 1970-71 era. We all remember Albert Apel's "war-like" stance in a 1963 photo showing him searching a captured VC when "Americans are only advisors." I would like to hear from some representative years about the various ROEs. Steve—Dallas

2210
From: Steve Stibbens
Subject: Rules of Engagement

This came from . . . guess-who . . .

'68 Cobra Platoon ROE's . . .

1. Don't ask, don't tell
2. If you see an EM (eligible male) shoot 'em.
3. If there's more than one, shoot 'em all. No witnesses
4. Always go for the "head shot".
5. Adjust your mission report to fit the AO.

2213
From: Dick Duerr
Subject: Rules of Engagement

Steve, I can't vouch for the accuracy much because of a mild case of CRS brought about by the ensuing years since 1967 but in 66 & 67 if we got shot at we returned fire without hesitation. There were also free fire zones where we could fire. Then of course there were also the complications brought about with the VN counterparts on board. They had the "final say" supposedly.

I was the Red Knight Slick Lead most of the time so I didn't do a lot of shooting but I was scheduled to take over the Lancer Platoon right after my arrival when it was formed and trained with the Cobras to get ready for taking it over. I was also assigned as the company Operations Officer early on so I had some experience in the offensive/shooting end of things. My impression is that we had a lot more latitude in '66 & '67 than they did later on. Thank God! I can't imagine fighting under the conditions Strobel describes. Hope this helps Steve but I plead ignorance on the subject of total accuracy.

Dick

2236
From: Clyde Scott
Subject: Rules of Engagement

As a slick driver most of the time we flew single or two ship

Missions. In the 1965/66 we had about the same thing except no card.

First try to make sure you were the first ship to fly your flight path that day. The VC worked at night so it was not polite to keep him awake all day.

We had 2 M-60's and a few cans with 250 rounds each. I found that that after the 1st 250 rounds doing a 180 for the other left us exposed with no covering fire at low speed (sitting duck) most of the time.

I amended <u>my</u> ROE (rules of engagement) ASAP. If fired upon let the gun that could see where it was coming shoot and then concentrate on not bending the up stick or if there was vegetation around get as low as possible an don't push the go stick through the chin bubble.

If you were going into an established location and you had rather the VC put some lead where the SIP usually chewed You would make a downwind, crosswind and a final into the wind.

White Knight 7 did not care which way the wind was blowing as long at you kept the IAS above translational lift speed If you were heavy make sure you had a place to land before slowing

below translational lift and treat the landing like a partial power auto rotation. I preferred the chewing out.

Clyde Scott
WK 7 65/66

2239
From: Gary Jones
Subject: Rules of Engagement

Clyde: The 65 war was a lot different from what I read that took place in the late 60's and early 70's. You and I and the other guys who flew in the 65 and earlier time frame had it made. I can remember being told go do this and do what ever you have to do but get the job done and bring the ship and crew home safely. I will tell you what I did, if shot at we got out of there and called the guns. I also flew real real low and/or 3000'. If we got shot at and had to get into a place, we got there from another direction and sometimes the approach and landing was not to pretty.

Again I'm so glad I flew with you and the other members of the 1965 Vinh Long gang. In 1968 when we went back flying the Chinooks in I corps that was a complete different type of mission. Everybody liked shooting at the flying barn but you couldn't hear the rounds so sometimes you didn't know you had been shot at until you landed at the end of the mission and counted the holes.

Gary 1965

2242
From: Frank Strobel

Just a short ROE clarification . . .

If someone shot at me I did return fire. I figured that we would sort it out later but I was willing to argue "self-defense"! There were several times when I received fire while I had a South Vietnamese Officer and his American counterpart on board and was told to stop firing. My personal rule was that I would fire the last shot, however long it took: but once they told me to stop, the responsibility was mine. A couple of times I thought I would hear about it later but that never happened. I truly believe that the people I was working for (the 114th and the people out in the AO) agreed with me. But, You never knew if it would continue to be that way! If someone was getting pressure from above, someone would be sacrificed!

Unfortunately for those of us out there everyday, if any of our actions were ever questioned there was great leeway to "disavow any knowledge or authorization" of the incident by the people we flew for.

I think this was after the Lt. Calley situation and nobody wanted to get in the middle of another one! That would have been a career crusher! The problem was guessing when that kind of a decision was going to be questioned.

Frank Strobel
"Knight Hawk 6"

2387 MOC HOA AKA . . . THE ADOPTION . . .

2389
From: John Laughinghouse
Subject: Moc Hoa & the Adoption . . .

Frank-Great story. It is also good that you and the others could not see how we reacted when reading the story. I don't cry but my eyes have a tendency to water very easily. My voice has a tendancy to show emotion at times. Col J.Y. Hammack could always tell when it was me on the radio and things were needing to be done "now". He was the Batallion Commander for awhile in 64. John

2390
From: Parker Evans
Subject: Moc Hoa,

Frank, What a wonderful, heart warming story. Thanks for sending it.

cobra599

2391
From: John Laughinghouse
Subject: Moc Hoa and the adoption . . . Photos

Frank- By the way, was that the uniform of the day that you were wearing in the photo? John

2393
From: Frank Strobel
Subject: Uniform of the Day?!

John,

Once you get to know me, you will find that I am not a real "formal" kind-a-guy! One nice thing about single ship missions there were No "Real Live Officers" watching all of the time. Much easier to hide that way!

Frank

2398
From: George Young
Subject: Moc Hoa & the Adoption . . .

Beautiful Story, Frank.

George Young

2404
From: Ginger Shannon
Subject: Moc Hoa & the Adoption

Email doesn't show the tears from the reader either, Frank, I know she has never forgotten you either,

Ginger Shannon

2405
From: John Laughinghouse
Subject: Stories

Thanks Frank for your contribution today. I have printed it to take home to the wife.

John Laughinghouse

2422 PERSONNEL RADAR UNITS

2424
From: John Laughinghouse
Subject: Things are too quiet . . . so here goes . . . again!

Frank- Looking at the subject of your message, I wonder, how did you feel on your night missions when "things were to quiet". Were you bored, concerned, content, restless or indifferent? I am sure the nights could be very long if nothing was going on. John

This was another very interesting and original story. You later guys got all of the more sophisticated toys. The newest thing that I can remember us getting was a Decca Navigation System that did not work except with tech rep on board during the day on a training mission. Our time, distance and heading was always more reliable.

2426
From: Parker Evans
Subject: Things are too quiet . . . so here goes . . . again!

Frank,

Once again, I'm impressed with your action. The only reason I left country when I did was because of being phased out to G models. I could have gone back to slicks but at that time there wasn't anyone doing the stuff you did. Had you been there, I'd have flown along with you anytime in a 'heart beat'. It sure sounds a lot more like gunship missions than waiting on the ground for a G model to land. Let them load their own damn rockets and ammo. That job just wasn't for me.

cobra599

2427
From: Miles Hedrick
Subject: Things are too quiet . . . so here goes . . . again!

Great story, Frank but I haven't the foggiest idea of the correct name of those radar units.

Miles

2428 RE: MESSAGE # 2424 BORING MISSION! AKA "CSING" MYSELF

2429
From: Parker Evans
Subject: I didn't let those missions get boring!

Frank,

Ah Ha!!! I knew I wasn't the only person at Vinh Long who did dumb things. Sir, you have made my day. :-)

cobra599

2447 VIETNAMIZATION

2448
From: Miles Hedrick
Subject: Vietnamization

Steve, During my tenure with the Knights (Oct 70-Apr 71) we began to be levied to turn aircraft over the VNAF by tail number. They generally had between 600 and 1000 hours on them. We were never asked for a new bird nor one with a lot time. They wanted the ones that were just broken in. When the first requisition came it, it was for a C & C bird. Needless to save the crew was chagrined but we had not choice. They removed all the extra radios and antennas, gave it a good once over and flew to the turn in location, where the birds were jointly inspected by the

VNAF and their USAF advisors (who apparently only new book knowledge of UH-1's and AH-1's at that time).

Our Bird was REJECTED for having unapproved modifications! When the crew chief joyfully showed me the points of rejection, it was obvious the USAF and VNAF were unaware of antenna mounts for C&C birds. So I had all our birds modified to be Command And Control birds. The 1st Avn Bde continued to levy us for birds and the VNAF continued to reject them.

Finally in early 1971, Col. (P) Samuel Cockerham, Deputy Bde CO and my former boss, paid me a visit. Cockerham was a transportation maintenance man and nearly split his pants laughing when I showed him why we never had a bird accepted even though we made over 90 per cent on a recent Command Maintenance Inspection. I was told never to prepare another bird for C&C unless it was to be designated as one! And also to never tell other companies what we had done.

In late, October 1970 we were given a secret mission to train 20 Cambodians, ranging from private to major, in maintaining the Hueys. They spoke no English and were not to let the Vietnamese know they were there. The Brigade also gave us a French Speaking Tech Inspector who would do the teaching. He translated the manuals as he went and we mimeographed them for the Cambodians. To try and keep them separated from the Vietnamese, his group became a night PE crew and became exceptionally proficient. We were sorry to see them go at the end of their training.

Frank also mentions VNAF pilots. The program called for selected individuals to go to Fort Wolters and Hunter AAF, GA to complete the regular rotary wing pilot course. They were then sent, in groups of 10, to US units were they were to pick up another 200 hours flying with our pilots before reporting to their

VNAF unit. Prior to my leaving Viet Nam we received at least two groups. Some were like Frank Strobel's night guy and some were pretty good. Hope this helps even if it is about a year beyond your blank period.

Miles Hedrick,
Miles
Knight 6 70-71.

2449
From: Frank Strobel
Subject: I now know why we kept you around!

Miles,

What a great explanation! I didn't know that <u>not any</u> of our ships were accepted. I remember some rejections but I assumed that I just didn't hear about the ones that were accepted! I love to hear when someone successfully (and legitimately) "works the system". Kudos to you! I knew there was a reason we kept you as CO!

Frank

2492 RUBBER DUCKEY

2497
From: Parker Evans
Jeez, Frank,

I wish you hadn't mentioned that "Rubber Ducky" song. My son played that song over and over and over when he was about 3 years old. So much so, I figured I'd remember the words right away but noooooo, I've been sitting here forever trying to remember with that damn tune going over and over in my head. Shame on you for causing an old man so much grief. lol

cobra599

PS, The situation you describe had to have been a real hoot.

2624 THE WATERMELON PATCH

2625
From: Parker Evans
Subject: Watermelons

Frank,

I'd love to have seen the look on their faces, too. Which reminds me of something. I'm sure when we were kids that we've all seen those little vegetable-fruit stands set up along the highways. Some had big signs that read "Iced Cold Watermelons" and "Fresh Vegetables".

Well, I recall seeing on occasion similar kinds of stands set up at staging areas. That Vietnamese fruit was sometimes unusual looking (like green oranges, green bananas, little bitty pineapplesand other stuff I couldn't name) but always good eatin'. Ya'll ever see that?

cobra599

2626
From: John Laughinghouse
Subject: Watermelons

More food-Toward the end of my tour (July/Aug 65) our whole company went up North and were camped out in the field a few miles inland from DaNang. Foxholes and the whole 9 yards. Well as Platoon Leader I had the occasion to go to DaNang for some reason that escapes me at the moment. While there, I happened to hear about a field bakery that was set up and operational. I went to them and told them how we were living in the field and how good their freshly baked bread smelled and how happy my troops would be to bite into some of it. Well, they gave me a chopper load of fresh baked unsliced bread AND a case of mayonnaise.

I went down the road about 1/2 mile by myself and bought a large sack of the best looking ripe tomatoes you have ever seen. When I arrived back at our area and started passing out the bread you should have heard some of the comments when they found out WE also had mayo and tomatoes. What a simple FEAST. Anyone on line remember this?

Red Knight Lead 64-65

2627
From: Frank Strobel
Subject: Bananas

Parker,

Can't say I saw anything like that, I never saw a tomato over there. On another occasion near the Southeast base of Nui Coto, we found a banana tree (bush, or whatever they are called) that had a large bunch of bananas just out of reach from the ground. Pas took off his combat boots, climbed up and severed a good sized portion of that bunch. They were a little bit green but we ate them anyway.

It was not near a house or in a grove and since no one was around, we did not pay for that harvest!

Frank

2628
From: Frank Strobel
Subject: Food!

John,

Tomato sandwiches with "mayo" and fresh onion, have always been one of my favorite summertime treats! In fact, about 3 years ago I ate so many, I grew a neck full of "zits", my doctor told me, "Too much acid from the tomatoes!" They will always be my weakness.

I was reading the stories earlier this week about the Vinh Long mess hall. Was going to keep quiet but that has never been my strength . . .

I never had a good experience with the Vinh Long mess hall. After my first month in Nam, I never went back! I ate at many good mess halls during my tour but not at Vinh Long. I remember playing football with a loaf of Vinh Long bread on several occasions and it held up very well. After my first month, 99% of my meals at Vinh Long were at the O'Club. I actually preferred C-Rations to the mess hall!

Of course, after telling my wife about some of the meals I ate in Viet Nam, she told me that I had better not complain about her cooking!

Frank

2629
From: Steve Stibbens
Subject: Care packages

While you guys were in the Land of Milk and Honey, as poets call the Delta, what kinds of things did you get from home?

All I ever asked for was bunches of Kool Aid for the canteen. (Remember, much of my times was up in I Corps, humpin' it with the grunts.)

Steve—Dallas

2630
From: Parker Evans
Subject: Care packages,

Steve,

I sure wish you hadn't brought that subject up. Orange "Breakfast Start" was the ticket. You just add it to Vodka (right into the bottle) and it's a poor boys screwdriver. My mom sent me a care package every month for 18 months and not one arrived intact. Usually, the only thing left of out good size package was the "Start" and cans of sardines in mustard sauce.

Big crushed boxes, with little in them. I never got the peanut butter, the jelly, the canned meats, the crackers, cookies, nothing but Start and Sardines in mustard sauce. Once, all I got was a crushed box. I learned to love sardines in mustard sauce.

My sister got me a subscription to "Playboy". I got a year's worth of those little manila sleeves they used to come in, with my name on them. Not one magazine. I'm afraid I felt the full brunt of the

"Black Market" in '67 and '68. It still upsets me that some a—got rich or fat or both on my stuff.

Parker

2631
From: John Laughinghouse
Subject: Care packages

Steve, One of the first things I received from my wife was a portable typewriter with a very durable carrying case. It had elite type and really wrote a nice looking letter. They were also legible when typed, otherwise?

I think you may have been referring to food, however, I also received another unusual gift from home. For Valentine Day I received a pair of boxer shorts with hearts on them. They came boxed with a plastic spring loaded heart in the box. You guessed it, when I opened it the heart started beating with a tic, tic, tic, tic. It did get my attention for a short while.

My homemade cookies came packed in large coffee cans. They usually arrived in good condition BUT did not last long when opened if the guys saw me open them. John

2632
From: Parker Evans
Subject: Care packages,

Steve,

One more thing. I did receive from home, upon request, a genuine, surplus Army issue K-Bar survival knife right after I started to fly. Seems there weren't any in supply. I carried it everywhere but when I tried to leave country with itand couldn't produce a receipt, I had to leave it in Long Binh. Some guy who pushed papers behind some desk at Long Binh got my knife. Parker

2712 TRAN AND HIS HUEY RIDE

2714
From: Parker Evans
Subject: Tran

Frank,

I'll bet Tran never forgot that experience. I'll also bet that he still tells the story. Strange though, that you should mention that story because the exact same thing happened to me (sitting in Tran's seat) when I experienced my "first" helicopter ride (on a Knight aircraft) from Can Tho to Vinh Long. I knew that very minute that no matter what it took, that ride wouldn't be my last.

Coming from stateside training like everyone else and just 19, those crew members on that aircraft looked so experienced and what I considered the first "Real Soldiers" I'd ever seen. Lotta years sure have passed since then.

cobra599 '67-'68

2715
From: Frank Strobel
Subject: Tran

Parker,

Might sound funny but I felt that my first "real ride" in a Huey was my ride in a Knight Chopper from Can Tho to Vinh Long too. Yes, I had flown them in the States in training but it is a great deal different out in the real world. Don't know quite how to say it but, training is like being in a fish hatchery, flying in Nam was like being dropped into the wide-open ocean. Anything can happen there!

I was told in flight school that, "We'll teach you how to keep a helicopter in the air here in the States. They'll teach you how to fly in Nam." How true that was!

Frank

2842 ROAD SERVICE—MOC HOA

2844
From: Carl Hess
Subject: Road Service

Great story, Frank! I've never had a fire caused by lightning but in Panama we had some pretty awesome build-ups and lightning. Sometimes, when IMC at night, the lightning would be so constant it would almost provide cockpit illumination by itself!

One interesting "war story" from Panama. We were returning from the Atlantic side to the Pacific side on one of our two airways IFR. Up ahead was a massive build-up. I kept asking the controllers if they were sure there was a "hole" for my Huey. They kept assuring me all was OK! Then we were in the middle of it. Big time rain, light rurbulence and moderate lightning. Then the cloud spit us out over the Pacific Ocean and the controller turned his attention to a Pan Am DC-8. He said, "Don't worry about that big cloud. I just put a little old helicopter through it!"

Best regards,
Carl Hess

2845
From: Parker Evans
Subject: "Bug"

Hey guys,

I don't want to bore anyone but I read in Gunn's journal yesterday that a young US Lieutenant, advisor on his first experience flying on a bug mission was unlucky enough to catch on fire when a flair ignited inside the aircraft. Gunn says the guy jumped out at about 2000 feet. Jeez, I don't remember that but I can see how it could happen.

Cobra599

2846
From: Frank Strobel
Subject: Weather

Carl, The fire was not caused by the lightning. I just had recognized the electrical arcing and fire as lightning.

When I first received my wings as a helicopter pilot I thought that it was pretty "neat" to be able to reduce some posted minimums in half that fixed wing pilots had to observe! That was before I had some controllers try to "squeeze" me through a hole between Pittsburgh International and Allegheny County Airport in

Pennsylvania, while flying for the National Guard! When you get bounced around a little in a small aircraft "in real life" and not in some kind of simulator or other training, it takes on a whole different appearance If you don't respect mother nature, mother nature always has a way to get back at you!

Shortly after I became an Aircraft Commander, the transition into the monsoon season in Viet Nam began. Feeling fat, dumb and happy, one day I flew between two large black clouds that were about 5 miles apart. I hit some clear air turbulence between them and boy did it wake me up in a hurry! We felt ourselves pressed back into our seats as we accelerated that is until we hit the still air. Our airspeed indicator flashed from 90 knots to above VNE (the aircraft's published Velocity Not To Exceed) when we were expelled from the mass of air that had accelerated us. The Huey felt and sounded as if it was beating itself apart. All of a sudden, 1500 feet AGL looked very high to me! I learned a lesson that day, "Don't fool with mother nature!"

Frank

2867
From: Carl Hess
Subject: Weather

Frank, that term "fat, dumb and happy" is still in use today here at Ft. Rucker. Both my students had a bad period this morning in nice smooth air. One of them used the term "fat, dumb and happy" and I said, "Two out of three isn't bad. Actually, only one of us was "happy" and that was me"! I still have a ball, wondering what I am going to "learn" next!

Best regards,
Carl

Note: Carl Hess was an instrument instructor in helicopters at Ft. Ruker, Alabama when he wrote this.

2847
From: Frank Strobel
Subject: "Bug"

Having a flare ignite inside your aircraft is not boring! I had it happen onceand it was kicked out quickly but burning white magnesium inside a Huey is not something that would give you a sense of security.

Maybe someone can verify or refute, (I'd like to hear!) this but I had a Maintenance Officer tell me once that, "If the magnesium in a Huey ignited while flying at 500 feet AGL only the 'stump' of the transmission would hit the ground, all else would be vaporized!"

If that is true, maybe that is why there is no emergency preceedure written for it!

Frank

2848
From: John Laughinghouse
Subject: "Bug",

Frank- All they have to do for safety is make all aircraft out of the same material they make those "little black boxes" out of. They seem to almost always survive the crash. JOHN

2849
From: Parker Evans
Subject: "Bug",

Frank,

I heard that same story from maintenance. I know it's a little before your time (and even early in mine) but when I first started flying on slicks, before the Cobras, there wasn't any designated flair ship. We'd stack the flairs on the floor and attach the lanyards to a floor ring or sometimes if you felt brave, you could hold on to the lanyard ring with a gloved hand. I remember when the guys in maintenance were working with the flight crews trying to figure out the best and safest way to deploy a flair "outside" the aircraft. I guess that dates me, doesn't it?

cobra599

2853
From: George Young
Subject: "Bug",

A little before your time Parker, (Bill might remember this) does anyone remember when we melted down the 3/4 ton flare truck caught fire somehow or other and the whole load went up?

George

2854
From: Bill Glasgow
Subject: And that's,

Parker,

We used to just stack the flares on the floor and use the lanyard like you said. I always wondered if those tubes they came in ever hit anything? George said we melted down a 3/4 ton flare truck. I can't remember how that started. I do know if the magnesium in a Huey catches fire it only takes two minutes and thirty five seconds until its just one white hot ball that doesn't appear graceful at all.

Bill

2857
From: Frank Strobel
Subject: Dedicated Flare Ship

Parker,

We had no dedicated flare ship in 1970. Whom ever had his "turn" that night, flew the mission with meand flew his ship. We just stacked those flares up in the cargo compartment and off we went! In most instances we connected the lanyard to one of the hold down O-rings, it seemed much safer that way. Rarely did we pull them with a gloved hand. I do remember complaints at times though from crew members that liked to pull the lanyard personally, by the end of the mission their hand was pretty sore!

I remember someone saying that those flares cost $80 each, on busy nights we sometimes used upwards 80-100 flares. That was a quite expensive night!

Frank

2858
From: Parker Evans
Subject: Dedicated,

Oh Frank,

You of all people would have loved the flair/smoke ship used in mid to late '68. Someone had finally developed a vertical "tube" set-up for flairs that was mounted outside the aircraft. (How well it worked and how long it was used, I don't recall) Also, it carried 5 crew just like yours and had a door mounted mini-gun (designed, developed and tested by the Cobra platoon, I might add) and of course the oil injector ring for the smoke behind the exhaust pipe.

I recall one mission where at least three slicks were downed just as they touched down in an LZ. Surviving crews and troops were running around all over. Practically every available gunship in the area was called in to give these guys support and keep the VC off of them until a rescue of some sort could be attempted.

The flair/smoke ship was called in to lay down a long trail of smoke between the good guys and the tree-line where the VC were concentrated. This could only be accomplished and made effective at 40 knots or so. Slow moving targets, huh?

Those brave crew members made, I think, 3 passes at that speed right down on the deck. The end result was not only the rescue of the guys on the ground but also a slick full of holes and some wounded crew. I saw that aircraft in the hanger and couldn't count all the bullet holes it had. Now, that aircraft had to be your predecessor.

cobra599

2860
From: Frank Strobel
Subject: Substantiation

Parker, Later in my tour we did have a "smoke" ship. I think Marvin Tabaka had that as a semi-permanent mission when the apparatus was mounted in his ship. If I recall correctly though, because of the weight of the oil tank that was carried internally, it was pretty much maxed out! Although, I was flying nights I recall seeing him "do his thing" along a tree line one day. Flying low and slow during the daytime did not look like a FUN thing to do! I remember thinking how much I would not like that mission! At least at night when things were dark . . . if/when they turned dicey, I could turn off my lights and make it harder if not impossible, for

Charlie to see me. Of course, there were guys that didn't like flying nights too . . . guess that's why it takes all kinds!

Frank

2863
From: Parker Evans
Subject: Subs,

Frank,

I tend to agree completely with you about the daylight low and slow smoke missions. It would take a brave AC and crew, regardless of weapons they carry, to do that. That's always been the amazing thing about this unit. Things just seemed to get done no matter what it took. There was always someone willing to take a risk (or two). It sure makes a man proud of his comrades.

cobra599

2864
From: John Laughinghouse
Subject: Subs

Parker- The thoughts you have about the smoke missions, low and slowand what could happen. That was the way I was thinking and feeling when Charlie Brown showed me how the Eagle Flight decoy worked. One slick down low to draw enough fire to commit the Eagle Flight. When you drew enough fire you dropped red smoke on the target and ran (flew) like hell. We didn't even have to go slow just low. That was during my first couple of weeks in country that I was shown this. I said to myself, am I going to be doing this for a whole year? John

2866
From: John Laughinghouse
Subject: Subs

Frank- I loved the way the reporters/newspapers gave accounts of the action in our area. They always referred to it as **"The Viet Cong Infested Mekong Delta"**. Every time we lost a ship the papers "back home" would report it as being shot down in the Viet Cong Infested Mekong Delta. Names of the crew are being withheld pending notification of next of kin. Every person State

side that had a friend or relative in the Delta would be on pins and needles until they heard from that person to know they were o.k. Those of us that were in the Delta had no way of knowing when these stories hit the local papers at home or we would have written home sooner in many instances. What a time that must have been for our dependants and friends. We knew we were okay but they did not. Good that it was only for a year at a time.

John

2868
From: Frank Strobel
Subject: Weather

Carl,

I have never been to Ft. Rucker, myself! However, I think I would enjoy doing what you're doing. It would put a whole new perspective on me and my training. Was always frustrated with instruments though, not because I didn't understand them, I just didn't do them often enough to feel real comfortable with them.

Every other aspect of flying helicopters fell in place while in Nam and I felt that I really knew the Huey in and out when I came back to the 'world' but instruments, well, not so much!

I flew for the PA Army National Guard for years but the only instrument time I would get is when I was preparing for a check ride. That frustrated me. I did get some real instrument time in Viet Nam but it was half an hour here and a half an hour there. I used to practice instrument approaches as often as I could but it wasn't ever enough for me.

Frank

3053 THE WHITE KNIGHT PUPPY—SAM

3054
From: Parker Evans
Subject: Mascot

Frank,

Jeez man, you are really making me feel sub-human! I mean, once again you've proven yourself to be a great individual. Lover of children AND dogs. I'm sure it will be a great pleasure (although a bit humbling) to meet you in Columbia at the reunion. I'll bet you don't even have any vises. :-)

Parker

3746 A NIGHT FIGHT WEST OF BA XOAI

3750
From: John Laughinghouse
Subject: A fight West of Ba Xoai

Frank- Sounds like you kept control pretty good for the circumstances. That does sound like a night that would be hard to forget. Not many of us had fights like that Frank. Us slick drivers spent more time on standby than we did in the heat of battle. This could make for some long boring days interrupted by phases of great pucker factor sessions then back to standby. I bet you and all of those involved were "beat" after a night like that. How long does it take to wind down before you can sleep after an event/ night like that, or did you just fall to sleep from sheer exhaustion? Are you sure you were a slick driver?

John

3751
From: Parker Evans
Subject: Ba Xoai

Frank,

This is another excellent story. I could sure picture the fight. But you with a shotgun, chasing down a VC? I do believe you did just that. Even though everyone knew we weren't supposed to have shotguns. (we did, of course)

As far as you losing control, I don't think so. You just took what you considered a necessary risk. No wonder you were so popular with the Special Forces!

Parker

From: Tom Nesbitt
Subject: Ba Xoai
Frank,

I think you maintained control much better than most could have. I may have used the shotgun had it been meand as for your back-seat VC, he should have also been taken prisoner and interrogated. Of course we all know that was out of your hands. I had a similar thing happen to me flying Nighthawk with the 335th Cowboys but in that case the Province Chief was the VC. Situations like that are really frustrating!

Tom

3756 SLICK DRIVERS

3757
From: Frank Strobel
Subject: Slick Drivers!

John,

Do you know why I know I'm a slick driver and not a gun driver? Slick drivers are much more compassionate than gun drivers. I never once had a crewmember get out of my ship and run alongside to help me attain translational lift, before I allowed them to get back in. Slick drivers had to be skillful enough to do it on their own!

Frank

3758
From: Tom Nesbitt
Subject: Slick Drivers!

Slick drivers had to be skillful enough to do it on their own!

Frank, by chunking a few ARVNs off till you could get TL ;-) Tom

3759
From: John Laughinghouse
Subject: Slick Drivers!

Frank- Well said, are you sure you were not a Red Knight? Your exploits make it sound like you are flying a gun ship and not a slick. It also sounds like you have no fear of the famous Cobras coming back at you for making such a statement. You know Frank, sometimes the truth hurts so you may have hurt a few of them.

I bet this is one way to generate some traffic on this net. The thing I keep thinking of is how so many of the Red Knights became Cobras. Must have been a good training ground somewhere. That's one slick driver to another.

John

3760
From: John Laughinghouse
Subject: Slick Drivers!

Tom—That doesn't take skill just good sense, get it light enough to fly. John

3761
From: Bill Glasgow
Subject: night flights

Frank

Your story sounded like it was a bit touchy that morning for awhile. You should have let the ARVN (cong) walk back. From about 3,000 ft. that is.

We been missing your stories. Bill

3762
From: Parker Evans
Subject: Slick Drivers!

You know you're heavy when a 6 inch hover meant picking up the 'back' of the skids while balancing on the front or scooting up that slight incline from the pad to the runway was a formidable task. And no ARVNs to throw out either. :-)

cobra599

3763
From: John Laughinghouse
Subject: Slick Drivers!

Parker- I bet it did not take a pilot to figure that out did it??? John

From: Parker Evans
Subject: Slick Drivers!
John,

I swear, the first time I saw one of our ships kinda bouncing up that incline a little at a time I thought the pilot was playing around. But you could bet that on a hot day someone (mostly my aircraft) would have problems. Even with reduced armament and only 1200 lbs. of fuel I've had to run along side. Actually, it was kinda cool, really. Left the ground crews thinking we were really loaded for bear.

Parker

3767
From: Charlie Brown
Subject: Slick Drivers!

I love that, Frank!

Charlie

3768
From: Charlie Brown
Subject: Slick Drivers!

Okay, who remembers not only the running take-off at the airfield but the running take-off wobbling from one skid to the other to have as little friction with the ground as possible while picking up speed? I saw this little trick a few times on the wagon roads outside of outposts.

Charlie

3780
From: Frank Strobel
Subject: Slick Drivers

John & Parker,

John, you are probably correct **them guns guys** do get mighty upset very easily . . . in fact, Parker, are you still packing a couple 2.75's (rockets) in your jean pockets? Wouldn't be too suprised!

guess I might be a little more careful in the future. If I receive a long cylindar in the mail soon, I'll handle it with great care!

Parker, Have to admit I did walk the skids of a "D" model many times and "yes" it was outside those tiny little outposts but an "H" model only once! You know, when you are flying trail, sometimes it's a little hard to tell the last ARVN in an LZ that we can't take his weight! Especially when they have a fully loaded M-16 or M-79 grenade launcher, or one of those over/under things that had both (M-179)!

Frank

3781
From: Frank Strobel
Subject: Night Flights

Bill,

I would have loved to have let him out for a walk while my skids were somewhat above a hover. I was chicken though, not for killing him because I truly believe in my heart that he was the enemy but for the politics involved. You never knew when one of the "good guys" would be sacrificed to protect someone else's back side or to placate an angry politican! I just knew it was not going to be me!

Think it couldn't happen? I remember a congressional inquiry of the 114th that took place in 1970 that I was told about. Seems one of our enlisted complained to their congressman that we couuldn't get M-60 replacement parts (Which was true!) and we were being sent out to fight with inferior equipment. All of a sudden, we had enough parts to rebuild all we had! Politics and war make strange bed-fellows! You just have to make sure you stay on the right side of any possible opinion. What a way to fight a war!

By the way, I still think we could have/should have won that war even before I had to go over there! You guys were plenty talented! When you fight a war, you fight a war! You don't make up rules to fight by that the other side wouldn't even consider, let alone adhere to! It's amazing, 30+ years later and I still feel we fought both sides from the middle!

Frank

3844
From: Dick Duerr
Subject: Slick Drivers!

Frank, I'll second that. Dick

3791
From: Tim Meitin
Subject: Slick Drivers

Those "over/under things are (were) called XM-179

Tim

3795
From: Frank Strobel
Subject: Slick Drivers

Tim!!! Hello, Haven't heard from you in awhile. Missed you at the reunion! Throughout the reunion, I kept looking at the door. Never was sure who would come through next. Thought one of those times it would be you. Another White Knight Lead can always be useful!

HMMMM . . . . XM179!?! I knew it would be something plain and simple as that!

Frank

3807
From: Roger D Winslow
Subject: Slick Drivers!

I did it many times with Father Hoas and in Ca Mau area. Density Altitude seemed to increase the farther South you flew in the Deltaand the loads increased based on non-availability of support aircraft. The look in the advisors eyes when you tried the running take off with the B model (loaded) with outpost stuff was overwhelming. Usually the advisor stood there and clinched his fists until lift off and T/L and then his hands and arms flung upwards in the touchdown sign—"YES".

Roger D Winslow

ANGELS POINT ZERO ZERO TWO FIVE

3844
From: Charlie Brown
Subject: RE: Allegedly True Aviation Encounters

Frank,

I love it! That is a really good short one.

Save this for our next book Frank. Charlie

3053 BACK HOME IN ERIE, PA AKA . . .
THE POPCORN INCIDENT

4181
From: Parker Evans
Subject: Quiet too Long!

Frank,

Thanks for sharing those thoughts. It will surely remind a lot of guys of coming home. What I remember most is the look of disbelief when I told my folks I was going back. These days, being a father myself, I think I can relate more to their reactions.

Being one of only a few returning soldiers on the flight back, you can imagine all the questions I tried to answer. "What's it like?, Did you do this", Did you see that?" And quite frankly, all I remember was thinking that I'd been gone for awhile and would I still be a Cobra. I wouldn't have extended for anything else. And to be more frank, when I arrived back at Vinh Long and reclaimed my bunk, it was like being home. Strange, isn't it??

cobra599

4184
From: Steve Stibbens
Subject: Quiet too long!

Frank, what a Norman Rockwell moment your arrival to this forum was . . .

Steve

4188
From: Ginger Shannon
Subject: Quiet too long!

My oh my Frank, once again you have filled all our hearts with the intensity and emotions of your story, Thank You, Ginger

APPENDIX 2

Rotor Roundup Information

From: "Frank Strobel"
Subject: Rotor-Roundup—Ship Number 69-15085, The Devil's Disciple

John, I hope this is what you need. If I'm missing something, just let me know,

Frank

Aircraft #: 69-15085

Assigned to 114th Assault Helicopter Company in March of 1970

First assignment . . .

Aircraft Commander:	WO1 Francis J. Strobel (1970 Apr-Dec)
Call sign: Knight Hawk 6 / Knight 27	
Crew Chief:	SP5 Pascual Mantanona
Gunner:	SP4 Smalley alternating with SP4 Stogner

Xeon Light & Starlight Scope Operator:	Pvt. Law
Aircraft was nicknamed:	The Devil's Disciple
Primary Mission:	Night Hunter-Killer, 1970 April to 1970 October (1011 Flight Hours)
Main Area of Operations	Cambodian Border Patrol, Moc Hoa Area and The Seven Mountains Area

Note: I received the aircraft when it had 20 flight hours on it. We did a number of modifications on it while it was used for the Night Hunter-Killer mission. The most major/permanent modification was the addition of two complete additional electrical circuits for the mini-guns mounted for the crew chief and gunner with emergency quick disconnects and an additional electrical circuit for the 1.5 million candle power xeon white/ infra-red light.

APPENDIX 3

My Glossary Therefore My Definitions!

This is a layman's compendium of Military Terms & Flying Jargon used by Army Aviation in Viet Nam.

These are <u>my</u> definitions . . . no one else's.

---

57 Recoilless Rifle	A 57 mm rocket supplied by the Soviet Union and Red China to the North Vietnamese, very powerful and very accurate.
106 Recoilless Rifle	A US Army issued jeep mounted launcher that fired a 106 mm rocket, more powerful and more accurate than the 57 Recoilless Rifle.
ARVN	The regular **Ar**my of (South) **Viet Nam**, often used in referring to an individual or group of soldiers
AGL	**A**bove **G**round **L**evel, "Your Altitude above the ground"
Angel(s)	1 Angel is 1,000 feet above the ground, 20 Angels is 20,000 feet above the ground.

Autorotation

The maneuver a helicopter uses to land safely after an engine fails by utilizing the power / energy remaining in the spinning rotor blades to cushion its touchdown.

Basaac River

The southern of the two main rivers that flowed southeastward across the Delta region. It flows past Can Tho.

Café Su

In Chau Duc, I drank *cafe su* (pronounced "sure" with a rising diacritical) with it, dark, bitter coffee dripped into a demitasse cup that was 1/3 filled with sweet condensed milk. Stirred, it was delicious.

CBR

Chemical, Biological and Radiological (warfare)

C-Rations

A boxed meal eaten by troops not near a mess hall. It was packaged in a way that could be stored successfully for years. It contained an entrée, usually a can of meat or meat based food (*i.e.* spaghetti or bacon & eggs), a can of bread, crackers or cake, sometimes a can of cheese spread or cans of peanut butter and a can of honey. It also had a package that contained salt & pepper, a box of three cigarettes, matchesand toilet paper. Nutrition wise, one box of C-rations consumed is enough to give an individual enough calories and vitamins for a whole day even though it would not satisfy a day's hunger.

C&C, C&C

Ship **C**ommand **&** **C**ontrol, a helicopter that usually flies high over a troop insertion, skirmish or fight to attempt to closely control the flow of the action. On Night Hunter-Killer missions, it is the low ship.

Call sign	A name given to an individual during radio communications to identify a person other than by his given name. In the case of a unit call sign, normally a number would be added to the call sign to indicate a specific individual. As an example the Commander or Commanding Officer would be designated with the number 6. The Commanding Officer of the 114th Assault Helicopter Company, the "Knights of the Air", would have the call sign Knight 6 (K6). The Platoon Leader of the White Knight Platoon would be White Knight 6 (WK6).
CO	**C**ommanding **O**fficer
Cong/Viet Cong/	South Vietnamese civilians that were fighting on the side of the North Vietnamese. Also called guerillas/Charlie
CYA	A colloquial expression meaning that a person would "politically" protect themselves possibly even to the detriment of another person, normally in other than a combat situation. **C**over **Y**our **A**—(Back End)
DEROS	**D**ate **E**stimated for an individual to **R**eturn from **O**verseas. Date to Go back "To The World" . . . to the States from Viet Nam.
EOD	Explosive Ordnance Disposal
Fuel Bladder	A large reinforced rubberized "balloon" that would be placed on top of the ground and filled with a liquid. In Viet Nam (in my references) it usually held fuel for jet engines called JP4. It was very practical and easy to use but it had no armor or protection from a nearby explosion or an attack.

GCA	A **G**round **C**ontrolled **A**pproach used by pilots in Instrument Flight Rules (IFR) weather. A pilot is given specific step by step, individual instructions on what to do and when to do it by a radar operator on the ground in order to make an approach to a landing.
Guns/Gunships	Helicopters armed specifically with rockets, machine or mini-guns and/or 40 MM grenade launchers. Later in the Viet Nam war they often came equipped with 20 mm rapid fire Vulcan Cannons. Those were usually the C or G model (Cobra) Hueys.
Ha Noi	A wonderful soup, which was as Chinese Soup and which, today, I can find on the menu of a local Vietnamese restaurants as Soup Ha Noi. It was a pork stock, full of rice noodles, scallions and slices of barbecued pork.
Highway 4 Ferry	Crossed the Mekong River NW of Vinh Long. It was used as our landing IP when landing from the west.
IFR	**I**nstrument **F**light **R**ules. The rules followed by pilots when flying in other than good weather. Additional training is required to be qualified to fly in IFR situations.
IP	**I**nstructor **P**ilot
JP4	Kerosene based jet fuel used by Army helicopters.

Knight Platoons	Duties
Gold	Company Commander
Blue	Maintenance Aircraft nicknamed . . . "Road Service"
Cobra	Gunships
Lancer	A second Gunship Platoon that served with the Knights for a short time in 1966 & 67
Red	1st Platoon, Slicks
White	2nd Platoon, Slicks
LRRP/LRRPl	**L**ong **R**ange **R**econnance **P**atrol. Usually five or six men (but could be any number based on the mission) that go out on a patrol, often for a week or more at a time. Normally <u>not</u> with the mission to get into a fight but to quietly gather information on enemy locations, strength and movements.
LZ	**L**anding **Z**one, an area that is designated for the insertion of ground troops or dropping off supplies by helicopters. An LZ could be prepared or unprepared, Hot (enemy firing) or Cold.
MACV	There were 2 MACV acronyms used by the military in Viet Nam: 1. US Air Force—Military Airlift Command, large aircraft for delivering personnel and suppliesand 2. US Army—Military Assistance Command Viet Nam, responsible mainly for placing and reading electronic sensors.

M-60	A World War II style machine gun that fired 600 rounds of 7.62 caliber NATO Standard) ammunition per minute. It operated on a gas fed piston to automatically load the next round and prepare the gun to fire continuously until the trigger is released.
Mekong River	The northern of the two main rivers that flowed southeastward across the Delta region. It flows past Vinh Long.
Med-i-vac	The emergency evacuation of a casualty for medical treatment.
Mini-gun	An electric motor driven rotating six barreled gun mechanism, for feeding 7.62 caliber ammunition into the barrel, rotating the barrel into firing positionand ejecting the spent cartridge. The mini-guns used with the Knights had a firing rate of 2,000 rounds per minute.
MRE	**M**eals **R**eady to **E**at. A freeze dried packaged meal used by the LRRP, the Green Beretsand the SEAL teams in Viet Nam. Newly introduced in Viet Nam, later they would replace the formerly standard C-ration. I never tasted them while in Viet Nam.
NDB/MDB	Navigational/Marine Directional Beacon (Radio) to assist navigation and flying particularly in bad (IFR) weather.
NVA	**N**orth **Vietnamese A**rmy, regular trained and equipped soldiers from North Viet Nam.

OPS	**Op**eration**s**, The scheduling of all missions and reports from all missions would be done through this area, within the Company.
Packs (PAX)	Acronym for passenger(s).
Peter Pilot	Slang for a New Pilot in-country, learning the ropes from the Aircraft Commander. AKA "NEWBY."
PBR	**P**atrol **B**oat **R**iver, U. S. Navy used in the Mekong River Delta in their "Brown River Navy." It was virtually formed 100% from foam and fiberglass. It was impossible to sink even with a large amounts of damage and was easy to repair. The later model PBR Mark II carried a .50 Caliber machine gun on the stern.
POL	**P**etroleum, **O**il and **L**ubricants. Fuel and Oil would be stored until need at a POL Dump.
PSP	**P**ierced **S**teel **P**lanking. Heavy corrugated metal strips, when interlocked, were used to make a landing strip, ramp or taxi way out in the field; extremely fast to assemble and durable.
Pucker Factor	A colloquial expression used among pilots when rating the stress of a situation. In a stressful or dangerous situation the cheeks of your buttocks would naturally squeeze together. The higher the danger, the tighter they would squeeze . . . thus the higher the "pucker factor"!

Ramp/Ramp 1	An area away from the main runway but used by aircraft at an Airfield or Taxiway. At Vinh Long, Viet Nam, there were three ramps parallel to the main runway. Ramp 1 (The Knight/Cowboy Ramp) was on the north side of the runway, Ramps 2 and 3 (The Air Calvary) were on the south side.
Revetment	Six foot high barriers, either two in parallel, or in an "L" shape, that were built to protect an aircraft from shrapnel from enemy attacks, normally from mortar rounds or rockets.
R&R	**R**est **&** **R**ecuperation. A short vacation from a combat zone.
RF/PF	Regional Forces / Popular Forces. The local South Vietnamese (militia) troops similar to the US Army National Guard. We called them "Ruff-Puff" soldiers for short.
RLO	Real Live Officer, normally used detrimentally in referring to a Commissioned Officer. It normally meant that he was a person who rigidly lived by the book and not too flexible in his thinking.
ROE	**R**ules **O**f **E**ngagement. The rules given to combat soldiers stating the Who, When, Where and How an American soldier could engage the enemy. There was no ROE for the North Vietnamese or the Viet Cong to follow. It was a set of rules of what was and wasn't allowed. The U.S has them but our enemies didn't.

Slicks	Lightly armed Huey helicopters (usually with two M-60 machine guns) used as transports (*i.e.* trucks) to ferry people and supplies where they were needed. These were the helicopters that normally were used for troop insertions.
Song Tien Giang	A river Americans commonly referred to as the Mekong River. It flowed closely past Vinh Long.
Translational Lift	Unlike fixed winged aircraft, helicopters do not inherently want to fly. It is commonly said that a helicopter's rotor blades "beat the air into submission" in the process of having a helicopter fly. There is a point, however, that after a helicopter begins to move, will actually become more efficient and begin climbing or going faster along the ground without adding any additional power. In a Huey, it is about 17 Knots (a little less than 20 miles per hour).
TO&E	**T**able of **O**rganization **&** **E**quipment. A listing developed by the Army to tell each military unit what people and equipment they are authorized to possess.
TW's	**T**ropical **W**eight. A tan two piece summer weight permanent press uniform.
USARV	**U**nited **S**tates **AR**rmy, **Viet Nam**. The senior United States Army Command and Control authority in Viet Nam; it was located just outside Saigon in Long Binh, Viet Nam.

USO	**U**nited **S**ervice **O**rganizations. A civilian organization that works to improve troop morale, especially overseas, by sponsoring visits by entertainers who give soldiers a temporary diversion with singing, dancing, *etc.*
VFR	**V**isual **F**light **R**ules. *i.e.:* Good flying weather
VNAF	South **Vietnamese** **A**ir **F**orce
XO	The e**X**ecutive **O**fficer. The number two Command Authority reporting to the Commanding Officer in a U. S. Army organization, Company level or higher.

APPENDIX 4

An Email I Received Just Before Publishing

I had never had any feedback as to how effective my night missions were. This is the one of the few comments on the value of the Night Hunter-Killer missions. I received this email over 40 years after I left Viet Nam.

Frank

From: FJStrobel@aol.com
Date: Mon, 12 Mar 2012 11:38:23 -0400
Subject: Hello
To: xxxxxxxxxx@hotmail.com

Dannie,

I saw your posting in the Knight guest book. I don't know if you remember me but I seem to recall we flew missions several times together before I returned home. I was White Knight 27 but mostly Knight Hawk 6. I usually flew night missions in the 7 mountains area of the western delta region.

Frank Strobel

From: xxxxxxxxx@hotmail.com
Date: Mon, 13 Mar 2012 01:18:26
Subject: Hello
To: FJStrobel@aol.com

Frank,

I do remember the night missions but I was usually assigned as co-pilot in the bug ship since I was new when the Knights were still responsible for that assignment. I also recall later on in my tour hearing that a diary found belonging to a senior NVA Officer describing how those missions really challenged VC activity in the 7 mountains area.

I am still flying, working for Columbia Helicopters in Papua New Guinea flying a Chinook supporting oil exploration. I am looking to retire by Dec 2013 as Joy and I have bought Lake Mayfield Resort and Marina near Mossyrock, Washington along with our Son Trent as Manager. It is proving to be quite a hand full during the summer season.

Stop by some day and I will shoot you a beer and talk about years gone by . . .

Dannie Richardson
xxxxxxxxx@hotmail.com

One last note before I quit

I was offered a direct commission while in Viet Nam but the Army did not have an aviation branch at the time. I would have had to become a Infantry or Armor Officer or some such! Maybe I should have accepted it and chosen the "Intelligence Branch". No, that wouldn't fit. My career would depend on that area not aviationand I wanted to fly. I figured that the Army was so flush with helicopter pilots, it was a way to weed some of them out. So I was weeded. I was released from the service a couple months later (actually April 1, 1971) and went back to finish my last year plus of college. I tried to enlist in the Air Force after College graduation to go to flight school and fly fighters but was told I was too old. I figured combat experience with a Distinguished Flying Cross, 37 Air Medals (2 "V" device's), a Bronze Star and the other salad on my chest and only having 29 months of active duty, it would make a difference but unfortunately it didn't! I was "Over the Hill" at age 26 ½.